Charles Wilson

A complete collection of the resolutions of the volunteers

Charles Wilson

A complete collection of the resolutions of the volunteers

ISBN/EAN: 9783337274276

Printed in Europe, USA, Canada, Australia, Japan

Cover: Foto ©Andreas Hilbeck / pixelio.de

More available books at **www.hansebooks.com**

A compleat Collection of the

RESOLUTIONS

OF THE

Volunteers, Grand Juries. &c. of Ireland,

Which followed the celebrated Resolves of the

FIRST DUNGANNON DIET.

To which is prefixed

A train of HISTORICAL FACTS relative to the Kingdom, from the Invasion of Henry II. down,

WITH THE

HISTORY OF VOLUNTEERING, &c.

" We know our Duty to our Sovereign, and are *loyal;* we know our Duty to *ourselves,* and are resolved to be FREE."

The PEOPLE.

By C. H. WILSON.

VOL. I.

DUBLIN:

PRINTED BY *JOSEPH HILL.*

M DCC LXXXII.

TO THE

VOLUNTEER BODY

OF

IRELAND.

SIR,

YOU have promifed and proved yourfelf to be the warmeft friend to Liberty and Religious Toleration. I truft I have fome claim to your friendfhip; like you, I have endeavoured for the benefit of my country; like you, in the midft of dangers, I fpeak bold *truths;* and ftill farther like you, I glory in the name of an *Irifh-man:* I, therefore, place this Work under your protection, as a lafting monument of your *public fpirit.*

C. H. WILSON.

Dublin,
Auguft 9, 1782.

HISTORICAL FACTS

RELATIVE TO

IRELAND.

‹‹‹‹‹‹‹‹‹ ‹✛✛› ›››››››‹

THAT the prefent fhining period of Irifh hiftory may not hereafter be clouded from the vague conjecture of literary pride, the affectation of uncommon difcernment, or the prejudice of party, I fhall make no apology for prefenting my countrymen with a full and compleat collection of their firm and liberal refolutions; to which I intend to prefix the Hiftory of Volunteering, and a retrofpect of this kingdom from the invafion of Henry II. &c. merely to exhibit our privileges, the innovation of our rights, the reftriction of our commerce, and the neceffity of our armed affociations; fo that by contrafting the paft time with the glorious profpect of the future, we may be the more truly fenfible of the bleffings we are about to enjoy, the obligations we are under of pioufly tranfmitting them to our children, and the gratitude we owe to Heaven, and thofe virtuous patriots,

a

whofe

whóſe firm exertions have reſtored us to that liberty, front which happinſs is inſeparable.

The Engliſh at every period appear to have entertained the higheſt contempt for the Iriſh *. Nor is there an hiſtorian among them who has treated us, or our affairs, with impar-tiality; nay, even Giraldus Cambrenſis, who attended Henry II. in his expedition here, as Hiſtoriographer, has aſcribed Mac Murragh's expulſion to an affair cf gallantry †, when in faƈt, it was the tyranny he exerciſed over his ſubjeƈts, as may more fully appear in Lord Lyttleton's hiſtory of Henry II. on authorities furniſhed by that venerable hiſtorian, Charles O'Conor, Eſq; from whoſe lips I have had a further corrobo-ration of this aſſertion.

King Henry having obtained a bull from Pope Adrian, his countryman, for the inveſtiture of this kingdom, I ſhall preſent it to my readers, as a proof of the miſerable ſuper-ſtition, grofs ignorance, and Papal authority of thoſe days; and, above all, the religious pretext for the invaſion.

" ADRIAN, Biſhop, ſervant of the ſervants of God, to his deareſt ſon in Chriſt the illuſtrious King of England, greeting and apoſtolic benediƈtion.

" Full laudably and profitably hath your magnificence con-ceived the deſign of propagating your glorious renown on earth, and completing your reward of eternal happineſs in Heaven; while, as a catholic prince, you are intent on en-larging the borders of the church, teaching the truth of the Chriſtian faith to the ignorant and rude, exterminating the roots of vice from the field of the Lord, and for the more

---

* Even the refined Cheſterfield, of graceful memory, who dwelt long amongſt us, in a letter to the Biſhop of Waterford, repreſents one of our provinces as then in a ſtate of the moſt profound ignorance and barbariſm.

† The cauſe of Dermod's expulſion, ſays the legendary monk, was in conſequence of his having carried off the wife of Tiergnan O'Rourke King of Breiffne. This lady is repreſented by the Poets and Annaliſts of thoſe days, as exceedingly beautiful, and of an amorous diſpoſition; her flight with Mac Murragh it is generally thought carried only the appearance of reluƈtance; her name was Dervorghal, her father was O'Mallaghlin, King of Meath; ſhe lived to the age of 90, and died in a Convent in Drogheda. Mr. Hume calls her Omach, and her huſband Ororic, King of Meath; miſtakes which, however trifling, ſhould awaken ſuſpicion to negligence, or ignorance in more impor-tant affairs.

convenient

convenient execution of this purpose, requiring the counsel and favour of the apostolic see. In which, the maturer your deliberation, and the greater the discretion of your procedure, by so much the happier, we trust, will be your progress, with the assistance of the Lord ; as all things are used to come to a prosperous end and issue, which take their beginning from the ardour of faith and the love of religion.

" There is indeed no doubt but that Ireland, and all the islands on which Christ the sun of righteousness hath shone, and which have received the doctrines of the Christian faith, do belong to the jurisdiction of St. Peter and of the holy Roman church, as your excellency also doth acknowledge. And therefore we are the more solicitous to propagate the righteous plantation of faith in this land, and the branch acceptable to God, as we have the secret conviction of conscience that this is more especially our bounden duty.

" You then, most dear son in Christ, have signified to us your desire to enter into the island of Ireland, in order to reduce the people to obedience unto laws, and to extirpate the plants of vice ; and that you are willing to pay from each house a yearly pension of one penny to St. Peter, and that you will preserve the rights of the churches of this land whole and inviolate. We therefore, with that grace and acceptance suited to your pious and laudable design, and favourably assenting to your petition, do hold it good and acceptable, that, for extending the borders of the church, restraining the progress of vice, for the correction of manners, the planting of virtue, and the encrease of religion, you enter this island, and execute therein whatever shall pertain to the honour of God and welfare of the land ; and that the people of this land receive you honourably, and reverence you as their lord : the rights of their churches still remaining sacred and inviolate ; and saving to St. Peter the annual pension of one penny from every house.

" If then you be resolved to carry the design you have conceived into effectual execution, study to form this nation to virtuous manners ; and labour by yourself, and others whom you shall judge meet for this work, in faith, word, and life, that the church may be there adorned, that the religion of the Christian faith may be planted and grow up, and that all things pertaining to the honour of God, and the salvation of souls, be so ordered, that you may be entitled to the fulness of eternal reward from God, and obtain a glorious renown on earth throughout all ages."

As

As the conqueſt of Ireland by Henry the Second, is an ex-
preſſion frequent in the mouths of the Engliſh, I ſhall ad-
duce Mr. Molyneux's obſervations on this ſubjeᴄt :

" I come to enquire, whether Ireland might be properly
ſaid to be conquered by King Henry II. or by any other
Prince in any ſucceeding rebellion. And here we are to un-
derſtand by conqueſt, an *acquiſition of a kingdom by force of*
arms, to which force likewiſe has been oppoſed ; if we are to un-
derſtand conqueſt in any other ſenſe, I ſee not of what uſe it
can be made againſt Ireland's being a free country. I know
conqueſtus ſignifies a peaceable acquiſition, as well as an hoſtile ſubjugating of an enemy. Vid. Spelman's Gloſ. And
in this ſenſe William I. is called the Conqueror, and many of
our Kings have uſed the epocha *poſt conqueſtum*. And ſo likewiſe Henry II. ſtiled himſelf *conqueſtor & dominus Hibernie ;*
but that his conqueſt was no violent ſubjugation of this kingdom, is manifeſt from what foregoes * : for here we have an
intire and voluntary ſubmiſſion of all the eccleſiaſtical and
civil ſtates of Ireland, to King Henry II. without the leaſt
hoſtile ſtroke on any ſide : we hear not in any of the chroni-
cles of any violence on either part ; all was tranſaᴄted with
the greateſt quiet, tranquility, and freedom imaginable. I
doubt not but the barbarous people of the iſland at that time,
were ſtruck with fear and terror of King Henry II's powerful force which he brought with him ; but ſtill their eaſy and
voluntary ſubmiſſions, exempts them from the conſequents of
an hoſtile conqueſt, whatever they are ; where there is no oppoſition, ſuch a conqueſt can take no place.

" I have before taken notice of Henry II's uſing the ſtile
of *conqueſtor Hibernie* † ; I preſume no argument can be drawn
from hence, for Ireland's being a conquered country ; for
we find that many of the Kings of England have uſed the
æra of *poſt conqueſtum ;* Edward III. was the firſt that uſed it
in England, and we frequently meet with *Henricus poſt con-*
queſtum quartus, &c. as taking the Norman invaſion of William I. for a conqueſt. But I believe the people of England
would take it very ill to be thought a conquered nation, in
the ſenſe that ſome impoſe it on Ireland : and yet we find the
ſame reaſon in one caſe, as in the other, if the argument
from the King's ſtile of *conqueſtor* prevail. Nay, England
may be ſaid much more properly to be conquered by Wil-

---

* See page 11 of this writer.

† Mr. Selden, will not allow that ever Henry II. uſed this ſtile. Tit.
Hon. Par. 2. C. 5. Seᴄt. 26.

liam

liam I. than Ireland by Henry II: for we all know with what violence and oppofition from Harold, King Wi liam obtained the kingdom, after a bloody battle nigh Haftings, Whereas Henry II. received not the leaft oppofition in Ireland ; all came in peaceably, and had large conceffions made them of the like laws and liberties with the people of England, which they gladly accepted, as we fhall fee hereafter. But I am fully fatisfied, that neither King William I. in his acquifition of England, or Henry II. in his acqueft of Ireland, obtained the leaft title to what fome would give to conquerors.   Though for my own part, were they conquerors in a fenfe never fo ftrict, I fhould enlarge this prerogative very little or nothing thereby.

" Another argument for Henry II's hoftile conqueft of Ireland, is taken from the oppofition which the natives of Ireland gave to the firft adventurers, Fitz-Stephens, Fitz-Gerald, and Earl Strongbow; and the battles they fought in affifting Mac Murragh, Prince of Leinfter, in the recovery of his principality.

" 'Tis certain there were fome conflicts between them and the Irifh, in which the latter were conftantly beaten ; but certainly the conquefts obtained by thofe adventurers, who came over only by the King's licenfe and permiffion, and not at all by his particular command (as is manifeft from the words of the letters patents of licenfe recited by *Giraldus Cambrenfis*, *Hib. expug*, page 760. *Edit. Francf.* 1603. *Angl. Norm. Hiber. Camd.*) can never be called the conqueft of Henry II. efpecially confidering that Henry II. himfelf does not appear to have any defign of coming into Ireland, or obtaining the dominion thereof, when he gave to his fubjects of England this licenfe of affifting Mac Murragh.   But I conceive rather the contrary appears, by the ftipulations between Mac Murragh, and the adventurers ; and efpecially between him and Strongbow, who was to fucceed him in his principality.

" From what foregoes, I prefume it appears that Ireland cannot properly be faid fo to be conquered by Henry II. as to give the parliament of England any jurifdiction over us; it will much more eafily appear, that the Englifh victories, in any fucceeding rebellions in that kingdom, give no pretence to a conqueft: if every fuppreffion of a rebellion may be called a conqueft, I know not what country will be excepted.   The rebellions in England have been frequent ; in the contefts between the houfes of York and Lancafter, one fide or other muft needs be rebellious.   I am fure the commotions

tions in King Charles I's time, are ftiled fo by moft hifto-
rians.   This pretence therefore of conqueft from rebellions,
has fo little colour in it, that I fhall not infift longer on it:
I know conqueft is an hateful word to Englifh ears, and we
have lately feen a book * undergo a fevere cenfure, for offering to broach the *doctrine of conqueft in the free kingdom* of *Eng-*
land.

  " But, to take off all pretence from this title by conqueft,
I come in the third place to enquire, *what title conqueft gives by*
the law of nature and reafon.

  " And in this particular I conceive, that if the aggreffor
or infulter invades a nation unjuftly, he can never thereby
have a right over the conquered : this I fuppofe will be readily granted by all men : if a villain, with a piftol at my
breaft, makes me convey my eftate to him, no one will fay
that this gives him any right : and yet juft fuch a title as this
has an unjuft conqueror, who with a fword at my throat
forces me into fubmiffion ; that is, forces me to part with my
natural eftate, and birth-right, of being governed only by
laws to which I give my confent, and not by his will, or the
will of any other.

  " Let us then fuppofe a juft invader, one that has right on
his fide to attack a nation in an hoftile manner ; and that thofe
who oppofe him are in the wrong : let us then fee what power
he gets, and over whom.

  " Firft, 'Tis plain he gets by his conqueft no power over
thofe who conquered with him ; they that fought on his fide,
whether as private foldiers or commanders, cannot fuffer by
the conqueft, but muft at leaft be as much freemen, as they
were before : if any loft their freedom by the Norman conqueft, (fuppofing King William I. had right to invade England) it was only the Saxons and Britains, and not the Normans that conquered with him.   In like manner fuppofing
Henry II. had right to invade this ifland, and that he had
been oppofed therein by the inhabitants, it was only the antient race of the Irifh, that could fuffer by this fubjugation ;
the Englifh and Britains, that came over and conquered with
him, retained all the freedoms and immunities of free-born
fubjects ; they, nor their defcendants, could not in reafon
lofe thefe, for being fuccefsful and victorious ; for fo, the
ftate of both conquerors and conquered fhall be equally fla-
vifh.   Now, it was manifeft that the great body of the pre-

  * Bifhop of Sallifbury's Paftoral Letter.

fent people of Ireland, are the progeny of the Englifh and Britains, that from time to time have come over into this kingdom; and there remains but a meer handful of the antient Irifh at this day; I may fay, not one in a thoufand: fo that if I, or any body elfe, claim the like freedoms with the natural born fubjects of England, as being defcended from them, it will be impoffible to prove the contrary. I conclude therefore, that a juft conqueror gets no power, but only over thofe who have actually affifted in that unjuft force that is ufed againft him.

" And as thofe that joined with the conqueror in a juft invafion, hath loft no right by the conqueft; fo neither have thofe of the country who oppofed him not: this feems fo reafonable at firft propofal, that it wants little proof. All that gives title in a juft conqueft, is the oppofers ufing brutal force, and quitting the law of reafon, and ufing the law of violence; whereby the conqueror is entitled to ufe him as a beaft; that is, kill him or enflave him.

" Secondly, Let us confider what power that is, which a rightful conqueror has over the fubdued oppofers: and this we fhall find extends little farther than over the lives of the conquered; I fay little farther than over their lives; for how far it extends to their eftates, and that it extends not at all to deprive their pofterity of the freedoms and immunities to which all mankind have a right, I fhall fhew prefently. That the juft conqueror has an abfolute power over the lives and liberties of the conquered, appears from hence, becaufe the conquered, by putting themfelves in a ftate of war, by ufing an unjuft force, have thereby forfeited their lives. For quitting reafon (which is the rule between man and man) and ufing force (which is the way of beafts) they become liable to be deftroyed by him againft whom they ufe force, as any favage wild beaft, that is dangerous to his being.

" And this is the cafe of rebels in a fettled commonwealth, who forfeit their lives on this account. But as for forfeiting their eftates, it depends on the municipal laws of the kingdom. But we are now enquiring what the confequents will be between two contefting nations.

" Which brings me to confider how far a juft conqueror has power over the pofterity and eftates of the conquered.

" As to the pofterity, they not having joined or affifted in the forcible oppofition of the conqueror's juft arms, can lofe no benefit thereby. It is unreafonable any man fhould be punifhed but for his own fault. Man being a free agent, is

only

only anfwerable for his own demerits; and as it would be highly unjuft to hang up the father for the fon's offence, fo the converfe is equally unjuft, that the fon fhould fuffer any inconvenience for the father's crime. A father hath not in himfelf a power over the life or liberty of his child, fo that no act of his can poffibly forfeit it. And though we find in the municipal laws of particular kingdoms, that the fon lofes the father's eftate for the rebellion or other demerit of the father, yet, this is confented and agreed to, for the public fafety, and for deterring the fubjects from certain enormous crimes, that would be highly prejudicial to the common-wealth. And to fuch conftitutions the fubjects are bound to fubmit, having confented to them, though it may be unrea-fonable to put the like in execution between nation and nation, in the ftate of nature: for in fettled governments, property in eftates is regulated, bounded and determined by the laws of the commonwealth, confented to by the people; fo that in thefe, 'tis no injuftice for the fon to lofe his patrimony for his father's rebellion or other demerit.

" If therefore the pofterity of the conquered, are not to fuffer for the unjuft oppofition given to the victor by their an-ceftors, we fhall find little place for any power of the con-querors over the eftates of the fubdued. The father, by his mifcarriages and violence, can forfeit but his own life; he involves not his children in his guilt or deftruction. His goods, which nature (that willeth the prefervation of all man-kind as far as poffible) hath made to belong to his children to fuftain them, do ftill continue to belong to his children. 'Tis true, indeed, it ufually happens that damage attends unjuft force; and as far as the repair of this damage requires it, fo far the rightful conqueror may invade the goods and eftate of the conquered; but when this damage is made up, his title to the goods ceafes, and the refidue belongs to the wife and children of the fubdued.

" It may feem a ftrange doctrine, that any one fhould have a power over the life of another man, and not over his eftate; but this we find every day; for though I may kill a thief that fets on me in the high-way, yet I may not take away his mo-ney; for it is the brutal force the aggreffor has ufed, that gives his adverfary a right to take away his life, as a noxious creature: but it is only damage fuftained, that gives title to another man's goods.

" It muft be confeffed, that the practice of the world is otherwife, and we commonly fee the conqueror (whether juft or or unjuft) by the force he has over the conquered, compels them with a fword at their breaft to ftoop to his conditions, and fubmit to fuch a government as he pleafes to afford them. But we enquire not now, what is the practice, but what right there is to do fo. If it be faid, the conquered fubmit by their own confent: then this allows confent neceffary to give the conqueror a title to rule over them. But then we may enquire whether promifes, extorted by force without right, can be thought confent, and how far they are obligatory; and I humbly conceive they bind not at all. He that forces my horfe from me, ought prefently to reftore him, and I have ftill a right to retake him: So he that has forced a promife from me, ought prefently to reftore it, that is, quit me of the obligation of it; or I may chufe whether I will perform it or not: for the law of nature obliges us only by the rules fhe prefcribes, and therefore cannot oblige me by the violation of her rules; fuch is the extorting any thing from me by force.

" From what has been faid, I prefume it pretty clearly appears, that an unjuft conqueft gives no title at all; that a juft conqueft gives power only over the lives and liberties of the actual oppofers, but not over their pofterity or eftates, otherwife than as before is mentioned; and not at all over thofe that did not concur in the oppofition.

" They that defire a more full difquifition of this matter, may find it at large in an incomparable treatife concerning the *true original, extent, and end of civil government*, chap. 16. This difcourfe is faid to be written by my excellent friend, John Locke, Efq. Whether it be fo or not, I know not; this I am fure, whoever is author, the greateft genius in Chriftendom need not difown it.

" But granting that all we have faid in this matter is wrong, and granting that a conqueror, whether juft or unjuft, obtains an abfolute arbitrary dominion over the perfons, eftates, lives, liberties, and fortunes of all thofe whom he finds in the nation, their wives, pofterity, &c. fo as to make perpetual flaves of them and their generations to come; let us next enquire whether conceffions granted by fuch a victorious hero, do not bound the exorbitancy of his power, and whether he be not obliged ftrictly to obferve thefe grants.

" And here I believe no man of common fenfe or juftice, will deny it: none that has ever confidered the law of nature and nations, can poffibly hefitate on this matter; the very propofing it, ftrikes the fenfe and common notions of all men fo forcibly, that it needs no farther proof. I fhall therefore

b

infift

infift no longer on it, but haften to confider how far this is the cafe of Ireland : and that brings me naturally to the' fourth particular propofed, viz. ' To fhew by precedents, re- cords, and hiftory, what conceffions and grants have been made from time to time to the people of Ireland, and by what fteps the laws of England came to be introduced into this kingdom.

" We are told by Matth. Paris, hiftoriographer to Henry III. that Henry II. a little before he left Ireland, in a public affembly and council of the Irifh at Lifmore, did caufe the Irifh to receive, and fwear to be governed by the laws of Eng- land : ' Rex Henricus (faith he) antequam ex Hibernia redi- ' ret apud Lifmore concilium congregavit ubi leges Angliæ ' funt ab omnibus graranter receptæ, & juratoria cautione ' preftita confirmatæ.' Vid. Matth. Paris, ad An. 1172. Vit. H. 2.

" And not only thus, but if we may give credit to Sir Ed- ward Cook, in the 4th inftit. cap. 1. and 76. and to the in- fcription to the Irifh *Modus tenendi parliamentum*, it will clearly appear, that Henry II. did not only fettle the laws of England in Ireland, and the jurifdiction ecclefiaftical there, by the vo- luntary acceptance and allowance of the nobility and clergy, but did likewife allow them the freedom of holding of parlia- ments in Ireland, as a feparate and diftinct kingdom from England ; and did then fend them a modus to direct them how to hold their parliaments there : the title of which modus runs thus :

' Henricus rex Angliæ conqueftor & dominus Hiberniæ,
   ' &c. mittit hanc formam archiepifcopis, epifcopis, ab-
   ' batibus, prioribus, comitibus, baronibus, jufticiariis,
   ' vicecomitibus, majoribus, præpofitis, miniftris, & om-
   ' nibus fidelibus fuis terræ Hiberniæ tenendi parliamen-
   ' tum.' In primus fummonitio parliamenti præcedere debet quadraginta dies. And fo forth.

" This modus is faid to have been fent into Ireland by Henry II. for a direction to hold their parliaments there. And the fenfe of it agrees for the moft part with the *modus tenendi parl.* in England, faid to have been allowed by William the conqueror, when he obtained that kingdom ; where 'tis alter'd, 'tis only to fit it the better for the kingdom of Ire- land.

" I know very well the antiquity of this modus, fo faid to be tranfmitted for Ireland by Henry II. is queftion'd by fome learned

learned antiquaries, particularly by Mr. Selden * and † Mr. Pryn, who deny alſo the Engliſh modus as well as this. But on the other hand, my Lord Chief Juſtice Cook, in the 4th inſtit. page 12, and 349, does ſtrenuouſly aſſert them both. And the late reverend and learned Dr. Dopping, Biſhop of Meath, has publiſh'd the Iriſh modus, with a vindication of its antiquity and authority in the preface.

" There ſeems to me but two objections of any moment raiſed by Mr. Pryn againſt theſe modi. The one relates both to the Engliſh and Iriſh modus ; the other chiefly ſtrikes at the Iriſh. He ſays the name *parliament*, ſo often found in theſe modi, was not a name for the great council of England known ſo early as theſe modi pretend to. I confeſs I am not pre-pared to diſprove this antiquary in this particular : but to me it ſeems reaſonable enough to imagine that the name *parlia-ment*, came in with William the conqueror : 'tis a word per-fectly French, and I ſee no reaſon to doubt its coming in with the Normans. The other objection affects our Iriſh modus, for he tells us, That Sheriffs were not eſtabliſh'd in Ireland, in Henry II's time, when this modus was pretended to be ſent hither ; yet we find the word *vicecomes* therein. To this I can only anſwer, that Henry II. intending to eſtabliſh in Ire-land the Engliſh form of government, as the firſt, and chief ſtep thereto, he ſent them directions for holding of parlia-ments, deſigning afterwards by degrees, and in due time, to ſettle the other conſtitutions, agreeable to the model of Eng-land. If therefore England had then Sheriffs, we need not wonder to find them named in the Iriſh modus, tho' they were not as yet eſtabliſh'd amongſt us, for they were deſigned to be appointed ſoon after, and before the modus could be put regularly in execution ; and accordingly we find them eſ-tabliſh'd in ſome counties of Ireland, in King John's time.

" This Iriſh modus is ſaid to have been in the cuſtody of Sir Chriſtopher Preſton of Clane in Ireland, An. 6. Hen. 4. and by Sir John Talbot, Lord Lieutenant of Ireland, under King Henry IV. It was exemplify'd by Inſpeximus under the great ſeal of Ireland, and the exemplification was ſome-times in the hands of Mr. Hackwel of Lincoln's Inn, and by him was communicated to Mr. Selden. The tenor of which exemplification runs thus :

' Henricus dei gratia rex Angliæ, & Franciæ, & dominus
' Hiberniæ, omnibus ad quos preſentes literæ pervene-

* Tit ·hon. par. 2. c. 5. ſect. 26. edit. Lond. an. 1672.
† Againſt Cook's 4th inſtit. c. 76.

' rint

' rint falutem infpeximus tenorem diverforum articulo-
' rum in quodam rotulo pergameneo fcriptorum cum
' Chriftophero Prefton, milite tempore arreftationis fuæ
' apud villam de Clare, per deputatum dilecti & fidelis
' noftri Johannis Talbot de Halomfhire chivaler locum
' noftrum tenentis terræ noftræ Hiberniæ nuper factæ in-
' ventorum ac coram nobis & concilio noftra in eadem
' terræ noftra apud villam de trim, Nono die Januarii
' ultimo præteriti in hæc verba,

" Modus tenendi parliamenta Henricus rex Angliæ con-
" queftor & dominus Hiberniæ, mittit hanc forman ar-
" chiepifcopis, &c." and fo as before, " Et omnibus
" fidelibus fuis terræ Hiberniæ tenendi parliamentum
" imprimis fummonitto, &c." and then follows the modus, agreeable in moft things with that of England, only
fitted to Ireland. Then the exemplification concludes:
' Nos autem tenores articulorum prædictorum de affenfu
   ' præfati locum tenentis & concilii prædicti tenore prefen-
   ' tium duximus exemplificandum & has literas noftras
   ' fieri fecimus patentes. Tefte præfato locum noftrum
   ' tenente apud Trim. 12 die Januarii anno regni noftri
   ' fexto.
    ' Per ipfum locum tenentem & concilium.'

" Now we can hardly think it credible (fays the Bifhop of
Meath) that an exemplification could have been made fo folemnly of it by King Henry IV. and that it fhould refer to a
modus tranfmitted into Ireland by King Henry II. and affirm
that it was produced before the Lord Lieutenant and Council
at Trim, if no fuch thing had been done : this were to call
in queftion the truth of all former records and tranfactions,
and make the exemplification contain an egregious falfhood
in the body of it.

" The Rev. Bifhop of Meath, in his fore-cited preface,
does believe, that he had obtain'd the very original record,
said by my Lord Cook to have been in the hands of Sir Chrif-
topher Prefton : it came to that learned Prelate's hands,
amongft other papers and manufcripts of Sir William Domvile, late Attorney General in this kingdom, who, in his life-
time, upon an occafional difcourfe with the Bifhop concerning it, told him, that this record was beftow'd on him (Sir
William Domvile) by Sir James Cuffe, late deputy Vice-trea-
furer of Ireland, that Sir James found it among the papers
of Sir Francis Aungier, mafter of the rolls in this kingdom ;
and the prefent Earl of Longford (grandfon to the faid Sir

Francis

Francis Aungier) told the Bishop, that his said grandfather had it out of the Treasury of Waterford.

" Whilst I write this, I have this very record now before me, from the hands of the said Bishop of Meath's son, my nephew, Samuel Dopping; and I must confess it has a venerable ancient appearance; but whether it be the true original record, I leave on the arguments produced for its credit by the said Bishop.

" This I am sure of, That whether this be the very record transmitted hither by King Henry II. or not; yet 'tis most certain, from the unanimous concessions of all the fore-mentioned antiquaries, Cook, Selden, Pryn, &c. that we have had parliaments in Ireland very soon after the invasion of Henry II. For Pryn confesses that * King Henry II. after his conquest of Ireland, and the general voluntary submission, homages, and fealties of most of the Irish kings, prelates, nobles, cities, and people, to him, as to their Sovereign Lord and King, anno 1170 (it should be 1172) held therein a general council of the clergy at Cashel, wherein he rectify'd many abuses in the church, and establish'd sundry ecclesiastical laws, agreeable to those in the church of England; ' Ecclesiæ illius statum ad Anglicanæ ecclesiæ forman redigere ' modis omnibus elaborando:' To which the Irish clergy promised conformity, and to observe them for time to come, as † Giraldus Cambrensis, who was then in Ireland, and other ‡ historians, relate: ' Et ut singulis observatio similis regnum ' colligaret utrumque' (that is England and Ireland) .' passim ' omnes unanimi voluntate communi assensu, pari desiderio ' regis imperio se subjiciunt, omnibus igitur hoc modo con- ' summatis, in concilio habito apud Lismore leges Angliæ ab ' omnibus sunt gratantur receptæ, & juratorio cautione præstita confirmatæ §,' says Matthew Paris.

" Can any concession in the world be more plain and free than this ? We have heard of late much talk in England of an

---

* Against the 4th instit. c. 76. p. 449.

† Topograph. Hibern. l. 3. c. 18. Hib. Expug. l. 11. c. 33, 34.

‡ Hoveden an. pars. p. 302. Brampton chr. col. 1071. Knighton de Even. Ang. l. c. 10. col. 2394, 2395. Pol. Virg. hist. Ang. l. 13. Rad. de Diceto. Walsingham, &c.

§ That each and singular every observation similar to one kingdom, should be extended to both (England and Ireland) every where with one common consent and one will, with the equal desire of the King they all form themselves into one empire; this therefore in all things being consummated in a council held at Lismore, the laws of England are received and confirmed by all, with due caution in law and proper confirmation.

original

original compact between the King and people of England;
I am fure 'tis not poffible to fhew a more fair original compact between a King and people, than this between Henry II.
and the people of Ireland, ' That they fhould enjoy the like
' liberties and immunities, and be govern'd by the fame mild
' laws, both civil and ecclefiaftical, as the people of England.''

The Magna Charta of Ireland coming next to hand, I
infert it with the tranflation, that my countrymen may fee
how far they have enjoyed thofe privileges, which a fifter
nation in herfelf holds facred.

At the inftance of William Earl Marfhal, this Charter was
granted us, by Henry III. who at the fame time, in the moft
folemn manner, ratified the Britifh one *.

MAGNA CARTA HIBERNIÆ.

REGIS HENRICI TERTII.

XII. DIE NOVEMBRIS, M,CCXVI. ANNO REGNI I.

Ex Libro rubro Scaccharii Dublin.

HENRICUS Dei gratia rex Anglie Dominus Hybernie
dux Normannie et Aquitanie et comes Andegavie archiepifcopis epifcopis abbatibus comitibus baronibus jufticiariis fo-
reftariis vicecomitibus prepofitis miniftris civibus ballivis et fidelibus fuis falutem. Sciatis nos intuitu Dei et pro falute ani-
me noftre et omnium antecefforum et fuccefforum noftrorum
ad honorem Dei et exaltationem fancte ecclefie et emendationem

* In the year 1253, there was affembled a very full parliament, to
whom King Henry III. promifed to ratify Magna Charta, and faithfully
to obferve all the articles of it, which King John and he at his coronation, and often fince, had fworn to obferve, and this was done in the
moft folemn and ceremonial manner that could be devifed; for the King,
with all the great nobility of England, all the Bifhops and chief Prelates
in their ornaments, with burning candles in their hands affembled to
hear the terrible fentence of excommunication upon all the infringers of
the fame, and at the lighting of thofe candles, the King bearing one in
his hand, gave it to one of the Prelates, faying, '' It becomes not me,
who am no Prieft, to hold this candle, my heart fhall be a greater teftimony;'' and withal laid his hand on his breaft the whole time the fentence was reading; which done, the Charter of King John's father was
read. In the end having thrown away their candles they cried out,
'' So let them who incur this fentence be extinct, and ftink in hell.''
Chron. de Marl. p. 228.

regni

regni noftri per confilium venerabilium patrum noftrorum domini Gaulonis titulo fancti Martini prefbiteri cardinalis apoftolice fedis legati Petri Winton' L. de fancto Afapho J. Bathon'
& Glafton' S. Exon' R. Ciceftr' W. Coventr' W. Roffen'
H. London' Menevens' Bangor' et S. Wygorn' epifcoporum
et nobilium virorum Willielmi Marifcalli comitis Pembroc'
Ranulfi comitis Ceftr' Willielmi de Ferrar' comitis de Derbia
Willielmi comitis de Aubomarle Huberti de Burgo Jufticiarii
noftri Savantii de Malo Leone Willielmi Bruerie patris Willielmi Bruerie filii Roberti de Curtenai Falkefii de Breante
Reginaldi de Vautort Walteri de Laci Hugonis de Mortuo
Mari Johannis de Monemute Walteri de Beuchamp Walteri
de Clifford Roberti de Mortuo Mari Willielmi de Cantelup'
Mathei filii Hereberti Johannis Marifcalli Alani Baffet Phi-
lippi de Albiniaco Johannis Extranei et aliorum fidelium noftrorum.

I. Imprimis conceffiffe Deo et hac prefenti carta noftra
confirmaffe pro nobis & heredibus noftris imperpetuum quod
Hybernicana ecclefia libera fit et habeat jura fua integra et
libertates fuas illefas. Conceffimus etiam omnibus liberis
hominibus de regno noftro pro nobis et heredibus imperpetuum omnes libertates fubfcriptas habendas et tenendas iis et
heredibus fuis de nobis et heredibus noftris.

II. Si quis comitum vel baronum noftrorum five aliorum
tenentium de nobis in capite per fervicium militare mortuus
fuerit et cum decefferit heres fuus plene etatis fuerit et relevium
debeatur habeat hereditatem fuam per antiquum relevium
fcilicet heres vel heredes comitis de baronia comitis integra
per centum libras heres vel heredes baronis de baronia baronis
integra per centum folidos ad plus et qui minus debuerit minus det fecundum antiquam confuetudinem feodorum.

III. Si autem heres alicujus talium fuerit infra etatem dominus ejus non habeat cuftodiam ipfius nec terre fue antequam
homagium ejus ceperit et poftquam talis heres fuerit in cuf-
dia ad etatem pervenerit fcilicet viginti et unius annorum habeat hereditatem fuam fine relevio et fine fine ita tamen quod
fi ipfe dum infra etatem fuerit miles nichilominus terra rema-
neat in cuftodia domini fui ufque terminum predictum.

IV. Cuftos terræ hujus et heredis qui infra etatem fuerit
non capiat de terra heredis nifi rationabiles exitus et rationabiles confuetudines et rationabilia fervicia et hoc fine deftruc-
tione vel vafto hominum vel rerum et fi nos commiferimus
cuftodiam alicujus talis terre vicecomiti vel alicui alii qui de
exitibus terre illius nobis refpondere debeat et ille deftructionem

de

de cuftodia fecerit vel vaftum nos ab eo capiemus emendam
et terre illa committatur duobus legalibus et difcretis hominibus de feodo illo qui de exitibus nobis refpondeant vel ei
cui nos affignaverimus et fi dederimus vel vendiderimus alicui cuftodiam alicujus talis terre et ille deftructionem inde fecerit vel vaftum amittat cuftodiam illam et tradatur duobus
legalibus et difcretis homimibus de feodo illo qui fimiliter nobis
inde refpondeant ficut predictum eft.

V. Cuftos autem quamdiu cuftodiam terre habuerit fuf-
tentet domos parcos vivaria ftagna molendina et cetera ad
illam terram pertinentia de exitibus terra ejufdem et reddet
heredi cum ad plenam etatem pervenerit terram fuam totam
inftauratam de carucis et omnibus aliis rebus ad minus fecundum quod illam recepit. Hec omnia obferventur de cuftodia
archiepifcopatuum epifcopatuum abbatiarum prioratuum eccle-
fiarum et dignitatuum vacantium excepto quod cuftodie hujus
vendi non debent.

VI. Heredes maritentur abfque difparagatione.

VII. Vidua poft mortem mariti fui ftatim et fine dilatione,
aliqua habeat maritagium fuum et hereditatem fuam nec ali-
quid det pro dote fua vel maritagio vel hereditate fua quam
hereditatem maritus fuus et ipfa tenuerunt die obitus ipfius
mariti et maneat vidua in domo mariti fui per quadraginta
dies poft mortem ipfius mariti fui infra quos ei affignetur dos
fua nifi prius ei fuerit affignata vel nifi domus illa fuerit caftrum
et fi de caftro recefferit ftatim provideatur ei domus competens
in qua poffit honefte morari quoufque dos fua ei affignetur
fecundum quod predictum eft.

VIII. Nulla vidua diftingatur ad fe maritandum duo voluerit vivere fine marito ita tamen quod fecuritatem faciat
quod fe non maritabit fine affenfu noftro fi de nobis tenuerit
vel fine affenfu domini fui fi de alio tenuerit.

IX. Nos vel ballivi noftri non faifiemus terram aliquam
nec redditum pro debitum aliquo quamdiu catalla debitoris
prefentia fufficiunt ad debitum reddendum et ipfe debitor
paratus inde fatisfacere nec plegium ipfius debitoris diftringatur
quamdiu ipfe capitalis debitor fufficit ad folutionem debiti et
fi capitalis debitor defecerit in folutione non habens unde reddat aut reddere noluerit cum poffit plegii refpondeant de du-
bito et fi voluerint habeant terras et redditus debitoris quoufque fit eis fatisfactum de debito quod ante pro eo folverunt
nifi capitalis debitor monftraverit fe effe quietum verfus eofdem
plegios.

X. Civitas

X. Civitas Dublin' habeat omnes antiquas libertates et liberas confuetudines fuas preterea volumus et concedimus quod omnes alie civitates ville et burgi et omnes portus habeant omnes libertates et liberas confuetudines fuas.

XI. Nullas diftringatur ad faciendum majus fervicium de feodo militis nec de alio libero tenemento quam inde debetur.

XII. Communia placita non fequantur curiam noftram fed teneantur in aliquo certo loco.

XIII. Recognitiones de nova diffeifina de morte antecefforis et de ultima prefentatione non capitantur nifi in fuis comitatibus et hoc modo Nos vel fi extra regnum fuerimus capitalis jufticiarius nofter mittemus duos jufticiarios per unumquemque comitatum per quatuor vices in anno qui cum quatuor militibus cujuflibet comitatus electis per comitatum capiant et in comitatu et in die et loco comitatus affifas predictas.

XIV. Et fi in die comitatus affife predicte capi non poffunt tot milites et libere tenentes remaneant de illis qui interfuerunt comitatui die illo per quos poffint fufficienter judicia fieri fecundum quod negotium fuerit majus vel minus.

XV. Liber homo non amercietur pro parvo delicto nifi fecundum modum delicti et pro magno delicto fecundum magnidudinem delicti falvo contenemento fuo et mercator eodem modo falva mercandafia fua et villanus eodem modo amercietur falvo wannagio fuo fi inciderit in mifericordiam noftram et nulla predictarum mifericordiarum ponatur nifi per facramentum proborum et legalium hominum de vifneto.

XVI. Comites et barones non amercientur nifi per pares fuos et non nifi fecundum modum delicti.

XVII. Nullus clericus amercietur nifi fecundum formam predictorum et non fecundum quantitatem beneficii fui ecclefiaftici.

XVIII. Nec villa nec homo diftringetur facere pontes ad riparias nifi qui ab antiquo et de jure facere debent.

XIX. Nullus vicecomes conftabularius coronatores vel alii ballivi noftri teneant placita corone noftre.

XX. Si aliquis tenens de nobis liacum feodum moriatur et vicecomes vel vallivus nofter oftendat literas noftras patentes de fummonitione noftra de debito quod defunctus nobis debuit liceat vicecomiti vel ballivo noftro attachiare et imbreviare catalla defuncti inventa in laico feodo ad valentiam illius debiti per vifum legalium hominum ita tamen quod nichil inde amoveatur donec perfolvatur nobis debitum quod clarum fuerit et refiduum relinquatur executoribus ad faciendum teftamentum

c   defuncti

defuncti et fi nichil debeatur abipfo omnia catalla cedant de-
functo falvis uxori fue et pueris fuis rationabilibus partibus
fuis.

XXI. Nullus conftabularius vel ejus ballivus capiat blada
vel alia catalla alicujus qui non fit de villa ubi caftrum fuum eft
nifi ftatim inde reddat denarios vel refpectum inde habere poffit
de voluntate venditoris fi autem de villa fuerit teneatur infra
tres feptimanas precium reddere.

XXII. Nullus conftabularius diftringat aliquem militem ad
dandum denarios pro cuftodia caftri fi ipfe eam facero voluerit
in propria perfona fua vel per alium probum hominem fi ipfe
eam facere non poffit propter rationabilem caufam et fi nos
duxerimus vel miferimus eum in exercitum erit quietus de
cuftodia fecundum quantitatem temporis quo per nos fuerit in
exercitu.

XXIII. Nullus vicecomes vel ballivus nofter vel alius capiat
equos vel carectas alicujus pro cariagio faciendo nifi reddat
liberationem antiquitus ftatutum fcilicet pro carecta ad duos
equos decem denarios per diem et pro carecta ad tres equos
quatuordecim denarios per diem.

XXIV. Nec nos nec ballivi noftri capiemus alienum bofcum
ad caftra vel alia agenda noftra nifi per voluntatem ipfius cujus
bofcus ille fuerit.

XXV. Nos non tenebimus terras illorum qui convicti fuerint
de felonia nifi per unum annum et unum diem et tunc reddan-
tur terre dominis feodorum.

XXVI. Et omnes kydelli deponantur de cetero per totam
Avenlich et per totam *Hyberniam* nifi per cofteram maris.

XXVII. Breve quod vocatur precipe de cetero non fiat
alicui de aliquo tenemento unde liber amittere poffit curiam
fuam.

XXVIII. Una menfura vini fit per totum regnum noftrum
& una menfura cervifie et una menfura bladi fcilicet quarterium
DUBLIN' et una latitudo pannorum tinctorum ruffettorum
haubergettorum fcilicit due ulne infra liftas de ponderibus autem fit ut de menfuris.

XXIX. Nichil detur de cetero pro brevi inquifitionis de
vita et membris fed gratis concedatur et non negetur.

XXX. Si aliquis teneat de nobis per feodi firmam vel fo-
cagium vel per burgagium et de alio terram teneat per fervicium militare nec habebimus cuftodiam heredis nec terre
fue que eft de feodo alterius occafione illius feodi firme vel
foccagii vel burgagii nec habebimus cuftodiam illius feodi firme vel foccagii vel burgagii nifi ipfa feodi firma debeat fervicium

cium militare. Nos non habebimus cuſtodiam heredis vel terre alicujus quam tenet de alio per ſervicium militare occaſi ne al cujus parve ſerjantie quam tenet de nobis per ſervicium reddendi nobis culteilos vel ſagittas vel hujuſmodi.

XXXI. Nullus ballivus ponat de cetero aliquem ad legem ſimplici loquela ſine teſtibus fidelibus ad hoc inductis.

XXXII. Nullus liber homo capiatur vel impriſonetur vel diſſeiſiatur aut utlegetur aut exulet aut aliquo alio modo deſtruatur nec ſuper eum ibimus nec ſuper eum mittemus niſi per legale judicium parium ſuorum vel per legem terre.

XXXIII. Nulli vendemus nulli negabimus aut differemus rectum aut juſticiam.

XXXIV. Omnes mercatores niſi publice antea prohibiti fuerint habeant ſalvum et ſecurum exire de HYBERNIA et venire in HYBERNIAM et morari et ire per HYBERNIAM tam per terras quam per aquas ad emendum et vendendum ſine omnibus malis toltis per antiquas et rectas conſuetudines preterquam in tempore guerre et ſi ſint de terra contra nos guerrina et ſi tales inveniantur in terra noſtra in principio guerra attachientur ſine dampno corporum vel rerum donec ſciatur a nobis vel a capitali juſticiario noſtro quomodo mercatores terre noſtre tractentur que tunc invenientur in terra contra nos guerrina et ſi noſtri ſalvi ſint ibi alii ſalvi ſint terra noſtra.

XXXV. Si quis tenuerit de aliqua eſcaeta ſicut de honore Walingeford Notingeham Bolon' Lancaſtr' vel aliis eſcaetis quæ ſunt in manu noſtra et ſunt baronie et obierit heres ejus non det aliud relevium nec faciat nobis aliud ſervicium quam faceret baroni ſi terra illa eſſet in manu baronis et nos eodem modo eam tenebimus quo baro eam tenuit.

XXXVI. Homines qui maneant extra foreſtam non veniant de cetero coram juſticiariis noſtris de foreſta per communes ſummonitiones niſi ſint in placito vel plegii alicujus vel aliquorum qui attachiati ſint pro foreſta.

XXXVII. Omnes homines qui fundaverint abbatias unde habent cartas regum Anglie vel antiquam tenuram habeant earum cuſtodiam cum vacaverint ſicut habere debeut et ſicut ſupra declaratum eſt.

XXXVIII. Omnes foreſte que afforeſtate ſunt tempore regis Johannis patris noſtri ſtatim deafforeſtentur et ita fiet de gruariis que per eundem Johannem tempore ſuo poſiti ſunt in defenſo.

XXXIX. Nullus capiatur vel impriſonetur propter appellum femine de morte alterius quam viri ſui.

XL.

XL. Omnes autem istas confuetudines predictas et liber-tates quas conceffimus in regno noftro tenendas quantum ad nos pertinet erga noftros omnes de regno noftro tam clirici quam laici conſervent quantum ad fe pertinet erga fuos.

XLI. Quia vero quedam capitula in priori carta contine-bantur que gravia et dubitabilia videbantur fcilicet de fcuta-giis et auxiliis affidendis de debitis Judeorum et aliorum et de libertate exeundi de regno noftro et redeundi in regnum nof-trum de foreſtis et foreſtariis de warrennis et warennariis de confuetudinibus comitatuum et de ripariis et earum cuſtodibus plaucit fupradictis prelatis et magnatibus ea effe in refpectu quoufque plenius confilium habuerimus et tunc faciemus ple-niffime tam de his quam de aliis que occurrerint emendanda id quod ad communem omnium utilitatem pertinuerit et pa-cem et ftatum noftrum et regni noftri. Quia vero figillum nondum habuimus prefentem cartam figillis venerabilis patris noftri domini Gualonis titulo fancti Martini prefbyteri cardi-nalis apoftolice fedis legati et Willielmi Marifcalli comitis Pen-brok' rectoris noftri et regni noftri fecimus figillari. Teftibus omnibus prenominatis et aliis multis. Dat' per manum pre-dictorum domini legati et Willielmi Marifcalli apud Briſtol-lum duodecimo die Novembris anno regni noftri primo.

Tranflation of the Magna Charta of Ireland, by Henry III. 12th day of November, 1216, An. regni 1. From the Red Book of the Exchequer.

HENRY by the grace of God, King of England, Duke of Normandy, &c. To the Archbiſhops, Biſhops, Abbots, Earls, Barons, Juſtices, Foreſters, Vifcounts, Provofts, Minifters, and to all his Bailiffs and his Lieges, greeting. Know ye, that We by the grace of God, and for the faving of our fouls, and the fouls of all our anceftors, and of our heirs, and for the honour of God, and the fafety of our holy church, and for the amendment of our government, by the advice of our venerable fathers, Saint Martin Lord of Gaul, &c. Peter Winton, L. of Saint Afaph, J. Bathon, and Glaftom, W. Coventr, S. Exon, R. Cicefter, W. Roffen, H. London, Menevens Bangor and S. Hygorn, and of Biſhops and Noble-men, William Marfhal Earl of Pembroc, Ranulph Earl of Chefter, William de Ferrar Earl of Derby, William Earl of Albemarle, Hubert de Burgo, &c.

I. Have

I. Have in the firſt place granted to God, and confirmed by this our preſent Charter, for us and for our heirs for ever, That the churches of Ireland ſhall be free, and ſhall enjoy their rights and franchiſes entirely and fully.

II. We have alſo granted to all the freemen of our kingdom, for us and for our heirs for ever, all the liberties hereafter mentioned, to have and to hold to them and their heirs of us and of our heirs.

III. If any of our Earls, our Barons, or others that hold of us in chief by the knight-ſervice die, and at the time of his death his heirs be of full age, and relief be due, he ſhall have his inheritance by the antient relief; to wit, the heir or heirs of an Earl, for an entire Earldom, C. pounds; the heir or heirs of a Baron, for an entire barony, C. marks; the heir or heirs of a knight, for a knight, for a whole Knight's fee, C. ſhillings at moſt: and where leſs is due, leſs ſhall be paid, according to the antient cuſtoms of the ſeveral tenures.

IV. The guardians of the land of ſuch heirs being within age, ſhall take nothing out of the land of the heirs, but only the reaſonable profits, reaſonable cuſtoms, and reaſonable ſervices, and that without making deſtruction or waſte of men or goods; and if we ſhall have committed the cuſtody of the land of any ſuch heir to a Viſcount, or any other who is to account to us for the profits of the land, and that ſuch committee make deſtruction or waſte, we will take of him amends, and the land ſhall be committed to two lawful and good men of that fee, who ſhall account for the profits to us, or to ſuch as we ſhall appoint. And if we ſhall give or ſell to any perſon, the cuſtody of the lands of any ſuch heir, and ſuch donee or vendee make deſtruction or waſte, he ſhall loſe the cuſtody, and it ſhall be committed to two lawful, ſage, and good men, who ſhall account to us for the ſame, as aforeſaid.

V. And the guardian, whilſt he has cuſtody of the heir's land, ſhall maintain the houſes, parks, ponds, pools, mills, and other appurtenances to the land, out of the profits of the land itſelf; and ſhall reſtore to the heir, when he ſhall be of full age, his land well ſtocked, with ploughs, barns, and the like, as it was when he received it, and as the profits will reaſonably afford.

VI. Heirs ſhall be married without diſparagement.

VII. A widow after the death of her huſband, ſhall preſently and without oppreſſion, have her marriage and her inheritance; nor ſhall give any thing for her marriage, nor for her

her dower, nor for her inheritance, which she and her husband were seized of the day of her husband's death: and she shall remain in her husband's house forty days after his death: within which time her dower shall be assigned her.

VIII. No widow shall be compelled to marry if she be desirous to live single, provided she give security not to marry without our leave, if she hold of us, or without the Lord's leave of whom she holds, if she hold of any other.

IX. We nor our Bailiffs will not seize the lands or rents of a debtor for any debt so long as his goods are sufficient to pay the debt : nor shall the pledges be distrained upon whilst the principal debtor have not wherewith to pay the debt, the pledges shall answer for it : and if they will, they shall have the lands and rents of the debtor till they have received the debt which they paid for him, if the principal debtor cannot shew that he is quit against his pledges.

X. The city of Dublin shall have all her ancient liberties and freedoms; besides we will and grant, that every city, town, and borough have their customs, and all the ports shall have their liberties, freedoms, and customs.

XI. None shall be distrained to do greater service for a Knight's fee, or for any other frank-tenement than what is due by his tenure.

XII. Common Pleas shall not follow our court, but shall be held in a certain place.

XIII. Recognizance of *novel Disseisin, Mordancester,* and *darrien Presentment,* shall be taken no where but in their proper counties, and in this manner : we, or our Chief Justice (if ourselves be out of the realm) will send two Justices through every county four times a year ; who, with four Knights of every county, to be chosen by the county, shall take the said assizes in the county.

XIV. At a day when the county-court is held, and in a certain place : and if the said assizes cannot be taken upon that day, so many Knights and Free-tenants of them that were present in the county-court that day, shall stay, as may give a good judgment, according as the concern may be greater or less.

XV. A freeman shall not be amerced for a little offence, but according to the manner of his offence ; and for a great offence he shall be amerced according to the greatness of his offence, saving his contentment; and so a merchant saving his merchandize ; and a villain in like manner shall be amerced

saving

faving his wainage, if he fall into our mercy: and none of the faid amercements fhall be affeered, but by oath of good and lawful men of the vicinage.

XVI. An Earl and a Baron fhall not be amerced but by their Peers, and according to the manner of their offence.

XVII. No clerk fhall be amerced but according to his lay-fee, and in like manner as others aforefaid, and not according to the quantity of his church-living.

XVIII. No ville nor any man fhall be diftrained to make bridges over rivers, but where they antiently have, and of right ought to make them.

XIX. No Vifcounts, Conftables, Coroners, or other our Bailiffs, fhall hold the pleas of our crown.

XX. If any that holds us a lay-fee die, and our She-riffs, or other our Bailiffs fhew our letters patents of fum-mons for a debt which the deceafed owed to us, our Sheriff or Bailiff may well attach and inventory the goods of the dead, which fhall be found upon his lay-fee, to the value of the debt which the deceafed owed to us, by the view of lawful men, yet fo as nothing be removed till fuch time as the debt, which fhall be found to be due to us, be paid; and the refi-due fhall go to the executors to perform the teftament of the dead : and if nothing be owing to us, all his goods fhall go to the ufe of the dead, faving to his wife and children their reafonable parts.

XXI. None of our Conftables, nor other our Bailiffs, fhall take corn, nor other the goods of any perfon, who may not be of the village where his caftle is, without paying for the fame prefently, unlefs he have time given him by confent of the vendor.

XXII. Our Conftables fhall deftrain no man who ho'ds by knight-fervice, to give money for Caftle-guard, if he has performed it himfelf in proper perfon, or by another good man, if he could not perform it himfelf for fome reafonable caufe : and if we lead him, or fend him into the army, he fhall be difcharged of Caftle-guard for fo long time as he fhall be with us in the army.

XXIII. No Vifcount, Bailiff of our or other, fhall take the horfes or carts of any to make carriage, unlefs he pays according to the antient liberty, to wit, for a cart and two horfes ten pence per day, and for a cart and three horfes four-teen pence per day.

XXIV. Neither ourfelves nor our Bailiffs fhall take an-other man's wood for our caftles, or other occafions, but by his leave whofe wood it is.   XXV.

XXV. We will hold the lands of such as shall be convict-ed of felony but a year and a day, and then we will restore them to the Lords of the fees.

XXVI. All wears shall, for this time forward, be wholly taken away in the Avenlich * and throughout all Ireland, except upon the sea-coast.

XXVII. The writ called *precipe* henceforth shall be made to none out of any tenement, whereby a freeman may lose his court.

XXVIII. One measure of wine shall be used throughout our kingdom, and one measure of ale, and one measure of corn, to wit, the London quart. And there shall be one breadth of dyed cloths, ruffets, and haubergets, to wit, two ells within the lifts : and concerning weights, it shall be in like manner as of measures.

XXIX. Nothing shall be given or taken henceforth for a writ of inquifition of life or member, but it shall be granted freely and shall not be denied.

XXX. If any hold of us by fee-farm, or by soccage, and hold likewife land of others by knight-service, we will not have the custody of the heir, nor of the land which is of the fee of another, by reason of such fee-farm, soccage, or bur-gage, unlefs such fee-farm owe knight-service.

XXXI. No Bailiff for the time to come shall put any man to his law upon his bare word, without good witnesses pro-duced.

XXXII. No freeman shall be taken, nor imprisoned, nor disseized, nor out-lawed, nor exiled, nor destroyed in any manner ; nor will we pass upon him, nor condemn him, but by the lawful judgment of his peers, or by the law of the land.

XXXIII. We will sell none, we will deny nor delay to none right and justice.

XXXIV. All merchants may, with safety and security, go out of Ireland, and come into Ireland, and stay, and pass through Ireland by land and water, to buy and sell without any evil tolls, paying the ancient and rightful duties, except in time of war ; and then if they are of the country with whom we are at war, and are found here at the beginning of the war, they shall be attached, but without injury to their bodies or goods, till it be known to us or to our Chief Justice, how our merchants are entreated which are found in our ene-

* River Liffey.

mies

mies country; and if our's be fafe there, they fhall be fafe in our Land.

XXXV. If any hold of an efcheat, as of the honour of Wallingford, Nottingham, Boloin, Lancafter, or of other efcheats which are in our hand, and are baronies, and die, his heirs fhall owe to us no other relief, nor do us any other fervice, than was due to the baron of fuch barony when it was in his hand; and we will hold the fame in like manner as the baron held it.

XXXVI. Men that dwell out of the foreft, fhall not appear before our juftices of the foreft by common fummons, unlefs they be in fuit themfelves, or bail for others who are attached for the foreft.

XXXVII. All that have founded Abbies, whereof they have charters from the kings of England, or ancient tenure, fhall have the cuftody thereof whilft they are vacant, as they ought to have.

XXXVIII. All the forefts that have been afforefted in our time, fhall inftantly be difafforefted; in like manner be it of rivers, that in our time and by us have been put in defence.

XXXIX. None fhall be taken nor imprifoned upon the appeal of a woman, for the death of any other than her hufband.

XL. Likewife all thofe cuftoms and liberties, which we grant in our faid kingdom, to be held as far as to us belongs towards all our faid kingdom, clericks as well as laicks, that they may conferve the fame, as far as to them belongs towards theirs.

XLI. But becaufe certain chapters contained in the former charter, may appear heavy and doubtful, to wit, concerning efcuages, aids of affeffing debts of Jews, and others, liberty of going out of our faid kingdom, and returning into our faid kingdom, forefts and forefters, warrens and warrenners, cuftoms of counties, rivers and their keepers, as they may feem fit to the aforefaid prelates and great men, until we fhall have thefe things examined in a more full council, and then we will make more fully, as well what concerns thefe things, as others that may hereafter occur to be amended; and whatever fhall pertain to the common utility of all, and the peace, and our ftate, and of our kingdom. And becaufe that we have not yet a feal, we caufe this prefent charter to be fealed, with the feals of our venerable father faint Martin, Lord of Gaul, &c. and William Marifchal, Earl of Pembrok our rector, and of our kingdom we caufe to be fealed. The

d   witneffes

witneſſes are the perſons above named and many others; given by the hand of the aforeſaid Lord Legate, and William Mariſcal at Briſtol, 12th day of November in the firſt year of our reign.

Soon after the Bill of Rights had paſſed in England, the following heads of a ſimilar one, for this kingdom, were preſented for tranſmiſſion by our parliament to Lord Capel, then Lord Deputy of Ireland, on the 14th of October, 1695, of which no more was heard.

HEADS of a BILL of RIGHTS.

I. That the pretended power of ſuſpending of laws, by regal authority, without conſent of parliament, is illegal.

II. That the pretended power of diſpenſing with laws, or the execution of laws by legal authority, as hath been aſſumed or exerciſed, is illegal.

III. That levying money for, or to the uſe of the crown, by pretence of prerogative, without grant of parliament, for longer time, or in other manner than the ſame is, or ſhall be granted, is illegal.

IV. That it is the right of the ſubjects to petition the King, or the chief governor, or governors of this kingdom, for the time being, and all commitments or proſecutions, or threats for ſuch petition, are illegal.

V. That the ſubjects which are proteſtants may have arms for their defence ſuitable to their conditions, and as allowed by law.

VI. That the elections of member of parliament ought to be free.

VII. That the freedom of ſpeech, and debates on proceedings in parliament, ought not to be impeached, or queſtioned, in any place out of parliament.

VIII. That juries ought to be duly impannelled and returned; and jurors which paſs upon men in trials for high treaſon, ought to be freeholders.

IX. That all grants and promiſes, fines and forfeitures of particular perſons before conviction, are illegal and void.

X. That for redreſs of all grievances in this kingdom, and for amending, ſtrengthening and preſerving the laws, parliaments ought not to be diſſolved, as they have been in the late reigns.

XI. That the free quartering of ſoldiers on any of this kingdom, in time of peace, is arbitrary and illegal.

The

The following Extract from a curious Record in the *Calender of Ancient Characters*, will best explain itself.

EDWARDUS Dei gratia rex Angliæ & Franciæ, & dominus Hiberniæ, venerabili in Christo patri M. eadem gratia Archiepiscopo Ardmachono salutem :

Cum alias oneravimus dilectum & fidelem nostrum Nicholaum Dagworth militem, nuncium nostrum versus terram nostram Hiberniæ per nos transmissum, quod ipse in quodam Parliamento in terra nostra prædicta, prætextu literarum nostrarum, dilecto & fideli nostro Willielmi de Wyndesore gubernatori & custodi dictæ terræ nostræ transmissarum, convocando, inter cætera in quadam indentura inter nos & dictum nuncium nostrum confecta, contenta, Prælatis, Magnatibus, & Communibus terræ nostræ prædictæ, ad dictum Parliamentum comparentibus, exponi faceret, quod cum nos, tam excessivas & intolerabiles expensas, circa guerras nostras in terra nostra prædicta, pro salvatione & defensione ejusdem, quales ante hæc tempora apposuimus, propter maximam effusionem expensarum quas circa guerras nostras aliunde necessario nos opponere oportebit, de cætero supportare minime valeamus ; iidem Prælati, Magnates & Communes et eorum quilibet, juxta facultates suas & status sui exigentiam, partem rationabilem hujusmodi expensarum super se capere recusarent, tunc dictus nuncium noster ipsos ex parte nostra oneraret, quod quilibet Episcopus duas personas ecclesiasticas idoneas protestatem sufficientiam pro se & clero suæ diocesis, per literas procuratorias ab ipsis episcopo & clero, ac communes cujuslibet comitatus dictæ terræ, duas personas laicas protestatem sufficientam tam pro seipsis, quam Magnatibus ejusdem comitatus, ac Cives & Burgenses cujuslibet Civitatis & Burgi ejusdem terræ, duos Cives & duos Burgenses potestatem sufficientem pro se, & Civibus & Burgensibus civitatum & burgorum prædictorum habentes, versus nos & consilium nostrum in Anglia, ad tractandum, consulendum & concordandum nobiscum, tam super gubernatione dictæ terræ, quam pro auxilio & sustentatione guerræ nostræ ibidem transmitterent. Et licet idem nuncius noster, præmissa omnia & singula Prælatis, Magnatibus & Communibus in Parliamento nostro apud Kilkenn. in octabis Sancti Michaelis proximis præteritis, ex causis præmissis summonito & tento, comparentibus, exposuerit, & ipsos in forma prædicta oneraverit ; ipsi tamen se per eorum insufficientiam excusarunt, quod aliquam partem sumptuum & expensarum, pro guerris nostris ibidem manutenendis, ad

præsens

præfens nequeant fuppo'tare : ob quod, hujufmodi perfonas verfus nos in Angliam, ex caufis prædiſtis, in forma fupradicta, tranfmitti volentes, vobis mandamus, quod convocato coram vobis Clero veſtræ diocefis, duas perfonas ecclefiaſticas hujuf-modi poteſtatem pro vobis & dicto clero veſtro optinentes, de aſſenfu ejufdem cleri eligi, & coram nobis, & dicto confilio noſtro in Anglia ad fumptus veſtros, & dicti cleri veſtri, citra quindenam purifications beatæ Mariæ proxim' futur', ubicun-que tunc fuerimus in Anglia, ad tractandum, confulendum & concordandum, ut prædictum eſt, tranfmitti faciatis, nobis in cancellaria noſtra Hiberniæ, de nominibus dictarum duarum perfonarum, fic per vos eligendarum, citra feſtum Sanctæ Katerniæ virginis prox' futur', ubicunque tunc fuerit fub fi-gillo veſtro certificantes, hoc breve nobis tunc ibidem remit-tentes & hoc fub pœna centum librarum de vobis & dicto clero veſtro, ad opus noſtrum levandarum, nullatenus omittatis.

Teſte Willielmo de Wyndefore gubernatore & cuſtode terræ noſtræ Hiberniæ, apud Kilkenn. xxv. die Octobris, anno reg-ni noſtri Angliæ quadragefimo nono, regni vero noſtri Fran-ciæ tricefimo fexto.

◄◄◄•►►◄•◄◄•►►◄◄•◄◄►

TRANSLATION.

Edward by the grace of God, King of England and France, and Lord of Ireland, to the venerable father in Chriſt, M. by the fame grace Archbiſhop of Armagh, greeting.

W HEN otherwife we charged our faithful and beloved Nicholas Dagworth, Knight, our Nuncio by us tranfmitted towards our land of Ireland, that he in a certain parliament aſſembled, in our land aforefaid under the pretext of our tranfmitted letters, to our faithful and beloved William de Wyndesford, governor and keeper of our faid land, among other things exhibited a certain indenture made and contained between us and our faid Nuncio, to the Prelates, Nobles, and Commons of our aforefaid land, at the fame parliament af-fembled, fhewing the exceffive and intolerable expences of our wars, heretofore in our land aforefaid, for the falvation and defence of the fame, and which on account of the greateſt effufion of the expences of our wars elfewhere, we are no longer able to fuſtain; that the Prelates, Nobles, Commons, and each of them, as far as in their power, grant a reafonable

part

part of the expences, for the fuſtenation of our ſaid war, and for the ſalvation of our aforeſaid land; and if the ſaid Prelates, Nobles, and Commons, ſhould refuſe to take on themſelves any reaſonable part of the expence for the ſuſtenation of the war there, and ſalvation of the aforeſaid land, then our ſaid Nuncio on our part ſhall inform them, that every Biſhop ſhall have ſufficient power for himſelf and the clergy of his dioceſe, by letters of procuration from the Biſhop and clergy themſelves, to tranſmit two eccleſiaſtical perſons to us and our council in England, to treat, conſult, and determine with us, as well for the aid and government of our ſaid land, as the ſuſtenation of our war there. And the Commons of every county of the aforeſaid land, ſhall have ſufficient power for themſelves, as the Nobles of ſaid county, to ſend two lay perſons for the ſame purpoſe, and the citizens and burgeſſes of every city and borough, two citizens, and two burgeſſes, &c. And although our ſame Nuncio, premiſed all and ſigular theſe things to our Prelates, Nobles, and Commons in our parliament at Kilkenny, in the eighth of St. Michael next paſt, ſummoned and held for the premiſed cauſes, neverthelefs they excuſed themſelves through inſufficiency, and at preſent deny to ſupport any part of the coſts and the expences of ſaid war to be maintained in our ſaid land there, on account of which, and for the cauſes aboveſaid, we will, that ſuch perſons aforeſaid, in the form aforeſaid, be tranſmitted to us into England. And we command you that you convocate yourſelves before the clergy of your dioceſe, chuſing for yourſelves and your clergy, two eccleſiaſtical perſons, to be elected by the aſſent of the ſame clergy, and before us, and our ſaid council of England, at your coſts, to appear, and your ſaid clergy within the fifth of the purification of the bleſſed Virgin next coming whereſoever we ſhall then be in England, to treat, conſult, and agree, as is above ſaid, that ye cauſe to be tranſmitted for us to our Chancellor of Ireland, the names of the aforeſaid two perſons, by you thus choſen, within the feaſt of the Holy Virgin St. Kathrine, whenſoever it ſhall then be, certified under your ſeal, under the penalty of one hundred pounds from you, and your ſaid clergy, to be levied for our uſe, on every ſuch omiſſion, &c.

Witneſs, William de Wyndeſore, governor and keeper of our ſaid land of Ireland, at Kilkenny, the 25th day of October, in the year of our reign of England forty-nine, but in our reign of France, thirty-ſix.

We

We have the anfwers of the Archbifhop of Armagh, and of
the county of Dublin, to this fummons, diftinctly recorded *,
" We are not bound," faid the Prelate, " agreeably to the li-
" berties, privileges, rights, laws and cuftoms of the church
" and land of Ireland, to elect any of our clergy, and to fend
" them to any part of England, for the purpofe of holding
" parliaments or councils in England. Yet, on account of
" our reverence to our Lord the King of England, and the
" now imminent neceffity of the land aforefaid, faving to us
" and to the Lords and Commons of the faid land, all rights,
" privileges, liberties, laws, and cuftoms before mentioned, we
" have elected reprefentatives to repair to the King in Eng-
" land, to treat and confult with him and his Council. Ex-
" cept, however, that we do by no means grant to our faid
" reprefentatives any power of affenting to any burdens or
" fubfidies to be impofed on us or our clergy, to which we
" cannot yield by reafon of our poverty and daily expence in
" defending the land againft the Irifh enemy."

In like manner we find the county of Dublin at firft electing their reprefentatives without power or authority to confent to the impofition of any burdens ; the Nobles and Commons " unanimoufly with one voice declaring, that accord-
" ing to the rights, privileges, liberties, laws and cuftoms of
" the land of Ireland, enjoyed from the time of the conqueft
" of faid land, they are not bound to fend any perfons from
" the land of Ireland to the parliament or council of our
" Lord the King in England, to treat, confult, or agree
" with our Lord the King in England, as the writ re-
" quires. Notwithftanding, on account of their reverence,
" and the neceffity and prefent diftrefs of the faid land, they
" have elected reprefentatives to repair to the King, and to
" treat and confult with him and his Council ; referving to
" themfelves the power of yielding or agreeing to any fub-
" fidies." At the fame time protefting, " that their prefent
" compliance is not hereafter to be taken in prejudice to the
" rights, privileges, laws, and cuftoms, which the Lords
" and Commons, from the time of the conqueft of the land
" of Ireland, have enjoyed, in confideration of the various
" burdens which the faid Lords and Commons have borne,
" and ftill do bear, and which for the future they cannot fup-
" port—*nifi Dominus Rex manum fuam melius apponere voluerit.*"

* MS. Rawlinfon.

In

In 13 year of King Edward I. the ſtatutes of Weſtminſter 1 anno 3 of Glouceſter, an. 6 and of merchants, and Weſtminſter 2. an. 13 of his reign, were by his command ſent to his chief juſtice in Ireland, to be there proclaimed and obſerved, as this one memorandum in the clauſe roll of that year aſſures us.

Memorandum, quod die Veneris in feſto exaltacionis ſanctæ crucis, anno, &c. 13 apud Wynton. liberata fuerunt Rogero Bretun Clerico venerabilis patris W. Waterfordenſes epiſcopi tunc Juſtic. Hibern. quædam ſtatuta per regem et conſilium ſuum edita et proviſa, viz. ſtatuta * Weſtm. ſtatim poſt coronationem edita, et ſtatuta Glouc. et ſtatuta pro mercatoribus facta, ac ſtatuta Weſtm. † in Parliamento regis Paſch. anno prædicto proviſa et facta, in Heibern. deferenda, et ibidem proclamanda et obſervanda.

Cl. 13. Ed. 1. dorſo m. 5. De Statutis leboratis.

Writs for free commerce between England and Ireland, as common one to another, 253. Raym. 4 Inſtit.

Richard II. made a voyage to this kingdom, the particulars of which Howe, the Engliſh hiſtorian thus relates.

Now ſomewhat of the former voyage of King Richard into Ireland, as the ſame was reported to Sir John Froiſart, by an Eſquire of England, named Henry Chriſtall. Sir John (quoth he) it is not in memory, that ever any King of England made ſuch proviſion for any journey into Ireland, nor ſuch a number of men of armes nor archers. The King was a nine moneths in the marſhes of Ireland to his great coſt, and charge to the realme, for they bare all his expences: and the marchant-cities, and good townes of the realm thought it well beſtowed, when they ſaw the King returne home againe with honour. The number that hee had thither, were foure thouſand men of armes, and thirty thouſand archers, well payed weekly. But to ſhew the truth, Ireland is one of the euill countries of the world to make warre upon or to bring under ſubiection, for it is cloſed ſtrongly and wildly with high forreſts, and great waters and mariſhes. It is hard to enter to doe any of the country any damage: nor yee ſhall find no towne, nor perſon to ſpeak withall. For the men draw to the woods, and dwell in caues or ſmall cottages, under trees and among buſhes, like wild and ſauage beaſts: and when they know that any man maketh warre againſt them, being

* Weſtm. 1. 3. Ed. 1.　　　　† Weſtm. 2.

entered

entred into their countries, then they draw together to the ftraits and paffages to defend them, fo that no man can enter into them. And when they fee their time they will foone take their advantage on their enemies, for they know the country, and are light people. For a man of armes, being neuer fo well horfed, and runne he neuer fo faft, the Irifh-men will run on foote as faft as hee, and ouertake him, yea, and leape up upon his horfe behinde him, and throw him from his horfe ; for they are ftrong men in their armes, and haue fharpe weapons with large blades, two edged, where-with they will flay their enemie, whom they neuer repute to be dead till they haue cut his throat, and opened his belly, and taken out his heart, which they carry away with them, fome fay they eate it, and haue great delight therein : they take no man to ranfome. And when they fee that they be ouer-matched, then they will depart and hide themfelues in bufhes, woods, and caues, fo that no man fhall finde them : Sir William Windfore, who had moft vfed the warres in thofe parts of any other Englifhman, could neuer learne the man-ner of the countrey. They be hard people, and of rude wit: and they fet nothing by iollity, nor frefh apparell, nor by nobleffe, for though their country be foueraignly governed by Kings, whereof they haue many, yet will they abide and continue in their rudeneffe.

Truth it is, that 4 of the principall Kings, and moft puif-fant after the manner of the countrey, are come to the obey-fance of the king of England, by loue and faire meanes, and not by battell, or conftraint. The Earl of Ormond, who marcheth upon them, hath taken great paine, and hath fo intreated them, that they came to Dubline, to the King, and fubmitted them to him, to be under the obeyfance of the crowne of England, wherefore the King and all the realme reputeth this for a great and honourable act. For King Ed-ward did never fo much upon them, as King Richard did in his voyage. The honour is great, but the profite is but fmall, &c. The names of the foure Kings were thefe, firft, the greate Oneale King of Meth, the fecond Otrine of Tho-mond, King of Thomond, the third Arthur of Mackquemur King of Leinfter, the fourth Ocomor King of Theuenes and Drape, they were made Knights by King Richard in the cathedral church of Dubline : thefe foure Kings watched all the night before in the church, and the next day at high maffe time, were made Knights, and with them Sir Thomas Orphew, Sir Iames Pado, and Sir Iohn Pado, his coufin.

Thefe

These Kings fate that day at the table with King Richard, they were regarded of many people, becaufe their behauiour was ftrenge to the manor of England.

When Sir Iohn Froifart defired to know how it came to paffe, that foure Kings of Ireland were fo foone brought to the obeyfance of King Richard, when King Edward the King's grand-father, who was fo valient a Prince, could neuer fubdue them: Sir Henry Chriftall anfwered, he could not tell, but as men faid, the great puiffance that the King had over with him, and remaining there nine moneths, abafhed the Irifhmen. Alfo the fea was clofed from them on all parts, whereby their marchandifes might not enter into their countries, though they that dwell farre within the realme cared little for it, yet fuch as live on the marches of England and by the fea coaft, vfe feare of merchandife.

King Edward in his time, had to anfwere fo many warres in France, Britaine, Gafcoigne, and Scotland, that his people were divided in divers places, wherefore he could not fend any great number into Ireland. But when the Irifhmen faw the great number of men of warre that King Richard had in this laft iourney, they aduifed themfelues, and came to obeyfance.

In thes Articles folowing been comprifed the Kyng's Will, Determination, Commandement, and Plefures, upon the Parliaments holdyn late at the Naafe and Drogheda; and upon the Parliament that fhall be now next holdyn within his lands of Ireland. Anno 1418, 19 Ed. IV. Rot. clauf.

WHERE as have been gret variences of late in our faid land of Ireland upon two parliaments ther laft holdyn; the oen at the Naafe, the other at Drogheda, whether of theym fhould be of auctorite; we have thereupon taken fuche directions as folowith:

Furft, We confider that in the faid two parliaments were communed and concludet principaly two acts, the oen touchyng the grauntes of certayn fubfidies for the wele and defence of our faid land, the fecund concerned refumptions afwell of offices as of our revenue.

As touching the fubfidies graunted in our parliament holdyn at Drogheda, for as moche as we underftand, that it was graunted, and alfo in gret part, as we ben enformed,

e   leveed

leveed for the wele and defence abovefaid, We will that the fame graunts with all that thereto apperteyneth be gode and effectuell, and alfo auctorifed by the parliament in our faid land now next to be holdyn.

As touching the acts of refumptions in eather of the faid parliaments paffed, which of partialte and malice been, and have been more hurtyng to our fubjects ther than to us or the wele of our faid land profitable; we will that the fame acts be maad void and of none effect in the lawe, except the refumption of offices and Chauncellerfhip and Treforefhip, made in the parliament holdyn at Drogheda, the which we will that hit ftand in his force and effect. Confidering that thereuppon, we have made the Bifhop of Meth, our Chanfeler, and Sir Rouland Euftace, Knyght, our Treforer there; and we will, that a general act of refumption fro the furft day of Kyng Herry the VIte, be had and made in the next parliament touching our revenue; and that fuch provifion be made upon the fame by our Depute Lieutenant there according to our plefure; which our plefure we have fhewed to our right trufty and welbeloved cofyn Therle of Kyldare, whom we have ordened to be Depute Lieutenant, and to the reverend father in God the Bifhop of Mythe, whom we have ordeyned as is above faid to be our Chanfeler.

As touching the refumpcion of offices, forafmoche as offices of Chanfeler and other in the Deputies commyfion to us oonly referved, we will that the offices of Chief of the Exchequer and the Maifter of our mint there be refumed in this fame parliament, and our leters patents be mad there uppon under our gret feall there, to thofe perfons to whom we have made our grauntes upon the fame.

And as to other offices to us in the faid commyfion not referved, we be contented that fuch of theym be refumed, and they for the wele of us and our faid land, by our faid Depute Lieutennant fo difpofed, as fhall be thought by him mofte expedient.

We will alfo, that at thys faid parliament be refumed the office of Senefchalfie of the liberte of Methe, with the fees, wages, and rewards therfor by us, or otherwife to any perfon graunted, and fo to remayn in our hands at our plefure. We will alfo, that if any act have be made to the prejudice of us, and in derogacion of our Corone in reftreyning of tonnage and pondage, it be utterly revoked and adnulled, and in this parliament the old graunt thereof reno-

                                                            velled

velled and eftablifhed, as fhall be beft for our right, wele and honor.

Item, the Kyng willeth, That fuch an act as herto before hath be made in the land there reftreyning, that noe man within that land fhall be called out of the faid land by any precept or commandement, made under the Kyng's grete feall, prive feall or fignet in England, be utterly revoked and adnulled.

Item, The Kyng willeth, that upon refumption of the Kyng's revenues to be made in this parliament, the townes of Divelyn * and Drogheda be providet fore al fuche grauntes as have ben made unto they by the Kyng's auctorite, his progenitours or predoceffours, fo that they promife to be redy to doo the Kyng fervice, at fuche tymes as by the Kyng's Lieutenant or his depute they fhall be defigned.

Thes articles folouying conteyne, the Kyng's comanndements and plefere, how his Chanfelere of Irland, Clerc of the Rolles, and the Clerk of the Hanaper ther, fhall demene them there in executyng of ther offices.

Furft, They and everithe of thems, fhall well and trewly ferve the Kyng and his liege peple of the fame land, in the doyng of their offices.

Item, That they ne none of them fhall affent to the hurt, damage, or alienacion of the Kyng's lands, revenues, or rights; but they fhall endevoer them felfe for the vauncyng and encrefyng therof, and lette all them to the beft of theire powere, that wold attempt the contrary therof.

Item, That the fead Chaunfeler do ferv alweyes in fuche place and tymes as the Clerc of the Rolles, the Clerc of the Hanaper, and other minifters of the Chaunfery, may be ther and then prefent.

Item, That the faid Chaunfeller do delyvre to the Clerc of the Rolles, all fuch warrants cummyng to his hands, fo as he may kepe them as the Kyng's recordes, according to his office.

Item, That the faid Chaunfeller fele no pardon under the grete fele, unto any man upon his provifione from the court of Rome, without the King's knowlege and confent.

Item, The Chaunfeller in perfon, fhall in true time make his abidyng in the place wher the Kyng's Courts be kept, un lefhe ther by a great and urgent caufe, by the depute with the advife of the more part of the Kyng's Confele, it be thought his abfence to be allowed.

Item,

* Dublin.

Item, That the Clerc of the Rolles do enroll all patents under the Kyng's grete feall, before that they be deliveret to the
parties, and kepe fo the Kyng's records, that none of them
be rafed, ne befoiled.

Item, That he fee and write at every fele, what profits
growith unto the Kyng thereof, and the fpecialtees of the
fame; fo that his boke fo made may be a controllment upon
the accompts of the Clerc of the Hanaper, to be made yerly
in the Kyng's Efchequer there.

Item, That no lyvere be made to the Kyng's tennant, nor
yet reftitution to be made to any Bifhop, Abbot, or Prior,
without that the Kyng be furft anfwered of his duete, accord-
ynge to the rate of the tyme that the landes have ben in the
Kyng's handes.

Item, That the Clerc of the Hanapier continueley receive
the fees of the fele of writts, commiffions and patents; and
alfo, all fuche fynes as fhall be made in the Chauncery, and
thereupon pay the Chaunceller his fees, wages, and rewards
accuftomed, and deliver the remenant unto the Kyng's Efchequer upon his accompts, which he fhall make yerly therof:
and to thentent that noone ignorance may be pretendit, what
fines ben to be made them within the Kyng's Chauncery, the
fpecialties of them hereafter enfueth.

	l.	s.	d.
All writs of covenant, every affife and writs in nature, affife and other writts of entry above the value of 40s. unto the value of 5 marks,	0	6	8
Every fpecial affife, be hit ever fo litell, it maketh a fyne, and ftreitly, every 5 marks,	0	6	8
Every formedonne above 40s. unto 8 marks,	0	6	8
Every pone of Juftices, pone of writts of right, every writt of confpirici, writts of atteynte, and writts of falfe judgment, the fine,	0	6	8
Every recordan of dett or trefpaffe, and every dedimus poteftatem upon a writt of covenant,	0	6	8
Every writt of dett or trifpaffe, exceeding the fome value or prife of 40l. unto the fome of 60l.	0	6	8

Alfo an attachments of the privilege of dett or
trifpaffe according to the fame, and if hit exceeds
more to pay more.

All refpite of homage 6s. 8d. or mark after the quantite
of the liveled; all oyer and determinor at the fuit of the
partie, if gretter trifpaffe the grett fyne. All manner of licence
to purchafe temperell livelod to mortmayne the firft yere
value of the fame. All manner licence of fpirituell livli-
hood, as appropriaciery of churches or of benefices, fpirituell

ef

of holy church, four yere value of the fame. All maner licence of alienacion by the Kyng's tenannt, the third part of the value thereof. All pardons of alienacions made by the Kyng's tenaunt, the value of a hole yere. All maner licence of marriage of the Kyng's widdows, the third part of their dower. All manner of confirmacions of offices, the third part or fourth part of the value thereof, by the yere. All confirmacions of libertees and franchifees, the third part, or the fourthe part of the profits or value of the fame franchifees. All patents of devyfing the third part of the value of his goods. All pardons of the Kyng's widdowes maried without licence, the value of her dower by the year.

Item, That the Clerc of the Kyng's Hanaper, leave for him a depute in the court of the Kyng's Bench, another in the court of the Common Place, which fhall receve for the Kyng all the profites growing of the Kyng's fele in either of the faid courts, and thereupon, fhall yeld his accompt in the Kyng's Efchequer.

Here folouyth the Kyng's comanndements and plefure, to be fhewed unto Sir Rouland Euftace, Knyght, whom his Highneffe hath deputed to be Treforer of his land of Irland.

Furft, The faid Sir Rouland, fhall well and trewly behave hym in the occupieng of his faid office, and juftely and rightouifly exercife it, as well betwix the Kyng and his fubjects, as betwix the Kyng's fubjects.

Item, He fhall not affent nore agre to the hurt, dammage, or difheretyng the Kyng of his lands, revenues, rights, regalie or prerogatifs, but in all that hym is, he fhall uphold, mayntene, encreafe and avaunce them.

Item, That the faid Sir Rouland continually endevour himfelf, that the Kyng be yerely anfuered of all fuch revenues and rights, as fhall belong unto his highnes within his land of Irland, and that he do fend unto the Kyng's goode grace yerly, a trew and pleyn vews thereof, compryfing the particulers and fpecialtees of the fame.

Item, That the fame Sir Rouland remytte and forgete all malice and evill will that he hath borne and berith to the Bifhop of Mythe, Bermyngham, the Juftice, and all other the Kyng's fubjects within the faid land; for the Kyng's highneffe hath comaundet them in femblable wife to do toward hym   Alfo the King vol that he delivre his grete fele, beying in his kepyng, unto the faid Bifhop of Mythe, whom he hath deputed and made to be his Chaunfeller of his faid land of Irland.

deputed

Item, That the faid Sir Rouland kepe the appointment by the Kyng, taken betwix hym and Sir Robert Euftace in thes articles folouying, beth comprifed the Kyng's comaundments and plefere, to be executed and accomplifhed by his Juges and Barons of the Efchequer within his land of Irland.

Furft, That this and every of them, duely and trewly have them as well towards the Kyng's higheneffe as towards his fubjects, in executyng and doyng of their offices, and after their cunyng and difcrecion, juftely and indefferently minifter juftice to all the Kyng's fubjects in theefe parties.

Item, That nether thei ne eny of them, affent nor agree to the hurtyng or damagyng of any fuche revenues, en his laws, prerogatifs, rights or intereft to the Kyng in any wife belongyng, but that thei and everith of theym endevoir theym to their power to the avauncing and encrecyng thereof.

Item, That they and everith of them, employ them as effectually as they can, that all fines, amerciaments, and all other iffues and profits, fhall or ought righturfly to grow within the Kyng's levity, whom they have or fhall have adminiftration of juftice, be truely and duely ceffed and ordered; and that thereof a due comptes be made yerly in the Kyng's Efchequer ther, fo that their fees, wages and rewards, may be paiet and contented of the fame, as farre as it fhall ftretche unto.

Item, In caas that eny variences growe amongft the Kyng's fubjects in thes parties, which God defends, whereby the Kyng or the comen wele of his land ther by eny liklyod fhold be hurted, that thei endevoir themfelf to the beft of ther power, to appeyfe thofe variences, and that fuche direction be taken therupon as fhall beft acorde to refon, and to the wele of the Kyng, and of his faid land of Irland.

Item, That the Juges of both the places, aid, affifte, and favoir, fuch perfons as the Clerke of the Hanaper fhall depute for hym ther, for the recevyng of profites of the Kyng's feles within the fame places, fo that the Kyng may be thereby anfwered thereof, as he ought to be.

In the articles folouying ben comprifed the Kyng's plefure, howe and in what forme Gerard Therle, of Kildare, depute unto his Lieutenant, fhall be demeaned in the peerceifing of his office of the faid depute, within his land of Irland.

Furft, The feid Erl fhall wel and trewly ferve the Kyng as depute to his Lieutenant of Irland, in all and every thing comprifed in his commiffion.

Item,

Item, He shall to the uttermost of his power, defend the Kyng's lands and his subjects within the said land, against the Kyng's rebells and Irish ennemyes.

Item, He shall not assent to the hurt, damage, or alienacion of the Kyng's lands, revenues, or rights within that land, but to the best of his power, avance and encres them, and hold all those that wold attempt to do the contrary.

Item, He shall not pardon thentre of any of the Kyng's tennants upon the Kyng's possession, nor yet graunt to deny them licence without a reasonable fyne.

Item, He shall graunt no pardon to any man upon his provision purchased or to be purchased from the court of Rome, ne therof he shall addresse no warrant unto the Chaunseler, without the Kyng's knowleche and assent.

Item, He shall favor, aide and assiste all the Kyng's officers within the same land, in the doing of their offices, and resist all therein that would maliciously attempt agens them for the doying of the saime.

Item, He shall effectuayly endevour himself, that Sir Rouland Eustace deliver unto the Bishop of Methe, whom the Kyng hath deputed to be his Chaunseler of the same land, the Kyng's grete sele.

Item, In neo parliament to be holdyn hereafter ther shall no subsidie be axed, ne graunted in the same upon the commounes ne levied but once in a yere, which shall not excede the extent of 1200 marks, as hath been accustumed.

Item, That noo thing that is or shall be commowned and concluded in Counsele, be taken in strenth as an act of Counsele, unless the Kyng's Lieutenant or his depute give his assent thereunto, by the advis of the more part of the Kyng's Counsele there, that is to say, the Chanselor, the Treforer, the Kyng's Chief Justys, the Chief Baron of the Kyng's Eschequer, the Clerc of the Rolls, the Kyng's Serjant.

Item, The Kyng will also, that the Maister of the Mint, work his cuniage oonly in the Castle of Divelin.

Item, That in the same cuinage touching the fynesse, it be according to the standart of England, and that an unce of sillver of that fynesse be coyned 4s. 8d. whereof to the merchant 4s. 2d. to the Kyng, the Maister of the Mynt, for hym, the odyr officers, and the Coyners 6d.

Item, That all and every of the peces to be coyned, ber a notable difference on eyther side; on the cross side a rose, and upon the pile side, a notable difference of the Kyng easy to be known to every body, accordyng to suche prints as ben delivered unto the Maister of the Mynt here.

* Such parliaments as have been held in Ireland, and such acts as have been made in them fince that year in the reigns of King Henry VI. Edward IV. Henry VII. VIII. Philip and Mary, Queen Elizabeth, and King James, and what elfe concerns the parliament of Ireland, their fummons, members privileges, jurifdictions, proceeding, acts and fettling of the Englifh laws, government, ftatutes in that realm, you may perufe at leifure in the ftatutes of Ireland, publifhed by Mr. Richard Bolton, Dublin, 1621, efpecially 25 Henry VI. c. 28, An act that the Lords of parliament in pleas fhall not be amerfed, otherwife than other perfons; 3 Edward IV. c. 5. An act whereby the Lords and Commons of parliament fhall have privilege for forty days before and after the parliament; 15 Edward IV. c. 2. An act concerning the chufing of knights and burgeffes of parliament; 10 Henry VII. c. 4. That no parliament be holden in this land, until the acts be certified into England; c. 16. An act declaring the effect of Poyning's act; 33 Henry VIII. c. 1. An act declaring how Poyning's act fhall be expounded; 4 Philip and Mary, An act authorifing ftatutes to be made in this parliament notwithftanding Poyning's act; 11 Elizabeth, feffi. 2. An act that there be no bill certified into England, for the repeal or fufpenfion of Poyning's act, before the fame be firft argued upon in a feffion of parliament holden in this realm.

Prefuming that the foregoing references relative to Poyning's act will be perufed, I fhall adjoin what Hume fays on this fubject.

The King's (Henry VII.) authority appeared equally prevalent and uncontroulable in Ireland; Sir Edward Poyning had been fent over with fome troops into that country, with an intention of quelling the partizans of the houfe of York, and of reducing the natives to fubjection : he was not fupported with forces fufficient for that important enterprife. The Irifh, by flying into their woods, moraffes, and mountains, in fome meafure eluded his efforts : but Poyning fummoned a parliament at Dublin, where he was more fuccefsful. He paffed that memorable ftatute, which ftill bears his name, and which eftablifhes the authority of the Englifh government in Ireland. By this ftatute all the former laws of England, were made to be of force in Ireland; and no bill can be introduced into the Irifh parliament, unlefs it previoufly receives the fanction of the council of England. This latter law feems calculated for enfuring the dominion of the Englifh over Ireland ; but was really granted at the defire of the Irifh commons, who propofed, by that means, to fecure themfelves from the tyranny of the Lords, particularly of fuch Lieutenants as were of Irifh birth †.

* Pryn, 4. inft.   † Sir J. Davies.

I come now to confider our Commercial Reſtrictions, which I find already ſo happily enumerated, in a work intitled " The Commercial Reſtraints of Ireland confidered, in a feries of letters to a noble lord," that I ſhall take the freedom with the judicious writer of giving his firſt letter entire, and the facts, &c. chiefly of the reſt.

FIRST LETTER.

MY LORD,

Dublin, 20th Aug. 1779.

YOU defire my thoughts on the affairs of Ireland; a ſubject little confidered, and confequently not underſtood in England. The Lords and Commons of Great Britain have addreſſed his Majeſty to take the diſtreſſed and impoveriſhed ſtate of this country into confideration; have called for information, and refolved to purſue effectual methods for promoting the common ſtrength, wealth and commerce of both kingdoms; and his Majeſty has been pleaſed to exprefs, in his ſpeech from the throne, his entire approbation of their attention to the preſent ſtate of Ireland.

The occaſion calls for the affiſtance of every friend to the Britiſh empire: thoſe who can give material information are bound to communicate it. The attempt however is full of difficulty; it will require more than ordinary caution to write with ſuch moderation as not to offend the prejudices of one country, and with ſuch freedom as not to wound the feelings of the other.

The preſent ſtate of Ireland teems with every circumſtance of national poverty. Whatever the land produces is greatly reduced in its value: wool is fallen one half in its uſual price; wheat one third; black cattle of all kinds in the ſame proportion, and hides in a much greater: buyers are not had without difficulty at thoſe low rates, and from the principal fairs men commonly return with the commodities they brought there: rents are every where reduced, in many places it is impoſſible to collect them: the farmers are all diſtreſſed, and many of them have failed: when leafes expire, tenants are not eaſily found: the landlord is often obliged to take his lands into his own hands, for want of bidders at reaſonable rents, and finds his eſtate fallen one fourth in its

f   value.

value. The merchant juftly complains that all bufinefs is at a ftand, that he cannot difcount his bills, and that neither money nor paper circulates. In this and the laft year, above twenty thoufand manufacturers, in this metropolis were reduced to beggary for want of employment; they were for a confiderable length of time fupported by alms; a part of the contribution came from England, and this affiftance was much wanting from the general diftrefs of all ranks of people in this country. Public and private credit are annihilated : parliament, that always raifes money in Ireland on eafy terms, when there is any to be borrowed in the country, in 1778 gave 7½l. per cent. in annuities, which in 1773 and 1775 were earneftly fought after at 6l. then thought to be a very high rate. The expences of a country, nearly bankrupt, muft be inconfiderable; almoft every branch of the revenue has fallen; and the receipts in the treafury for the two years, ending lady-day, 1779, were lefs than thofe for the two years, ending lady-day, 1777, deducting the fums received on account of loans in each period, in a fum of 334,900l. 18s. 9½d: there was due on the 25th of March laft, on the eftablifhments, and for extraordinary expences, an arrear amounting to 373,706l. 13s. 6½d. : a fum of 600,000l. will probably be now wanting, to fupply the deficiencies on the eftablifhments and extraordinary charges of government: and an annual fum of between 50 and 60,000l. yearly, to pay intereft and annuities : in the laft feffion 466,000l. was borrowed.; if the fum wanting could now be raifed, the debt would be increafed in a fum of above 1,000,000l. in lefs than three years, and if the expences and the revenues fhould continue the fame as in the laft two years, there is a probability of an annual deficiency of 300,000l. The nation in the laft two years has not been able to pay for its own defence; a militia law, paffed in the laft feffion, could not be carried into execution for want of money. Inftead of having forces abroad *, Ireland has not been able in this year to pay the forces kept in the kingdom : it has again relapfed into its ancient ftate of imbecility, and Great Britain has been lately obliged to fend over money to pay the army †, which defends this impoverifhed country.

---

* On account of the inability of Ireland, Great Britain fince Chriftmafs, 1778, relieved her from the burthen of paying forces abroad.

† A fum of 50,000l. has been lately fent from England for that purpofe.

Our

Our diftrefs and poverty are of the utmoft notoriety; the proof does not depend folely upon calculation or eftimate, it is palpable in every public and private tranfaction, and is deeply felt among all orders of our people.

This kingdom has been long declining. The annual deficiency of its revenues, for the payment of public expences, has been, for many years, fupplied by borrowing. The American rebellion, which confiderably diminifhed the demand for our linens; an embargo on provifions continued for three years *, and highly injurious to our victualing trade; the increafing drain of remittances to England for rents, falaries, profits of offices, penfions and intereft, and for the payment of forces abroad, have made the decline more rapid, but have not occafioned it.

If we determine to inveftigate the truth, we muft affign a more radical caufe: when the human or political body is unfound or infirm, it is in vain to inquire what accidental circumftances appear to have occafioned thofe maladies which arife from the conftitution itfelf.

If in a period of fourfcore years of profound internal peace, any country fhall appear to have often experienced the extremes of poverty and diftrefs; if at the times of her greateft fuppofed affluence and profperity, the flighteft caufes have been fufficient to obftruct her progrefs, to annihilate her credit, and to fpread dejection and difmay among all ranks of her people; and if fuch a country is bleffed with a temperate climate and fruitful foil, abounds with excellent harbours and great rivers, with the neceffaries of life and materials of manufacture, and is inhabited by a race of men, brave, active, and intelligent, fome permanent caufe of fuch difaftrous effects muft be fought for.

If your veffel is frequently in danger of foundering in the midft of a calm; if by the fmalleft addition of fail fhe is near overfetting, let the gale be ever fo fteady, you would neither reproach the crew, nor accufe the pilot or the mafter; you would look to the conftruction of the veffel, and fee how fhe had been originally framed, and whether any new

---

* By a proclamation, dated the 3d of February, 1776, on all fhips and veffels, laden in any of the ports in this kingdom, with provifions of any kind, but not to extend to fhips carrying falted beef, pork, butter and bacon into Great Britain, or provifions to any part of the Britifh Empire, except the colonies mentioned in the faid proclamation. 4th of January, 1779, taken off as far as it relates to fhips carrying provifions to any of the ports of Europe.

works

works had been added to her, that retard or endanger her course.

But for such an examination more time and attention are neceffary than have been ufually beftowed upon this fubject in Great Britain; and as I have now the honour to addrefs a perfon of rank and ftation in that kingdom on the affairs of Ireland, I fhould be brief in my firft audience, or I may happen never to obtain the favour of a fecond.

I have the honour to be, my lord, &c.

SECOND LETTER.

MY LORD,

Dublin, 23d Auguſt, 1779.

FROM the time that king James the firſt had eſtabliſhed a regular adminiſtration of juſtice in every part of the kingdom, until the rebellion of 1641, which takes in a period of between thirty and forty years, the growth of Ireland was conſiderable *. In the act recognizing the title of king James, the Lords and Commons acknowledge " that many bleffings " and benefits had, within thefe few years paſt, been poured " upon this realm † ;" and at the end of the parliament in 1615, the commons return thanks for the extraordinary pains taken for the good of this republic, whereby they fay " we " all of us fit under our own vines, and the whole realm " reapeth the happy fruits of peace ‡." In his reign the little that could be given by the people, was given with general confent §: and received with extraordinary marks of royal favour ; he defires the lord-deputy to return them thanks for their fubfidy, and for their granting it with univerfal confent ‖ ; and to affure them that he holds his fubjects of that kingdom in equal favour with thofe of his other kingdoms ; and that he will be as careful to provide for their profperous and flouriſhing ſtate, as for his own perfon.

---

* Its tranquility was fo well eſtabliſhed in 1611, that king James reduced his army in Ireland to 176 horfe, 1450 foot. Additional judges were appointed; circuits eſtabliſhed throughout the kingdom, 2d Cox, 17 ; and Sir John Davis obferves, that no nation under the fun loves equal and indifferent juſtice better than the Iriſh. Davis, p. 184, 196.

† 13 Jac. ch. i.   ‡ Vol. Com. Journ. p. 92.
§ Ib. 61.   ‖ Ib. p. 88.

Davis mentions the prosperous state of the country, and that the revenue of the crown, both certain and casual, had been raised to a double proportion.   He takes notice how this was effected, " by the encouragement given to the maratime " towns and cities, as well to increase the trade of merchan- " dize, as to cherish mechanical arts;" and mentions the consequence, " that the strings of the Irish harps were all " in tune."

In the succeeding reign, Ireland for fourteen or fifteen years appears to have greatly advanced in prosperity.   The commons granted in the session of 1634, six entire subsidies, which they agreed should amount in the collection to 250,000l. * ; and the free gifts previously given to king Charles the first, at different times, amounted to 310,000l.† ; in the session of 1630, they gave four entire subsidies, and the clergy eight ; the customs which had been framed at 500l. yearly, in the beginning of this reign, were in the pro- gress of it set for 54,000l

The commodities exported were twice as much in value, as the foreign merchandize imported, and shipping is said to have increased an hundred fold §.   Their parliament was en- couraged to frame laws conducive to the happiness and pros- perity of themselves and their posterities, for the enacting and " consummating" whereof the king passes his royal word ; and assures his subjects of Ireland that they were equally of as much respect and dearness to him as any others‡.

In the speaker's speech in 1639, enumerating the national blessings, he mentions as one, "that our in-gates and out-gates do stand open for trade and traffic**" and as the lord chancel- lor declared his excellency's " high liking of this oration," it may be considered as a fair account of the condition of Ireland at that time.   When the commons had afterwards caught the infection of the times, and were little disposed to pay compliments, they acknowledge, that this kingdom, when the earl of Stratford obtained the government, " was " in a flourishing, wealthy and happy estate ††.

After the restoration, from the time that the acts of set- tlement and explanation had been fully carried into execu-

* Cox's Hist· of Ireland, 2 Vol. 61.
‡ †. Some of these subsidies, from the subsequent times of confusion, were not raised.
§ Lord Stafford's Letters, 2d Vol. p. 297.
‡ Leland's Hist, of Ireland, 3d Vol. 41.
** Ir. Com. Jour. 1st Vol. p. 228, 229.
†† Lord Clarendon.   Cox, ib.   Ir. Com. Journ. 1 Vol. p. 280, 31:.

tion, to the year 1688, Ireland made great advances, and
continued, for several years, in a moft profperous condition*.
Lands were every where improved; rents were doubled; the
kingdom abounded with money; trade flourifhed to the envy
of our neighbours; cities encreafed exceedingly; many places
of the kingdom equalled the improvements of England; the
king's revenue increafed proportionably to the advance of
the kingdom, which was every day growing, and was *well
eftablifhed in plenty and wealth* †; manufactures were fet on foot
in divers parts; the meaneft inhabitants were at once en-
riched and civilized: and this kingdom is then reprefented to
be the moft improved and improving fpot of ground
in Europe. I repeat the words of perfons of high rank,
great character and fuperior knowledge, who could not be
deceived themfelves, and were incapable of deceiving others.

James, the firft duke of Ormond, whofe memory fhould be
ever revered by every friend of Ireland, to heal the wound
that this country had received by the prohibition of the export of her cattle to England, obtained from Charles the Se-
a letter ‡, dated, the 23d of March, 1667, by which he directed that all reftraints upon the exportation of commodities,
of the growth or manufacture of Ireland, to foreign parts,
fhould be taken off, but not to interfere with the plantation
laws, or the charters to the trading companies, and that this
fhould be notified to his fubjects of this kingdom; which was
accordingly done by a proclamation from the lord lieutenant
and council; and at the fame time by his majefty's permiffion, they prohibited the importation from Scotland of linen,
woollen, and other manufactures and commodities, as drawing
large fums of money out of Ireland, and a great hindrance
to its manufactures. His grace fuccefsfully executed his
fcheme of national improvement, having by his own conftant
attention, the exertion of his extenfive influence, and the
moft princely munificence, greatly advanced the woollen, and

---

* Archbifhop King, In his ftate of the proteftants of Ireland, p. 52,
53, 445, 446. Lord Chief Juftice Keating's addrefs to James the Second, and his letter to Sir John Temple, ib.
The prohibition of the exportation of our cattle to England, though a
great, was but a temporary diftrefs; and in its confequences greatly promoted the general welfare of this country.

† Lord Sydney's words in his fpeech from the throne, in 1692, from
his own former knowledge of this country. Ir. Com. Journ. 2d Vol. p.
577.

‡ Carte, 2 Vol. p. 342, 344.

revived

revived * the linen manufactures, which England then encouraged in this kingdom, as a compenſation for the loſs of
that trade of which ſhe had been deprived; this encouragement, from that time to the revolution, had greatly increaſed
the wealth, and promoted the improvement of Ireland.

The tyranny and perſecuting policy of James the ſecond †
after his arrival in Ireland, ruined its trade and revenue; the
many great oppreſſions which the people ſuffered during the
revolution had occaſioned almoſt the *utter deſolation* of the
country. § But the nation muſt have been reſtored in the
reign of William to a conſiderable degree of ſtrength and
vigour: their exertions in raiſing ſupplies to a great amount,
from the year 1692 to the year 1698, are ſome proof of it.
They taxed their goods, their lands, their perſons, in ſupport
of a prince whom they juſtly called their deliverer and de-
fender, and of a government on which their own preſerva-
tion depended. Thoſe ſums were granted ‖, not only without
murmur, but with the utmoſt chearfulneſs, and without any
complaint of the inability, or repreſentation of the diſtreſſed
ſtate of the country.

The money brought in for the army at the revolution, gave
life to all buſineſs, and much ſooner than could have been expected retrieved the affairs of Ireland. This money furniſhed capitals for carrying on the manufactures of this kingdom. Our
exports increaſed in 96, 97 and 98, and our imports did not
riſe in proportion, which occaſioned a great balance in our
favour; and this increaſe was owing principally to the woollen manufacture. In the laſt of thoſe years the ballance in favour of Ireland in the accounts of exports and imports was
419,442l. **.

But in the latter end of this reign a law was made in England,
reſtraining, in fact prohibiting the exportation of all woollen
manufactures from Ireland. From the time of this prohibition no parliament was held in Ireland until the year 1703.
Five years were ſuffered to paſs before any opportunity was

* Lord Strafford laid the foundation of the linen manufacture in Ireland, but the troubles which ſoon after broke out had entirely ſtopped
the progreſs of it.
 † Harris : life of K. W. 116.
 § The Words of Lord Sydney, in his ſpeech from the throne in
1692. Com. Jour. 2 Vol 576.
 ‖ Ir. Com. Jour. 3 Vol. 45 and 65, that great ſupplies were given
during this period.
 ** Dobbs, p. 5, 6, 7, 19.

given

given to apply a remedy to the many evils which such a prohi‑
bition must necessarily have occasioned. The linen trade was
then not thoroughlyestablished in Ireland ; the woollen manu‑
facture was the staple trade, and wool the principal material
of that kingdom. The consequences of this prohibition ap‑
peared in the session of 1703 *.

In an addrefs to the queen †, laid before the duke of Or‑
mond, then lord lieutenant, by the house with its speaker,
they mention the distressed condition of that kingdom, and
more especially of the industrious proteftants, by the almost
total lofs of trade and decay of their manufactures, and to
preferve the country from utter ruin, apply for liberty
to export their linen manufactures to the plantations.

In a subsequent part of this session ‡, the commons resolve,
that by reafon of the great decay of trade and discouragement
of the manufactures of this kingdom, many poor tradefmen
were reduced to extreme want and beggary. This refolution
was nem. con. and the speaker, Mr. Broderick, then his ma‑
jefty's folicitor general, and afterwards lord chancellor, in
his speech at the end of the session §, informs the lord lieute‑
nant, that the reprefentation of the commons was, as to the
matters contained in it, the unanimous voice and confent of a
very full house, and that the foft and gentle terms used by the
commons in laying the distressed condition of the kingdom
before his majefty, shewed that their complaints proceeded
not from queruloufnefs but from a necessity of feeking redrefs ;
he adds, " it is to be hoped they may be allowed fuch a por‑
" tion of trade, that they may recover from the great poverty
" they now lie under ;" and in presenting the bill of fupply
fays, the commons have granted it " in time of extreme po‑
" verty." The impoverished state of Ireland, at that time,
appears in the speech from the throne at the conclufion of the
session, in which it is mentioned that the commons could not
then provide for what was owing to the civil and military
lifts **.

The fupply given for two years, commenced at Michaelmas
1703 ††, was a fum not exceeding 150,000l. which, confider‑
ing that no parliament was held in Ireland fince the year
1698, is at the rate of 30,000l. yearly, commencing in 1699,
and ending in the year 1705.

---

* Com. Jour. 3 Vol. 45.   § Ib. 207, 208.
† Com. Jour. 3 Vol. p. 149.   ** Ib. p. 210.
‡ Ir. Com. Jour. 3 Vol. p. 195.   †† Ib. 79, 94.

The

The great diſtreſs of Ireland, from the year 1699, to the year 1703, and the cauſe of that diſtreſs, cannot be doubted.

Let it now be conſidered, whether the ſame cauſe has operated ſince the year 1703. In the year 1704 * it appears, that the commons were not able, from the circumſtances of the nation at that time, to make proviſion for repairing the neceſſary fortifications; or for arms and amunition for the public ſafety: and the difficulties which the kingdom then laboured under, and the decay of trade, appear by the addreſſes of the commons † to the queen, and to the duke of Ormond, then lord lieutenant, who was well acquainted with the ſtate of this country; by the queen's anſwer ‡, and the addreſs of thanks for it.

In the year 1707 §, the revenue was deficient for payment of the army, and defraying the charges of government; and the commons promiſed to ſupply the deficiency " as far as " the preſent circumſtances of the nation will allow."

In 1709, it appears ** by the unanimous addreſs of the commons to the lord lieutenant, that the kingdom was in an impoveriſhed and exhauſted ſtate: in 1711 ††, in their addreſs to the lord lieutenant, at the cloſe of the ſeſſion, they requeſt, that he ſhould preſent to her majeſty, that they had given all the ſupplies which her majeſty deſired, and which they, in their preſent condition, were able to grant ‡‡: and yet theſe ſupplies amounted, for two years, to a ſum not exceeding 167,023l. 8s. 5d §§; though powder magazines, the council chamber, the treaſury office, and other offices were then to be built.

This laſt period, from the year 1699 to the death of queen Anne, is marked with the ſtrongeſt circumſtances of national diſtreſs and deſpondency.

That the woollen manufactures were the great ſource of induſtry in Ireland, appears from the Iriſh ſtatute of the 17th and 18th of Charles II. ch. 15 ***; from the reſolutions of the commons in 1695 †††, for regulating thoſe manufactures; the reſolutions of the committee of ſupply in that ſeſſion ‡‡‡;

---

* Com. Jour. 3 Vol. p. 298.   † Ib. 225, 266.
‡ Ib. 253, 258.   § Ib. 364, 368, 369.
** Ib. 3 Vol. p. 573.   †† Ib. 827.
‡‡ Ib. 929.   §§ Ib. 876.
*** In the ſame ſeſſion an act was made for the advancement of the linen manufacture, which ſhews that both kingdoms then thought (for theſe laws came to us through England) that each of theſe manufactures was to be encouraged in Ireland.
††† Ir. Com. Jour. 2 Vol. p. 725.   ‡‡‡ Ib. 733.

and

and from the preamble to the Englifh ftatute of the 10th and 11th of William III. ch. 10, in which it is recited, that great quantities of thofe manufactures were made, and were daily increafing in Ireland, and were exported from thence to foreign markets.

Of the exportation of all thofe manufactures the Irifh were at once totally deprived : the linen manufacture, propofed as a fubftitute, muft have required the attention of many years before it could be thoroughly eftablifhed. What muft have been the confequences to Ireland in the mean time, the journals of the commons in queen Anne's reign have informed us. Compare this period with the three former, and you will prove this melancholy truth ; that a country will fooner recover from the miferies and devaftation occafioned by war, invafion, rebellion, maffacre, than from laws reftraining the commerce, difcouraging the manufactures, fettering the induftry, and above all, breaking the fpirits of the people.

T H I R D   L E T T E R.

To an inquirer after truth, hiftory fince the year 1699 furnifhes very imperfect, and often partial views of the affairs of Great Britain and Ireland. The journals of parliament evince the poverty of Ireland for the firft fourteen years of this century. That this poverty continued in the year 1716, appears by the unanimous addrefs of the houfe of commons to George the firft*. A fmall debt of 16,106l. 11s. 0½d. †, due at Michaelmas 1715, was, by their exertions to ftrengthen the hands of government in that year, increafed at midfummer 1717, to a fum of 91,537l. 17s. 1d. ‡, which was confidered as fuch an augmentation of the national debt, that the lord lieutenant, the duke of Bolton, thought it neceffary to take notice in his fpeech from the throne, that the debt was confiderably augmented, and to declare at the fame time that his majefty had ordered reductions in the military, and had thought proper to leffen the civil lift.

In 1721, the fpeech from the throne §, and the addreffes to the king and to the lord lieutenant, ftate, in the ftrongeft

* Com. Jour. 4 Vol. p. 249,   † Ib. 296.
‡ Ib. 335.   § Ib. 694, 700, 701.

terms,

terms, the great decay of her trade, and the very low and impoverished state to which she was reduced.

It is a melancholy proof of the desponding state of this kingdom, that no law whatever was then proposed for encouraging trade or manufactures, unless that for amending the laws as to butter and tallow casks deserves to be so called. The remedy proposed by government, and partly executed, by directing a commission under the great seal for receiving voluntary subscriptions *, in order to establish a bank, was a scheme to circulate paper without money; and considering that it came so soon after the south sea bubble had burst, it is more surprising that it should have been at first applauded †, than that it was in the same session disliked, censured and abandoned ‡. The total inefficacy of the remedy proved however the inveteracy of the disease, and furnishes a farther proof of the desparate situation of Ireland, when nothing could be thought of for its relief, but that paper should circulate without money, trade or manufactures.

In the following session of 1727, our manufacturers, and the lowest classes of our people, were greatly distressed; the duke of Grafton, in his speech from the throne, particularly recommends to their consideration the finding out of some method for the better employing of the poor §; and though the debt of the nation was no more than 66,318l. 8s. 3½d. ‖ and was less than in the last session; yet the commons thought it necessary to present an address to the king, to give such directions as he, in his great goodness should think proper, to prevent the increase of the debt of the nation. This address was presented ** by the house, with its speaker, and passed nem. con. and was occasioned by the distressed state of the country, and by their apprehensions that it might be further exhausted by the project of Woods's half-pence.

But notwithstanding the success of the linen manufacture, Ireland was in a most miserable condition. The great scarcity of corn had been so universal in this kingdom in the years 1728 and 1729, as to expose thousands of families to the utmost necessities, and even to the danger of famine; many artificers and house-keepers having been obliged to beg for bread in the streets of Dublin. It appeared before the house of commons, that the import of corn for one year and six months, ending the 29th day of September, 1729, amounted

* Ir. Com. Jour. 4 Vol. p. 694.   † Ib. 720.
‡ Ib. 832.   § Ib. 5 vol. p. 12.
** Ib. 108.   ‖ Ib. 102.

in value to the fum of 274,000l. an amazing fum compared with the circumftances of the kingdom at that time! and the commons refolve that public granaries would greatly contribute to the increafing of tillage, and providing againft fuch wants as have frequently befallen the people of this kingdom, and hereafter may befal them, unlefs proper precautions fhall be taken againft fo great a calamity.

The great fcarcity which happened in the years 28 and 29, and frequently before and fince, is a decifive proof that the diftreffes of this kingdom have been occafioned by the difcouragement of manufactures.

In the year 1731 there was a great deficiency in the public revenue, and the national debt had confiderably increafed. The exhaufted kingdom lay under great difficulties by the decay of trade, the fcarcity of money, and the univerfal poverty of the country, which the fpeaker reprefents * in very affecting terms, in offering the money-bills for the royal affent, and adds, " that the commons hope from his majefty's " goodnefs, and his grace's free and impartial reprefentation " of the ftate and condition of this kingdom, that they may " enjoy a fhare of the bleffings of public tranquillity, by " the increafe of their trade, and the encouragement of their " manufactures."

But in the next feffion, of 1733, they are told in the fpeech from the throne what this fhare was to be. The lord lieutenant informs them, that the peace cannot fail of contributing to their welfare, by enabling them to improve thofe branches of trade and manufactures † which are properly their own, meaning the trade and manufacture of linen. Whether this idea of property has been preferved inviolate, will hereafter appear.

The years 40 and 41 were feafons of great fcarcity, and in confequence of the want of wholefome provifions, great numbers of our people perifhed miferably; and the fpeech from the throne recommends it to both houfes, to confider of proper meafures to prevent the like calamity for the future. The employment of the poor and the encouragement of tillage, are the remedies propofed by the lord lieutenant, and approved of by the commons; but no laws for thofe purpofes were introduced.

* Ir. Com. Jour. 6 Vol. p. 143.   † Ib. 189.

For

For above forty years after making those reftrictive laws *
Ireland was always poor, and often in great want, diftrefs
and mifery †, tho' the linen manufacture had made great progrefs during that time.   In the war before the laft, fhe was
not able to give any affiftance.   The duke of Devonfhire, in
the year 1741, takes notice from the throne, that during a
war for the protection of the trade of all his majefty's dominions, there had been no increafe of the charge of the eftablifhment ; and in the year 1745 the country was fo little able
to bear expence, that lord Chefterfield difcouraged and prevented any augmentation of the army, tho' much defired by
many gentlemen of the houfe of commons, from a fenfe of
the great danger that then impended.   An influx of money
after the peace, and the further fuccefs of the linen trade, encreafed our wealth, and enabled us to reduce by degrees,
and afterwards to difcharge the national debt.   This was not
effected until the firft of March 1754.   This debt was occafioned principally by the expences incurred by the rebellion
in Great Britain in the year 1715 ; an unlimited vote of credit was then given ‡.   From the lownefs of the revenue, and
the want of refources, not from any further exertions on the
part of the kingdom in point of expence, the debt of 16,106l.
11s. 0½d. due in 1715, was encreafed at Lady Day, 1733,
to 371,312l. 12s. 2½d.

After the payment of this debt, the wealth and ability of
Ireland were greatly over-rated, both here and in Great Britain.

A large redundency of money in the treafury, gave a de-
lufive appearance of national wealth.   At Lady Day, 1755,
the fum in credid to the nation was 471,404l. 5s. 6½d§, and the
money remaining in the treafury of the ordinary unappro-
priated revenue on the 29th day of September, 1755,
457,959l. 12s. 7½d.   But this great increafe of revenue arofe
from an increafe of imports, particularly in the year 1754,
by which the kingdom was greatly overftocked, and which
raifed the revenue in that year 208,309l. 19s. 2d. higher
than it was in the year 1748, when the revenue firft began
to rife confiderably ‖ ; and though what a nation fpends is
one method of eftimating its wealth ; yet, a nation, like an

* The act intitled an act for better regulation of partnerfhips, and to
encourage the trade and manufactures of this kingdom, has not a word
relative to the latter part of the title.
† Com. Jour. 6 Vol. 694; 7 Vol. 742.   ‡ Ib. 4 Vol. p. 195.
§ 9 Vol. p. 35.   ‖ Ib. 10 Vol. p. 751.
individual,

individual, may live beyond its means, and fpend on credit which may far exceed its income. This was the fact as to Ireland in the year 1754, for fome years before and for many years after; it appeared in an enquiry before the houfe of commons in the feffion of 1755, that many perfons had circulated paper to a very great amount, far exceeding not only their own capitals*, but that juft proportion which the quantity of paper ought to bear to the national fpecie. This gave credit to many individuals, who without property became merchant importers, and at the fame time increafed the receipts of the treafury and leffened the wealth of the kingdom. At the very time that fo great a balance was in the treafury, public credit was in a very low way, and the houfe of commons was employed in preparing a law to reftore it. In 54 and 55 three principal banks † had failed, and the legiflature took up much time in enquiring into their affairs, and in framing laws for the relief of their creditors.

LETTER IV.

THE revenue, for the reafons already given, decreafed in 1755, fell lower in 1756, and ftill lower in 57. In the laft year the vaunted profperity of Ireland was changed into mifery and diftrefs; the lower claffes of our people wanted food‡; the money arifing from the extravagance of the rich was freely applied to alleviate the fufferings of the poor. One of the firft fteps of the late duke of Bedford's adminiftration, and which reflects honour on his memory, was obtaining a king's letter, dated 31ft March, 1757, for 20,000l. to be laid out as his grace fhould think the moft likely to afford the moft fpeedy and effectual relief to his majefty's poor fubjects of this kingdom. His grace, in his fpeech from the throne, humanely expreffes his wifh, that fome method might be found out to prevent the calamities that are the confequences of a want of corn, which had been in part felt the laft year, and to which this country had been too often expofed; the commons acknowledge that thofe calamities had

* Com. Jour. 9 Vol. p. 818.
† March 6, 1754, Thomas Dillon, and Richard Ferral, failed. 3d March, 1755, William Lennox and George French. Same day John Wilcocks and John Dawfon.
‡ Com. Jour. 10 Vol. p. 16. Speech from the throne, and ib. 25, addrefs from the houfe of commons to the king.

been

been frequently, and were too fenfibly and fatally experienced in the courfe of the laft year; thank his grace for his early and charitable attention to the neceffities of the poor of this country in their late diftreffes, and make ufe of thofe remarkable expreffions, "that they will moft chearfully embrace * every *practicable* method to promote tillage †." They knew that the encouragement of manufactures were the effectual means, and that thefe means were not in their power.

The ability of the nation was eftimated by the money in the treafury, and the penfions on the civil eftablifhment, exclufive of French, which at Lady-day, 1755, were 38,003l. 15s. od. amounted at Lady-day, 57, to 49,293l. 15s. od ‡.

The fame ideas were entertained of the refources of this country in the feffion of 1759. Great Britain had made extraordinary efforts, and engaged in enormous expences for the protection of the whole empire. This country was in immediate danger of an invafion. Every Irifhman was agreed that fhe fhould affift Great Britain to the utmoft of her ability, but this ability was too highly eftimated. The nation abounded rather in loyalty than in wealth §. Our brethren in Great Britain had, however, formed a different opinion, and furveying their own ftrength, were imcompleat judges of our weaknefs. A lord lieutenant of too much virtue and magnanimity to fpeak what he did not think, takes notice from the throne, " of the profperous ftate of this country, " improving daily in its manufactures and commerce ‖." His grace had done much to bring it to that ftate, by obtaining for us fome of the beft laws * * in our books of ftatutes. But this part of the fpeech was not taken notice of, either in the addrefs to his majefty, or to his grace, from a houfe of commons well-difpofed to give every mark of duty and refpect, and to pay every compliment confifting with truth. The event proved the wifdom of their referve. The public expences were greatly increafed, the penfions on the civil eftablifhment, exclufive of French, at Lady-day, 1759, amounted

* Com. Jour. 10 Vol. 25.
† They brought in a law for the encouragement of tillage, which was ineffectual (fee poft 42) but the preamble of that act is a legiflative proof of the unhappy condition of the poor of this country before that time. The preamble recites, " the extreme neceffity to which the poor of this " kingdom had been too frequently reduced for want of provifions. "
‡ Com. Jour. 10 Vol. 285.
§ 11 Vol. 472, Speaker's fpeech.   ‖ Ib. 16.
** The acts paffed in 58, giving bounties on the land-carriage of corn, and on coals brought to Dublin.

to 55,497l. 5s. 0d. * there was at the fame time a great augmentation of military expence †. Six new regiments and a
troop were raifed in a very fhort fpace of time. An unanimous and unlimited addrefs of confidence to his grace ‡, a
fpecific vote of credit for 150,000l. ‖, which was afterwards
provided for in the loan-bill § of that feffion ; a fecond vote of
credit in the fame feffion for 300,000l. **, the raifing the rate
of intereft paid by government, one per cent. and the payment out of the treafury †† in little more than one year, of
703,957l. 3s. 1½d. ‡‡ were the confequences of thofe encreafed
expences. The effects of thefe exertions were immediately and
feverely felt by the kingdom. Thefe loans could not be fupplied by a poor country, without draining the bankers of their
cafh; three of the principal houfes §§ among them ftopped
payment; the three remaining banks in Dublin difcounted no
paper, and in fact, did no bufinefs. Public and private credit,
that had been drooping fince the year 1754, had now fallen
proftrate. At a general meeting of the merchants of Dublin,
in April 1760, with feveral members of the houfe of commons, the inability of the former to carry on bufinefs was univerfally acknowledged, not from the want of capital, but from
the ftoppage of all paper circulation, and the refufal of the remaining bankers to difcount the bills even of the firft houfes.
The merchants and traders of Dublin, in their petition ‖‖ to
the houfe of commons, reprefent " the low ftate to which
" public and private credit had been of late reduced in this
" kingdom, and particularly in this city, of which the fuc-
" ceffive failures of fo many banks, and of private traders in
" different parts of this kingdom, in fo fhort a time as fince
" October laft, were inconteftable proofs. The petitioners,
" fenfible that the neceffary confequences of thefe misfortunes
" muft be the lofs of foreign trade, the diminution of his ma-
" jefty's revenue, and what is ftill more fatal, the decay of
" the manufactures of this kingdom, have in vain repeatedly
" attempted to fupport the finking credit of the nation by af-
" fociations and otherwife ; and are fatisfied that no refource
" is now left but what may be expected from the wifdom of
" parliament, to avert the calamities with which this king-
" dom is at prefent threatened."

* Com. Jour. 11 Vol. p. 212.   † Ib. from 826, to 837.
‡ Ib. p. 141.   ‖ Ib. 408.   § Ib. 473.
** Ib. 862.   †† Ib.   ‡‡ Ib. 982, from 25th of March 59, to 21ft
of April 60, exclufive.
§§ Clements's, Dawfon's, and Mitchell's.
‖‖ Com. Jour. 11 Vol. 966. April 15. 1760.
The

The committee, to whom it was referred, refolve * that they had proved the feveral matters alledged in their petition ; that the quantity of paper circulating was not near fufficient for fupporting the trade and manufactures of this kingdom ; and that the houfe fhould engage, to the firft of May 62, for each of the then fubfifting banks in Dublin, to the amount of 50,000l. for each bank ; and that an addrefs fhould be prefented to the lord lieutenant, to thank his grace for having given directions, that bankers notes fhould be received as cafh from the feveral fubfcribers to the loan ; and that he would be pleafed to give directions, that their notes fhould be taken as cafh in all payments at the treafury, and by the feveral collectors for the city and county of Dublin. The houfe agreed to thofe refolutions, and to that for giving credit to the banks, nem. con.

The fpeech from the throne takes notice of the care the houfe of commons had taken for eftablifhing public credit, which the lord lieutenant fays, he flatters himfelf will anfwer the end propofed, and effect that circulation fo neceffary for carrying on the commerce of the country †.

The great law which we owe to his interpofition (I fpeak of that which gives a bounty on the land carriage of corn and flour to Dublin ‡) has faved this country from utter deftruction ; this law, which reflects the higheft honour on the author and promoter, is ftill a proof of the poverty of that country where fuch a law is neceffary. Its true principle is to bring the market of Dublin to the door of the farmer, and that was done in the year, ending the 25th of March, 1777, at the expence of 6,789l. 18s. 6d. to the public ; a large, but a moft ufeful and neceffary expenditure §.

In the beginning of the next parliament, the rupture with Spain occafioned a new augmentation of military expence. The ever loyal commons return an addrefs of thanks to the meffage mentioning the addition of five new battalions ‖, and unanimoufly promife to provide for them ; and with the fame unanimity pafs a vote of credit for 200,000l **. The amount of penfions on the civil eftablifhment, exclufive of French, had for one year, ending the 25th of March, 1761, amounted to 64,127l. 5s. †† and our manufacturers were then

* Com. Jour. 11 Vol. p. 993, 994.　† Ib. 1049.
‡ Brought in by Mr. Pery, the prefent Speaker.
§ In the year ending lady-day, 1778, it amounted to 71,533l. 1s. and in that ending lady-day, 1779, to 67,864l. 8s. 10d.
‖ Com. Jour. 12 Vol. p. 700.　** Ib. 728.　†† Ib. 443.

diftreffed

diftreffed by the expence and havock of a burthenfome war *.

The ftate of penfions remained nearly the fame †; by the peace the military expences were confiderably reduced; of the military eftablifhment to be provided for in the feffion 1763, compared with the military eftablifhment as it ftood on the 31ft of March, 1763, the net decreafe was 119,037l. os. 10d. per annum; but as a peace eftablifhment it was high, and compared with that of the 31ft of March, 1756 ‡ being the year preceding the laft war, the annual increafe was 110,422l. 9s. 5d. the debt of the nation at Lady-day 1763, and which was entirely incurred in the laft war, was 521,161l. 16s 6d §. and would have been much greater, if the feveral lord lieutenants had not ufed with great œconomy the power of borrowing, which the houfe of commons had from feffion to feffion given them.

The fame miftaken eftimate of the ability of Ireland, that occafioned our being called upon to bear part of the Britifh burthen during the war, produced fimilar effects at the time of the peace, and after it. The heavy peace eftablifhment was increafed by an augmentation of our army in 1769, which induced an additional charge, taking in the expences of exchange and remittance, of 54,118l. 12s. 6d. yearly, for the firft year; but this charge was afterwards confiderably increafed, and amounted from the year 1769, to Chriftmas 1778, when it was difcontinued, to the fum of 620,824l. os. 9d. and this increafed expence was more felt, becaufe it was for the purpofe of paying forces out of this kingdom.

As our expences increafed our income diminifhed; the revenue for the two years, ending the 25th of March, 1771 ‖, was far fhort of former years, and not nearly fufficient to pay the charges of government, and the fums payable for bounties and public works **. The debt of the nation at lady-day, 1771, was increafed to 782,320l. os. 0d ††. The want of income was endeavouring to be fupplied by a loan. In the money-bill of the October feffion, 1771, there was a claufe impowering government to borrow 200,000l. Immediately

* Com. Jour. 929, Speech of Lord Hallifax from the throne, 30th of April, 1762.
† For a year ending 25th March, 1763, they were 66,477l. 5s.; they afterwards rofe to 89,095l. 17s. 6d. in September 1777 at the higheft; and in this year, ending the 25th of March laft, amounted to 85,971l. 2s. 6d.
‡ Com. Jour. 13 Vol. p. 576.   § Ib. 574. 621.
‖ Ib. 14 Vol. 715.   ** Ib. 15 Vol. 710.   †† Ib. 153.

after

after the linen trade declined rapidly; in 1772, 1773, and 1774, the decay in that trade was general in every part of the kingdom where it was eftablifhed; the quantity manufactured was not above two-thirds of what ufed formerly to be made, and the quality did not fell for above three-fourths of its former price; the linen and linen yarn exported for one year, ending the 25th of March, 1773 *, fell fhort of the exports of one year, ending the 25th of March 1771, to the amount in value of 788,821l. 1s. 3d.   At lady-day, 1773 †, the debt increafed to 994,890l. 10s. 10d. 1-8th.   The attempt in the feffion of 1773 ‡, to equalize the annual income and expences failed, and borrowing on tontine in the feffions of 1773, 1775 and 1777, added greatly to the annual expence, and to the fums of money remitted out of the kingdom.   The debt now bearing intereft amounts to the fum of 1,017,600l. befides a fum of 740,000l. raifed on annuities, which amount to 48,900l. yearly, with fome incidental expences.   The great increafe of thofe national burdens, likely to take place in the approaching feffion, has been already mentioned.

The debt of Ireland has arifen from the following caufes : the expences of the late war, the heavy peace eftablifhment in the year 1763, the increafe of that eftablifhment in the year 1769, the fums paid from 1759 to forces out of the kingdom, the great increafe of penfions and other additional charges on the civil eftablifhment, which however confiderable, bears but a fmall proportion to the increafed military expences, the falling of the revenue, and the fums paid for bounties and public works; thefe are mentioned laft, becaufe it is apprehended that they have not operated to increafe this debt in fo great a degree as fome perfons have imagined; for though the amount is large, yet no part of the money was fent out of the kingdom, and feveral of the grants were for ufeful purpofes, fome of which made returns to the public and to the treafury exceeding the amount of thofe grants.

When thofe facts are confidered, no doubt can be entertained but that the fuppofed wealth of Ireland has led to real poverty; and when it is known, that from the year 1751 to Chriftmas 1778, the fums remitted by Ireland to pay troops ferving abroad, amounted to the fum of 1,401,925l. 19s. 4d. it will be equally clear from whence this poverty has principally arifen.

* Com. Jour. 16 Vol. p. 372.   † Ib. p. 190. 191, 193.   ‡ Ib. 256.

In 1762, lord Hallifax, in his fpeech from the throne*, acknowledges that our manufactures were diftreffed by the war. In 763, the corporation of weavers, by a petition to the houfe of commons, complain that, notwithftanding the great increafe both in number and wealth of the inhabitants of the metropolis, they found a very great decay of feveral very valuable branches of trade and manufactures † of this city, particularly in the filken and woollen.

In 765, there was fo great a fcarcity of potatoes, fpring corn, &c. that it was thought neceffary to appoint a committee ‡ to inquire what may be the beft method to reduce it; and to prevent a great dearth, two acts paffed early in that feffion, to ftop the diftillery, and to prevent the exportation of corn, for a limitted time.

In 1778 and 1779 there was great plenty of corn, but the manufacturers were not able to buy, and many thoufands of them were fupported by charity; the confequence was that corn fell to fo low a price that the farmers in many p'aces were unable to pay their rents, and every where were under great difficulties.

FIFTH LETTER.

FOR feveral years the exportation of live cattle to England § was the principal trade of Ireland. This was thought moft erroneoufly ‖, as has fince been acknowledged**, to lower the rents of lands in England. From this; and perhaps from fome lefs worthy motive †† a law paffed in England ‡‡, to reftrain and afterwards to prohibit the exportation of cattle from Ireland. The Irifh, deprived of their principal trade, and reduced to the utmoft diftrefs by this prohibition, had no

---

* Com. Jour. 12 Vol. p. 928.   † Ib. 13 Vol. p. 987.

‡ Ib. 11. Vol. p. 69, 1 4, 151.

§ Carte, 2 Vol. 318,   19.

‖ Sir W. Petty's Political Survey, 69, 70.   Sir W. Temple, 3 Vol. 22, 23.

** By feveral Britifh acts (32 G. 2, ch. 11. 5 G. 3, ch. 10, 12. G. 3, ch. 56.) allowing from time to time the free importation of all forts of cattle from Ireland.

†† Perfonal prejudice againft the duke of Ormond. (2 Carte, 332, 337.

‡‡ 15 Ch. 2, ch. 7. 18 Ch. 2, ch. 2.

refource

refource but to work up their own commodities, to which they applied themfelves with great ardor *. After this prohibition they increafed their number of fheep, and at the revolution were poffeffed of very numerous flocks. They had good reafons to think that this object of induftry was not only left open, but recommended to them. The ineffectual attempt by lord Strafford in 1639, to prevent the making of broad cloaths in Ireland †, the relinquifhment of that fcheme by never afterwards receiving it, the encouragement given to their woollen manufactures by many Englifh acts of parliament from the reign of Edward the 3d, ‡ to the 12th of Ch. 2d, and feveral of them for the exprefs purpofe of exportation; the letter of Charles the 2d, in 1667, with the advice of his privy council in England, and the proclamation in purfuance of that letter, encouraging the exportation of their manufactures to foreign countries; by the Irifh ftatutes of the 13th Hen. 8, ch. 2, 28th Hen 8, ch. 17, of the 11th Elizabeth, Ch. 10, and 17 and 18 Ch. 2, ch. 15, (all of which, the act of 28 Henry 8th excepted, received the approbation of the privy council of England, having been returned under the great feal of that kingdom) afforded as ftrong grounds of affurance as any country could poffefs for the continuance of any trade or manufacture.

An act, in its title, profeffes the encouraging the importation of wool from Ireland.

By a report from the commiffioners of trade in that kingdom, dated on the 23d December 97, and laid before the houfe of commons, in 1698, they find that the woollen manufacture in Ireland had increafed fince the year 1665, as follows:

Years.	New draperies. Pieces.	Old draperies. Pieces.	Frize. Yards.
1665	224	32	444,381
1687	11,360	103	1,129,716
1696	4,413	34½	104,167

The bill for reftraining the exportation of woollen manufactures from Ireland, was brought into the Englifh houfe of commons on the 23d of Feb. 97, but the law did not pafs until the year 1699, in the firft feffion of the new parliament. I have not been able to obtain an account of the exportation

* 2 Carte, 332.
† Com. Jour. 1 Vol. p. 208, by a claufe to be inferted in an Irifh act.
‡ See poft, thofe acts ftated.

of

of woollen manufactures for the year 1697 *, but from the
25th of December 1697, to the 25th of December 1698,
being the first year in which the exports in books extant, are
registered in the custom-house at Dublin, the amount appears
to be of

New drapery.	Old drapery.	Frize.
Pieces.	Pieces.	Yds.
23,285½	281h	666,901

Though this encrease of export shews that the trade was advancing in Ireland, yet the total amount, or the comparative
increase since 1687 could scarcely "sink the value of lands,
" and tend to the ruin of the trade and woollen manufactures
" of England †.

King William in his answer, says, " his majesty will take
" care to do what their lordships have desired ;" and the lords
direct, that the lord chancellor should order that the address
and answer be forthwith printed and published ‡.

Of what Ireland gains it is computed that one-third cen-
ters in Great Britain §. Of our woollen manufacture the
greatest part of the profit would go directly there. But the
manufacturers of Ireland would be employed.

Mr. Dobbs, who wrote in 1729 ||, affirms, that by this law
of 1699, our woollen manufacturers were forced away into
France, Germany and Spain ; that they had in many branches
so much improved the woollen manufacture of France, as
not only to supply themselves, but to vie with the English in
foreign markets, and that by their correspondence, they had
laid the foundation of the running of wool thither both from
England and Ireland. He says that those nations were then
so improved, as in a great measure to supply themselves with

* In a pamphlet cited by Dr. Smith, (v. 2, p. 244) in his memoirs
of wool, it is said that the total value of those manufactures exported in
1697, was 23,614l. 9s. 6d. namely, in frizes and stockings 14,625l. 12s; in
old and new draperies 8,988l. 17s. 6d. and that though the Irish had been
every year increasing, yet they had not recovered above one-third of the
woollen trade which they had before the war (ib. 243). The value in
1687, according to the same authority, was 70,521l. 14s. of which the frizes
were 56,483l. 16s. Stockings 2,520l. 18s. and old and new drapery (which
it is there said could alone interfere with the English trade) 11,514l. 10s.
 † Preamble of English act of 1699.
 ‡ Lords Jour. page 315.
 § Sir M. Decker's decline of foreign trade, p. 155, and Anderson on
commerce, 2 vol. p. 149.
 || Essay on the trade of Ireland. p. 6, 7.

many

many forts they formerly had from England, and fince that time have deprived Britain of millions, inftead of the thoufands that Ireland might have made.

It is now acknowledged that the French underfel the Englifh; and as far as they are fupplied with Irifh wool, the lofs to the Britifh empire is double what it would be, if the Irifh exported their goods manufactured.   This is mentioned by Sir Matthew Decker[*], as the caufe of the decline of the Englifh, and the increafe of the French woollen manufactures; and he afferts that the Irifh can recover that trade out of their hands.   England, fince the paffing this law, has got much lefs of our wool than before[†].   In 1698, the export of our wool to England amounted to 377,520 ftone; at a medium of eight years, to lady-day 1728, it was only 227,049 ftone, which is 148,000 ftone lefs than in 1698, and was a lofs of more than half a million yearly to England.   In the laft ten years the quantity exported has been fo greatly reduced, that in one of thefe years [‡] it amounted only to 1007ft. 11lb. and in the laft year did not exceed 1665ft. 12lb.§.   The price of wool, under an abfolute prohibition, is 5ol. or 6ol. per cent. under the market price of Europe, which will always defeat the prohibition [∥].

The impracticability of preventing the pernicious practice of running wool is now well underftood.   Of the thirty-two counties in Ireland, nineteen are maritime, and the reft are wafhed by a number of fine rivers that empty themfelves into the fea.   Can fuch an extent of ocean, fuch a range of coafts, fuch a multitude of harbours, bays and creeks be effectually guarded?

The prohibition of the export of live cattle forced the Irifh into the re-eftablifhment of their woollen manufacture; and the reftraint of the woollen manufacture was a ftrong temptation to the running of wool.   The fevereft penalties were enacted, the Britifh legiflature, the government and houfe of commons of Ireland, exerted all poffible efforts to remove this growing evil, but in vain, until the law was made in Great Britain[**] in 1739, to take off the duties from

---

[*] Decline of foreign trade, p. 55, 56, 155.   [†] Dobbs, p. 76.

[‡] In 1774.

[§] Nor was this deficiency made up by the exportation of yarn. The quantities of thefe feveral articles exported from 1764 to 1778, are mentioned in the appendix, Numb.

[∥] Smith's Memoirs of Wool, 2 Vol. p. 554.   The only way to prevent it, is to enable us to work it up at home. ib. 293.

[**] This was done for the benefit of the woollen manufacture in England.   Eng. Com. Jour. 22 Vol. p. 442.

woollen

woollen or bay yarn exported from Ireland, excepting worſted yarn of two or more threads, which has certainly given a conſiderable check to the running of wool, and has ſhewn that the policy of opening is far more efficacious than that of reſtraining. The world is become a great commercial ſociety, exclude trade from one channel, and it ſeldom fails to find another.

To ſhew the abſolute neceſſity of Great Britain's opening to Ireland ſome new means of acquiring, let the annual balance of exports and imports, returned from the entries in the different cuſtom-houſes, in favour of Ireland, on all her trade with the whole world, in every year from 1768 to 1778, be compared with the remittances made from Ireland to England in each of thoſe years, it will evidently appear that thoſe remittances could not be made out of that balance. The entries of exports made at cuſtom-houſes are well known to exceed the real amount of thoſe exports in all countries, and this exceſs is greater in times of diffidence, when merchants wiſh to acquire credit by giving themſelves the appearance of being great traders.

This balance in favour of Ireland on her general trade, appears by thoſe returns to have been in 1776, 606,190l. 11s. 0d. in 1777, 24,203l. 3s. 10d. in 1778, 386,384l. 5s. 7d. and taken at a medium of eleven years, from 1768 to 1778, both incluſive, it amounts to the ſum of 605,083l. 7s. 5d. The ſums remitted from Ireland to Great-Britain for rents, intereſts of money, penſions, ſalaries, and profits of offices, amounted, at the loweſt computation, from 1768 to 1773, to 100,000l. yearly* ; and from 1773, when the tontines were introduced, from which period large ſums were borrowed from England, thoſe remittances were conſiderably increaſed, and are now not leſs than between 12 and 13,000l. yearly. Ireland then pays to Great-Britain double the ſum that ſhe collects from the whole world in all the trade which Great Britain allows her. It will be difficult to find a ſimilar inſtance in the hiſtory of mankind.

What was the information given by the trading towns in 1697 and 1698, on the ſubject of the woollen manufacture of Ireland? ſeveral of their† petitions ſtate that the woollen manufacture was *ſet up* in Ireland, as if it had been lately intro-

* This is ſtated conſiderably under the computation made in the liſt of abſentees, publiſhed in Dublin in 1769, which makes the amount at that time 1,208,982l, 14s, 6d.
† Eng. Com. Jour. 12 Vol, 64, 68.

duced there; and one of them goes fo far as to reprefent the
time and manner of introducing it. "Many of the poor of
"that kingdom (fays this extraordinary petition) during the
"late rebellion there, fled into the Weft of England, where
"they were put to work in the woollen manufacture to learn
"that trade, and fince the reduction of Ireland, endeavours
"were ufed to fet up thofe manufacturers there."

Would any man fuppofe that this could relate to a manufacture, in which this kingdom excelled before the time of
Edward the 3d, which had been the fubject of fo many laws
in both kingdoms, and which was always cultivated here, and
before this rebellion with more fuccefs than after it? the trading towns gave accounts totally inconfiftent of the ftate of this
manufacture at that time in England: from Exeter it is reprefented as greatly decayed and difcouraged * in thofe parts,
and diminifhed in England. But a petition from Leeds reprefents this manufacture as having very much increafed †
fince the revolution in all its feveral branches, to the general
intereft of England; and yet, in two days after the clothiers
from three towns in Gloucefterfhire affert, that the trade
has decayed, and that the poor are almoft ftarved‡. The
commiffioners of trade differ in opinion from them, and by
their report, it appears that the woollen manufacture was then
very much increafed and improved §. The traders have fometimes miftaken their own interefts on thofe fubjects; in 1698,
a petition for prohibiting the importation from Ireland of all
worfted and woollen yarn, reprefents that the poor of England
are ready to perifh by this importation ‖; and in 1739, feveral petitions were preferred againft taking off the duties **
from worfted and bay yarn exported from Ireland to England.
But this has been done in the manner before-mentioned, and
is now acknowledged to be highly ufeful to England. Trading people have ever aimed at exclufive privileges; of this
there are two extraordinary inftances; in the year 1698, two
petitions were preferred, from Folkeftone and Aldborough,
ftating a fingular grievance that they fuffered from Ireland,
"by the Irifh catching herrings at Waterford and Wexford††,
"and fending them to the Streights, and thereby foreftalling
"and ruining petitioners markets;" but thefe petitioners had
the hard lot of having motions in their favour rejected.

* Englifh Com. Jour. Vol. 12, p.7.   † Ib. 527.   ‡ Ib. 530.
§ Ib. 434.   ‖ Ib. 387.
** Ib, vol. 22.   †† Ib. 178.

In

It is hoped, many of the excellent obfervations contained in the remainder of thefe letters, will not appear improperly applied to the fupport of a few remarks fuggefted from a review of the foregoing pages.

In the mean time I fhall lay the following letter before my readers, as no unpleafing picture to an Irifhman of the confequence of his country.

LETTER II. of the juftly efteemed OWEN ROE O'NIAL
To the Men of Ireland.

S*UÆ quifque faber fortunæ eft*, is one of thofe truths which the experience of ages has handed down as a proverb.

What is true of every individual muft be fo of nations— " Their fortune muft depend upon *themfelves*."

It is a truth well worthy the deep confideration of Ireland —I have, in my former letter, endeavoured to convince her by reafoning, and an appeal to hiftorical facts, of what fhe fhould long ere this have learned from experience ; that whatever juftice or generofity exifts among individuals, it is vain to lcok for it in the mutual intercourfe of nations. Their principle is policy.

It is time for Ireland to take thought for herfelf.

That Ireland hath been, and is, fubordinate to, and dependent on the imperial crown of Great Britain, and that the King's Majefty, with the confent of the Lords and Commons of Great Britain in Parliament, hath power to make laws to bind the people of Ireland *, is a truth too melancholy to admit contradiction. That it of right " ought" to be fo, was referved for the modefty and good fenfe of an Englifh parliament to affert, and would therefore be a *blunder* in Irifhmen to deny.

That no nation can by conqueft, or by any other means, acquire a right of perpetual dominion over another ; that no confent or contract, however exprefs or folemn, can bind pofterity to their injury; that no prefcription or length of time can fanctify oppreffion ; that little deference is due to names impofed by the oppreffors upon the act of affuming rights unalienable in their nature, and only overborne by force, or overlooked by folly ; thefe are propofitions which I fhall not attempt to enlarge upon. Time, with moft minds, gives a facrednefs to error : enquiry then bears the name of impiety : but the idols of one age are trampled under foot in another, and the prejudices which once required a Locke to remove, are in thefe days but themes to the fchools.

* 5 Geo. I. c. 5.

I shall not then war with the dead; nor shall I offend the delicacy of an English Judge, by doubting the propriety, or disputing the omnipotence of an English act of parliament. That would be " to oppose my private Irish judgment to public English authority *." And, in so plain a case, the opposition " must be virulent and factious †." Authority must be ever in the right! The demand of Magna Charta was but a successful rebellion; the reformation was an impious defection from the church; and the author of Christianity was an heretic and a traitor! Ireland then, by right, ought to be, nay more, for ever must be, subordinate to the sovereign legislative parliament of Great Britain. I acknowledge it! my reason is a strong one; she thinks so herself; and who dare deny the competency of her judgment? She thinks herself formed by nature an humble attendant upon England. She crouches under what she calls necessity. Her loyalty dares not form a wish for the preservation of her crown in the house of Hanover, united with the separate independency of her own legislature: because she looks upon that wish as hopeless. The very thought to her seems madness! the attempt, she apprehends, would be ruin!

I owe a deference to the general opinion, and shall submit to it; yet, as all sound judgment on this question can only be built upon experience, it seems not unreasonable to enquire, were it but as matter of speculation, into the fate of other countries, which having been nearly in the same situation with Ireland, endeavoured to mend their condition. One advantage will certainly result from the enquiry, which cannot fail of proving acceptable to a people, who have hitherto appeared more delighted with their fears, than with any other feelings of the human heart. It will lead us, by the consideration of our superior resources, to estimate infallibly the quantum of national punishment, likely to be superadded to our present burdens, by our masters, the parliament of Great Britain, for the efforts of this day, when their leisure and security shall permit them to turn their thoughts to us. In proportion to our superior power of resisting, will the means be of preventing, in future, the possibility of the operation of such a resistance.

A late respectable writer (Guatimozin) has already enumerated the natural advantages of Ireland. It appears that

* 6 George I. ch. 5.
† See Blackstone's Comment. book 4, p. 50, Irish edition.

she

she poffeffes within herfelf, or immediately within her reach, almoft every advantage that nature or fituation can give, or that is neceffary to make a nation rich, great, and happy.

A climate of the fineft temperature ; a foil of moft extraordinary fertility ; mines that encouragement might convert into fources of national induftry and national fuperiority ; feas that teem with fifh ; harbours numerous, fafe, commodious, and well fituated for commerce ; and, to conclude, a people with capacity for every thing, and who want but leave to acquire habits of induftry, as perfevering as fpirited.

Thefe are the natural advantages of Ireland. How few nations can boaft fo many and fo great ? Compare her rank and confequence in the world, with what thefe advantages might entitle her to. Enquire then, whence arifes the difference, and thank England, if you can, for the generofity of her protection !

Are either the United Provinces, or Switzerland, to be compared to Ireland in natural advantages? I cannot think they are. The former is but one-third, the latter only one-half her fize. Ireland is an ifland, and fuch an one as I have defcribed ; rich in climate, foil, mines, and harbours. Switzerland is in the heart of the Continent, and is poor in all thefe,—the latter fhe cannot poffefs at all. The Duch States are joined to the Continent ; their fhore is dangerous from its flats ; does not afford them a fingle good harbour ; and the froft binds up their commerce during a confiderable part of the winter. I need not mention the fifh which the lakes of Switzerland afford. The fifheries of Holland lie upon our coaft. They enjoy more from their unchecked induftry, than we from nature and the protection of England. The Dutch have no mines. The Swifs don't work theirs, except for their neceffary inftruments of war and agriculture. Neither Holland nor Switzerland produces corn for half their inhabitants. In the latter half the harveft produced by a ftubborn foil is often deftroyed by ftorms, and but part of the remainder is allowed by the climate to ripen.

The Swifs may be faid to have neither commerce nor navigation, fince the latter they have only on their lakes, the former is concerned wholly in neceffaries.

Of the timber of the Swifs I need not fpeak. They can have no navy, nor do they require one. As to Holland, the fpongy produce of marfhes is ufelefs in trade or navigation. Her navy muft be purchafed by induftry. Ireland may be as induftrious as Holland, but fhe requires it lefs. She may
                                                                    raife

raife a navy at home, if fhe cannot with more advantage bring marerials from abroad. The climate of Switzerland may make an hardy race of foldiers or hufbandmen, but to a nation that would aim at more than a penurious exiftence, it cannot be a fubject of envy. The climate of Holland, marfhy in its foil, and interfected by fo many ftagnated canals, is not wholefome. Some of their towns are formed on the foil left by the ftagnation of rivers. In others the folid foundations of the earth feemed to have forfaken them, and they laid new ones. The fea threatens to overwhelm them. They oppofe it with mounds, which require a continual repair, and dream not of danger, though the failure of a bank would give them a fecond deluge.   -

✦ Labour and induftry are in Holland neceffary. They cannot otherwife exift. This, it is true, will keep them laborious and induftrious. But what they are from neceffity, other nations may be from nobler motives ; and Ireland fets out from a point which, in Holland, it required the labour and induftry of years to gain.

Holland muft be a drudge, as fhe fubfifts on the wants of other nations, and thefe, we know, are moftly artificial. She is their factor and carrier. She may fuffer from their caprice. She muft languifh in their ill-humour. Their induftry, or even frugality, would ftarve her. Ireland is more independent. She can fubfift by her internal refources, though the world fhould refufe her either commerce or employment. She is rich in herfelf. Nature, that made her an ifland, and gave her fertility, qualified her equally for abfolute independence, and unlimited intercourfe with other nations. She can fubfift without other nations. She can trade with them to mutual advantage.

Such are the natural advantages of Holland and Switzerland, and fuch are they compared with Ireland. America I fhall briefly confider hereafter. Each of the former is furrounded by powerful empires. Each of them was once oppreffed by all the rigours of flavery. Each of them burft her fhackles, and baffled the moft inveterate attacks of enemies, whofe power feemed to approach them with the irrefiftability of fate.

Holland, inferior to Ireland in every natural advantage, and equal to but a third of her in fize, threw off the yoke of the moft powerful monarch then in Europe. The firmnefs and courage which fhe. difplayed, will appear incredible to thofe who are unacquainted with the power of enthufiafm.

The

The feven provinces we are fpeaking of furmounted every difficulty—they thought they could defend themfelves. The ten other provinces, fays Voltaire, would have a foreign Prince to protect them, and are in flavery to this day.

One Prince [Henry the IVth of France] to whom they applied for affiftance, was himfelf engaged in civil wars, and yet tottered on his throne. The extreme caution of another, [Queen Elizabeth] in foreign enterprize, correfponded but ill with her magnanimity and refolution in domeftic affairs; and from the reprimands fhe was daily giving to the Houfe of Commons, for prefuming to judge of the duty they were called to, fhe feemed little likely to tempt the wrath of a powerful tyrant or turn abettor of rebellion. The fuccours received by the States were accordingly for a long time feeble and clandeftine. To obtain open affiftance from Elizabeth required a longer ftruggle: and even the offer of their fovereignty. But before any affiftance had been received by the States, they had gotten poffeffion of what Doctor Johnfon calls "the choice of evil:" Their darling object *liberty*. The very women had formed regiments for the defence of their cities; and, rather than again fall under the hated tyranny of Spain, the dykes and fluices had been opened, and the very Peafants, fays Hume, had been active in ruining their own fields by an inundation; they preferred the mercy of the waters to that of tyrants.

Thefe fame people have fince withftood the moft formidable attacks of a Monarch, who thought his power equal to univerfal empire. They have fupported themfelves with more than equal honour againft the combined fleets of France and England. They have fwept the channel of England, and their infults in the Thames have carried confternation to the capital.

In little more than half a century from the time, at which, unprepared as they muft have been, they firft ventured to take up arms againft Spain in defence of their liberty, they beat one of her formidable Armadas*. They obliged it to take fhelter in the Downs under the Englifh flag. They retire for a reinforcement;—they refolve—that the fleet of England fhall no longer protect their enemy; they return to the charge; and the Spanifh navy, in its flight, received from them a blow which at this day, after near a century and an half, it has

* The Duke of Alva left the Low Countries in the year 1574. They beat the Spanifh Armada in 1639.

not

not fully recovered. A few years more, affifted by a few
more defeats, foftened the obftinacy of Spain. She acknowledged the independence of the States *, and in twenty years
after they protected her provinces againft France †.

The Swifs, now that they are free, are more fecure from
attacks, than when they were dependent. They are defended
by their mountains and the barrennefs of their country ; by
their poverty, by their valour, and, by the mutual jealoufies
of the neighbouring empires. A partition is not eafily agreed
upon, and none will confent to their becoming an acceffion to
the power of another, if fuch an acceffion were practicable.
But it muft be confeffed that of all the advantages I have mentioned, their valour alone, at the time they threw off the
yoke, feemed moft in their favour. The enemy had poffeffion
of their country. The balance of power was then lefs underftood, or lefs attended to, and their poverty and commercial
infignificance muft have been feeble inducements to the protection of their neighbours. Accordingly they had to work
out their own liberty, and above three centuries elapfed before the Houfe of Auftria acknowledged their independence ‡.

I believe there are few will deny that America has already
eftablifhed her independence. She would not come over and
proftrate herfelf at the feet of England ; fo England, with
the magnanimity of a conqueror, appointed ambaffadors to
her by act of Parliament. Upon England's condefcending
" to treat with armed rebels," they refufed to treat with England. They had procured friends, and they preferred them
to mafters. For the fituation of America in the beginning of
the conteft, hear her own unexaggerated defcription : " Without arms, ammunition, difcipline, revenue, government, or
ally, almoft tota.ly ftript of commerce, and in the weaknefs
of youth, as it were, " with a ftaff and a fling only," fhe
dared, " in the name of the Lord of Hofts," to engage a
gigantic adverfary, prepared at all points, boafting of his
ftrength, and of whom even mighty warriors were greatly
afraid."

When to this enumeration of difficulties, which, one is
tempted to think, requires little addition, we fubjoin the fol-

* Treaty of Münfter, 1648.   † Triple alliance in 1668.
‡ They took up arms in the year 1308. Their independence was acknowledged in 1648, by the treaty of Munfter, the fame by which Spain
acknowledged the independence of the United Provinces.
It would be fingular enough if the fame period which eftablifhes American independence, fhall be found to have deftroyed the ufurpation of the
Britifh Parliament over the legiflative rights of Ireland.

lowing; that thefe Colonies were not more difunited by diftance of place, than by difference of opinion, manners, fpirit,
religion and government ; that they were fo difunited in all
thefe, that it feemed the dream of a dotard to think of connecting them in one intereft, or of bringing them to co-operate, if they could be convinced that their intereft was the
fame ; that they were expofed to the navy and arms of England on their fea-coafts, to the incurfions of Indiars (perhaps
too juftly enraged) on their rear; and, in fome provinces,
to the more dangerous infurrections of their domeftic flaves,
whofe difpofitions to revenge muft have been expected to burft
on their more immediate oppreffors; when all thefe particulars, I fay, are confidered, befides thofe which America herfelf has enumerated, I think fcarce any nation on the earth
fhould abfolutely defpair.

Let us confider the prefent fituation of Ireland. I need
fcarce fay, that there is not a maritime power in Europe to
which her alliance would not, in itfelf, be an object of emu-
lation. What then would it appear to the enemies of England? If Ireland fhould afk their protection, would they
require to be founded at a diftance, or to be affailed by pre-
paratory arguments and leading propofitions? Would they
think it prudent to act as they did by America, to ftand by,
cool fpectators of our ftruggle, till they judged how far we
fhould be able to perfevere or be likely to fucceed? or, if they
determined to affift Ireland, would they be obliged to have
recourfe to art in order to deceive a credulous minifter, and
to mafk their intentions until they could declare them with
fafety? No, my countrymen: diftant propofitions, prepara-
tory arguments, negociation, art,—all thefe are to us unneceffary! Conviction has long been confirmed. Their refolution is already taken. Their arms are already in their hands.
They have croffed the Atlantic for their own intereft and for
the humiliation of England. Will a few leagues terrify them
when their fcheme is fo near arriving at almoft unhoped-for
perfection? They were then at peace, yet, they engaged in
war. They are now at war, will they not carry it on? The
fole queftion with them at prefent muft be this : will they
chufe to vifit us as enemies, or as friends? For vifit us they
probably will. Will they attempt a conqueft to which they
are probably unequal; or will they chufe the eafier road, and
offer an alliance, which will have every real advantage to be
expected from dominion, without the danger of an unfuccefs-
ful attempt, or the inconveniencies and hazards of the moft
                                                    fuccefsful

fuccefsful execution? Will they not offer an alliance fuch as
their good fenfe has been content with from America, and
which they have thought worthy of fupporting by a war with
England? fuch an alliance as, from its liberality, it will be
the intereft of the other European powers, at leaft, by a tacit
acquiefcence, to fupport? An alliance that will not contribute
more to the weakening of an haughty adverfary, and the dif-
appointment of an infatiable monopolift, than to their own regal power, aggrandifement and glory.

And here, my countrymen, occurs an awful paufe! What
inducements hath Britifh policy fuffered to take root in the
hearts of Irifhmen, to enable them to refift fuch neceffary and
proffered protection. None, my friends! Loyalty, the faireft
flower that can ornament the bofom of a Prince, finds in Ireland
its happieft foil. Perfonal attachment to the King of Ireland,
and his illuftrious houfe, is the cord which binds us to our
burden, and furnifhes to a Britifh people the occafion of load-
ing us without bounds or mercy. Had we as little attachment to the Houfe of Hanover as Scotland, or Manchefter,
we had long fince in defpair implored the protection of other
powers, for fo long as the "Parliament of Great Britain can
bind us in all cafes whatfoever," the worft that could happen
to us would be to change our mafters*. The word is not
my own. It is by an Englifh Judge and commentator directly applied to the fituation of this kingdom, and its fubordination to England by right of conqueft.

But has England learned nothing from her late experience
in America? Will fhe for ever truft to our loyalty alone, and
will our King for ever leave us at the mercy of a Britifh Parliament? As to the Englifh people, the power of God has been

* It may be feen by Blackftone, b. I. p. 100, what an Englifh lawyer
thinks the *neceffary* confequence of *all* dependence upon *England!* We are
bound by *every law* fhe, in her wifdom or wantonnefs, *thinks proper* to
prefcribe. We fhall foon, I fuppofe, be on a footing with thofe flaves of
the Romans who were *bound to the glebe*, or foil. England will *think proper*
that we fhould not *depart* from the foil, but be transferred with it by *deed*,
roll, or *indenture*. This will fave us a multitude of difputes about *our property*, for we fhall then, like the Roman flaves, become perfect THINGS,
and ceafe to be PERSONS. The Englifh prints will then afford entertain-
ment to thofe who can relifh it. If any of us are miffing from our *ftalls*
or *lumber-rooms*, we fhall be *advertifed* for, and defcribed, as "LOST,
STRAYED, STOLEN, or MISLAID."—We fhall be taken *damage feafant*
(perhaps *rider* and all!) and if we happen to die of cold and hunger, in
an *open pound*, it will be at the fuit of *the owner!*—O Ireland! Ireland!
Doft thou retain one fpark of feeling, to make the oppreffion of thee *a
crime?*

difplayed

difplayed to them in vain.   They feem to have revived the age of miracles, and to have left the Egyptians at a diftance.   All that fhould have infpired them with awe, humility, and wif- dom, feems but to have darkened their underftandings and hardened their hearts ! But let it be our duty, my country- men, to confider the crifis, and profit of it ! Let us adore that wonder-working God, who in the intoxication of our oppref- fors has laid the foundation of our relief, and who in the mif- carriages of Britifh tyranny beyond the Atlantic, has taught Irifhmen the practicability of their own emancipation from the authority of an ufurping Englifh Parliament.

But we are nearer to England.   I hear my countrymen lament it, and often have lamented it myfelf ! Yet, (indulge me, my countrymen, while I explain my paradox!) *on that very proximity does the weal of Ireland depend.*

We are near to England ; but we are near to affiftance alfo.   The Atlantic rolls not between us and England; but neither does it roll between us and her enemies.   Thefe ene- mies are on the way.   Before the wind changes they are here. Our proximity to England is to us, in the prefent pofture of affairs, what the diftance of America was in the beginning of the conteft, to her.   The latter was a barrier againft Bri- tain ; the former is a bridge for her foes.   In this refpect then we are equal to America.   We have however an advantage from our proximity, which fhe never can derive from her diftance.   It is a *perpetual guarantee* againft the oppreffion of any felf-created protector.   It is perpetual, becaufe it depends not on the policy or caprice of kings or of nations.   It is fixed in the nature of things.

America might have been ruined by the treachery of France, or fhe may yet fall by Congrefs, as England has done by a parliament.

Let Ireland be fubject to her own legiflation only, and one might venture to fay fhe is free for ever.   Her fituation and fize fit her for that moderate degree of ftrength and power which is moft likely to be permanent.

Let thefe things be weighed, and perhaps that man could not be acquitted of prefumption, who would venture to point out another fpot upon the globe, to which Ireland fhould now wifh to be removed.

From this proximity of England, I would deduce *this truth*, which I wifh to be engraven on the heart of every Irifh- man : *England is the only power that can enflave us further, or keep us as we are.*   And this is the important mo- ment

ment when our own firm conftitutional refiftance will derive additional fupport from the dread of her enemies, towards fhaking of the fhackles off an ufurping Englifh people.

But, unlefs we entertain for each other a mutual and general confidence, unlefs we lay afide all rancour of prejudice on account of diftinctions either political or religious, to attempt fuch a relief from thofe fhackles would be only to folicit confufion.

There are, however, many inftances of ftates differing very much in religion, and yet united in ftrict civil confederacy and union. Scarce fix of the Cantons of Switzerland are Proteftants, the feven remaining are Roman Catholics; and, what feems a little extraordinary, the greater number of the Roman Catholic Cantons are democratical, that of the Proteftant Cantons ariftocratical in their government. In the United Provinces the majority of the people are either Prefbyterians or Roman Catholics, and though Prefbyterianifm is the eftablifhed religion, yet, the toleration or connivance which all fects meet with from the government, has produced a general moderation and peace, and, in its natural confequences, has added power, grandeur, and ftability to the ftate. The ftate of Pennfylvania is equally various in its religion. The laws of this province are more liberal than the fpirit of any other province. They give no preference to any fect. They tolerate all fects. All fects are therefore not only peaceable, but content. Moft of the other ftates of America, fo firm in their union againft England, are fcarcely more oppofite than they are inveterate in the feveral prejudices and opinions which they carried with them from Europe. In fhort, from all the facts we can collect, our uniform conclufion muft be, that that nation is moft likely to be great, powerful, and happy, which finds political and civil moderation neceffary to its very being. Where there are no fects or parties, I may venture to fay there cannot be fenfe, fcience, liberty, or commerce. Where, from circumftances internal or external, different fects are nearly ballanced in power, the laws muft be moderate, and the fpirit of the laws will become the fpirit of the people. The nation will be in harmony within itfelf, and that moderation and good fenfe which will diftinguifh it in its internal government and policy, muft characterife it in its conduct towards other nations.

It is very fenfibly obferved by a Roman Catholic Prieft *, in a late addrefs to thofe of his own perfuafion in Ireland,

* Rev. Arthur O'Leary.

that

that " conquerors, (and, let me add, traders and politicians) are of no religion." The Englifh eftablifhed popery in Canada. The French entered into alliance with Prefbyterians in North America ; and, I dare fay, would have done the fame, if their Deity had been the fun or a ferpent, an onion or a monkey. The Dutch, it is faid, tread upon the crofs at Japan, and the Englifh make alliances with Moors and with Indians.

The French are, perhaps, even in religion, as liberal a nation as any in Europe. I judge not of them by their creeds, confeffions, or articles of belief: God forbid that I fhould judge by thefe alone of the hearts or underftandings of any people upon earth, who have public creeds, confeffions, or articles ! Thefe are not always formed by the wifeft or moft religious people of a nation. The wifeft and moft religious are generally better employed. I judge of the French nation by the general conduct of the people ; and I believe it will be owned that they are more liberal to Englifhmen, than Englifhmen are to them. The abfurdity of fuppofing that even conquerors would make violent alterations in private property, and involve themfelves in the perplexed difputes and antiquated claims of families, that have fuffered by for-feiture, has been well expofed by the Reverend Divine juft mentioned. Were the queftion indeed between two pretenders to the crown, the cafe might be different. He who fucceeded muft reinftate fome of his adherents, and gratify others. This muft be done at the expence of the oppofite party. But a conqueror, who is not able to crufh the fubdued nation at a fingle effort, will think himfelf happy in prevailing upon the people to remain quiet as he found them. He will make no alteration which he can avoid ; he will avoid every alteration which can difguft or difpleafe. What then is to be expected from even a powerful protector, that offers independence to a nation fo divided into parties that no one of them has power to crufh the others, fupported as they would be, by the nation that formerly enflaved them ? I fay that, in this cafe, we might expect fuch a moderation as would over-rule every petty diftinction or jealoufy, and would unite the nation by com-munity of intereft. To make an alteration in the eftablifhed religion, or to deny to all denominations of Proteftant Dif-fenters that toleration which they at prefent enjoy, would be the madnefs of folly. Thofe we fpeak of are neither fools nor madmen.

The

The Roman Catholics might, with juſtice indeed, expect a more compleat toleration. But it would require peculiar delicacy to grant this without offending thoſe Proteſtants who at preſent enjoy but a toleration themſelves. The interference of Roman Catholic protectors, conſcious of the prudence their ſituation required, muſt be of the moſt temperate kind. The alterations made would be gentle, gradual, and rather the effect of an inſenſible alteration of opinion and removal of prejudice, than an act of force or power in the ſtate. And, from the co-operation of all theſe cauſes, I am inclined to think there would naturally ariſe a mildneſs of government, and a benevolence of toleration which is unknown to the laws of any other country in Europe, and which enthuſiaſm itſelf has ſcarce dared to think conſiſtent with the littleneſs of human nature.

But whatever may be the natural dignity and ſtrength of Ireland, or whatever advantages ſhe might derive from the preſent poſture of affairs, there are ſome who cannot readily give up their attachment to the people of England, or think themſelves juſtified in reſiſting them in their preſent ſtate of misfortune, while there are others who yet dread her power, and tremble at her name. To the former I ſhall ſpeak more particularly hereafter, and hope to ſhew that we are not bound by any ties of duty, gratitude, or honour, to remain in ſubjection to the parliament of England.

At preſent I would addreſs myſelf to the latter. That the power of England is not yet an imagination I readily will own. Great even yet is the power of England, and great is the memory of her glory ! but her glory lives but in memory, and the ſinews of her power are withered. Exhauſted and foiled by America, whom, in the hour of her inſolence, ſhe treated with a contempt that would have robbed victory of its honour, but has covered defeat with aggravated diſgrace, returning reaſon can ſuggeſt but one conſolation for her folly; that ſomething yet remains for madneſs to ſquander, that there is yet a remnant which penury may ſave. The arbitreſs of empires may yet exiſt among nations ! the patroneſs of nations may yet be an houſe-wife !

There was a time when the world and the Roman Empire were ſynonimous terms.

There was a time too when the very name of Rome kept the Provinces in awe, though ſhe could ſcarce have defended her walls ; England has fallen by her own weight which ſhe
wanted

wanted wisdom to balance. Those days are past in which her history went hand in hand with romance. France has struck terror into *her conquerors*, and has shaken the throne of *her* King! The English channel has become a term of mockery. It has seen the navy of England in its *flight!* The navy of England has left her coasts to be insulted! That the navy of England was able to secure the protection of a port has, to a sovereign of England, become a theme of congratulation!

While England thus protects herself, need I ask what protection she is likely to afford to Ireland? If we remain by her bad policy in our present impoverished state, can she protect us from the arms or insults of her enemies?

Have we not men in arms already? Men whom England, and the slaves of England, would long ere this have disarmed, had they dared to do so! Men whose spirit they now affect to approve, because they find their approbation is indifferent to them! Men whose spirit must obtain a momentary protection, and to whom a very little time will render protection unnecessary! Men who may yet teach England that the soil of their own country benumbs not their courage; that it is not on the plains of Flanders or America alone that *Irishmen* can *conquer!*

The subject, my countrymen, has risen upon me. I have (I hope you will think unavoidably) been led into some details. My indignation, upon other occasions, I have found it difficult to repress. You will consider the design, and pardon any involuntary failure in the execution. But, before I take my leave for the present, allow me to ask one short question:

Shall we trust to other nations for a temporary protection, which (judging from human nature, and their particular line of conduct) I aver it to be equally their interest and their inclination to give, and the bounds of which, as I have endeavoured to prove, they cannot exceed; or, shall we depend to eternity on the generosity of a nation, who has shewn herself as incapable of generosity as of justice, and whose folly has disabled her from performing the duties of either? She thunders forth the mandates of her *omnipotence;* but, is her providence so particular, so watchful, so active, and so benevolent, that we should leave to her more than the God of Nature demands for himself, that we should leave agency to her, and address her but in prayer? Is the night of religious superstition passed away, and must that of political idolatry usurp the rightful vicissitude of day? Our night of both has been sufficiently long? But the sun of England, in whose

meridian

meridian beams our feebler light was loft, is now fet, perhaps, for ever : and the Hefperian ftar of America, which
fet with England, for a time, is now rifen, a Lucifer to light
us into day.   It has moved, 'till it is vertical in glory, and
points to *our political falvation !*

OWEN ROE O'NIAL.

As the author of the foregoing excellent letter, in enumerating the natural advantages of Ireland, juft mentions her
mines, it may not be thought unneceffary to add what Mr.
O'Halloran fays on this fubject :

Thus Gerard Boate * tells us, " All the mines which are at
" this day found out in Ireland, have been difcovered by the
" new Englifh, that is, fuch of them as came here in, and
" fince the days of Queen Elizabeth, and thefe, he tells us, are
" Iron, Lead and Silver. As to the Irifh themfelves (he
" fays) *being one of the moft barbarous nations of the whole earth,*
" they have been, *at all times,* fo far from feeking out any,
" that even in thefe laft years, and fince the Englifh have be-
" gun to difcover fome, none of them all, great or fmall,
" have applied themfelves to, or furthered that bufinefs." In
the next fection, he thinks mines of Gold are in Ireland ; and
he mentions a drachm of pure gold being got in a rivulet in
the county of Tyrone, from which he prefumes that the adjacent mountains are replete with this metal.   In cap. 18, he
mentions a filver mine, in the county of Antrim, fo very rich
that every 30 pounds of ore yielded one of pure filver. This
candid writer was ftate phyfician to the common-wealth juftices of Ireland ; and was too well acquainted with the fentiments of his mafters, to lofe any opportunity of infulting a
nation, fo remarkably attached to Monarchy.

Let us now fee, how far doctor Boate's cenfure is fupported by truth and hiftory. Stanihurft, who wrote a century
earlier, and no very warm Irifhman, tells us, that Ireland
was then known to be rich in mines of different metals ; and
Adrianus the Dutchman, ftill earlier, thus celebrates them,

. . . . . . *Stannique fodinas*
Et puri argenti venas.——

Cambrenfis himfelf bears teftimony to our mines † ; and
Donatus, bifhop of Feficoli, who wrote about 1100 years ago,

* Natural Hiftory of Ireland, cap. 16. fect. 11.
† Topograph. Hibern. Dift. 3. cap. 10.

fhews

shews that Ireland was even then highly renowned on the same account,

Insula dives opum, gemmarum, vestis & auri.

From these foreign evidences, let us now recur to the accurate pages of the Irish History. In the reign of Tighernmas, who flourished about 1000 years before Christ, we are told that the first gold mine found in Ireland, was discovered near the banks of the Liffy: and our annalists have been minute enough to tell us, that Juachadhan of Cualane, in the county of Wicklow, was the principal conductor of these works *, whose knowledge in metals and colours, they have not neglected to mention. In more than a century after we find that targets of pure silver were fabricated, and distributed to the bravest of the soldiery; and in the reign of Muincamhuin, who founded the order of the Golden Collar (so called from each knight wearing a collar of gold hung round his neck by a chain of the same metal) helmets were made with the neck and fore-pieces of pure gold. The handles of the swords of our antient knight, were made of pure gold, and the blades of a mixt brass, numbers of which have been and are daily discovered in bogs and other recesses. It appears among the hostages delivered to the Emperors of Ireland by the provinces, as well foreign as domestic, that those of Orgial were particularly distinguished from the rest, by having their shackles of pure gold, and the very word signifies the Golden Hostage. Part of the *Boirimhe-Laighen*, or tax on the kingdom of Leinster, and regularly paid into the monarch's treasury, for near 400 years, was 6000 ounces of pure silver. These facts it should seem are sufficient proofs of the great riches of antient Ireland, and her superior knowledge and industry to the modern. But if her own history will not be allowed as evidence in her favour, without modern collateral proofs, we are even abundantly furnished with these.

Mr. ò Flaherty †, from Nenius, an author of the 9th century, and from old manuscripts, gives an account of the antiently supposed wonders of Ireland, some of which have been found true, others false. Among others we find the following account of mines about Louch-Lene, or Killarney in the county of Kerry.

Mamoniæ stagnum Lochlenius undique Zonis
Quatuor ambitur : prior est ex ære ; secunda
Plumbea ; de rigido conflatur tertia ferro :
Quarto residenti pallescet linea Stanno.

* Keating p. 1. ò Flaherty, p. 195.   Gràt. Lucius, &c.
† Ogygia, p. 220.

We alfo find, that in faid lake, large quantities of pearls have been found.

It is net above thirty years fince a very rich copper mine was difcovered on the border of this lake, and worked with very great profit to the proprietors for many years ; but what is greatly to our purpofe, is, that on pufhing on their works, they found fhafts had been regularly funk, and implements of mining were found. Thefe works were ignorantly imputed to the Danes, who, it appears, had very inconfiderable fettlements here, and who, it muft be confefled, feem to have been little qualified for fuch undertakings. As to the lead mine it is an uncontroverted fact, that about fifty years ago, an Englifh company worked one at Caftle Lyons, on the fide of the Lake ; and many years after, the fame works were refumed under the infpection of one Longftaff, from which they extracted large quantities of filver. Though the tin mine has not been yet found, nor, I fuppofe, fearched for, yet Smith * confeffes to have found near the lake an ore which contained tin ; and as for the iron mines, the proofs that they were largely carried on here are many, and at this day one is worked near Mucrofs. A. C. 1094, we read of an elegant prefent of Kerry pearls, from Gilbert Bifhop of Limerick, to Anfelm Archbifhop of Canterbury †. At this day pearls are frequently found in the lake; nor can it be denied but the fineft amethyfts, emeralds, and other precious ftones, and the hardeft, are found in this country ; and the common Kerry ftone nearly approaches the diamond in luftre and hardnefs. Yet it is not above fifty years fince fuch have been difcovered ; though we read, that our early princes and nobles wore them in their ears and on their cloaths ; and that the Bifhop of Feficoli has mentioned thefe among the other productions of Ireland ! In opening of many other mines, old fhafts have been difcovered, and implements of mining found, particularly in a rich lead one, on the eftate of Thomas Weftrop, Efq; in this county, and bordering on the Shannon. In working the lead mines of Knocaderry, fince called Silver Mines, in the county of Tipperary, in the beginning of the laft century, fhafts were feen, and every other proof of its being worked centuries earlier. The rich copper mines in the county of Wicklow, and thefe latter ones in the county of Tipperary, are ftill further proofs of the great plenty of this metal formerly ; and will explain why

* Nat. Hiftory county of Kerry, p. 125.
† Epift. Hibern, 5yl. p. 81, &c.

l

the

the fharp edges of the blades of our antient fwords, &c. were of a mixt brafs; and how the people of Leinfter were ena-bled to give fix thonfand copper cauldrons to the Monarch's tax-gatherers, every fecond year, being a part of their famous tribute, the caufe of fo much bloodfhed in Ireland.

When the Spaniards, in Queen Elizabeth's days, landed at Smerwic bay, in the county of Kerry, on erecting a fort near it, from the many pieces of gold they found here they called it Fort de l'or; and fome years ago fome country peo-ple, in trenching potatoes near it, found feveral corfelets of pure gold. Mr. Smith * fuppofes this to be part of the trea-fures fent from Spain, in thefe days; but is it probable that gold corfelets were fent to relieve a diftreffed people, who only wanted powder and ball, and which they fought for at an immenfe expence? Befides, Sir George Carew, then pre-fident of Munfter, and an indifputable authority, tells us †, that thefe treafures were in money, fafely landed by Mac Eagan, Apoftolic Vicar, and by him diftributed to the Irifh chiefs; nay, he is even minute enough to tell us each per-fon's fhare. But numbers of thefe, as well as handles of fwords, and gold of a particular colour and hardnefs, made for the purpofe of lodging the poll-axes of our antient *Marc-Sloigh*, or cavalry, have been frequently found. Of thefe corfelets alone, I have feen above twenty, and purchafed one, the gold cf which was fo ductile as to roll up, like paper. Thefe likewife prove the reality of our Niagha-Nafc, or Knights of the Golden Collar, as well as the fuperior know-ledge of our anceftors in the natural hiftory of their country. They fhew the care taken to advance nothing but what was ftrictly true, in our antient hiftory; and at the fame time, point out to the public, the great lofs the learned world, as well as this kingdom, has fuftained by the deftruction of fo many of our antient annals, and the neceffity of attending more diligently to what remain. Even our old odes and bal-lads, fhould not be too flightly regarded. The Bifhop of London, in his edition of Cambden, p. 1411, tells us, " That " The Bifhop of Derry being one day at dinner, an Irifh harp-" er came in, and fung an old ode to the harp, the fubftance " of which was, that in fuch a place, pointing to the very " fpot, near Ballyfhannon, a man of gigantic figure lay bu-" ried; and that over his breaft and back were plates of pure " gold, and on his fingers rings of the fame; the place was

---

* Hiftory of Kerry, p. 186.   † Pacat. Hibern. p. 306.

" fo

" fo minutely defcribed, that two of the company were
" tempted to examine into it, and did accordingly find two
" thin pieces of pure gold," a figure of one of which, Mr.
Harris gives. The great plenty of gold in antient Ireland
cannot be contefted. We have feen that part of the furniture
of Tara was of pure gold, as was moft of the church plate
through the kingdom: even the bells for the altars were of
gold, or of filver inlaid with gold, and ornamented with precious ftones, many of which exifted in the laft century, as
the learned Colgan witneffes *; and we yet call them Muil-
lean-oir. Nay this luxury extended to private life; thus,
the ô *Cowhig*'s, a family in the county of Cork, are, in a very
antient poem, diftinguifhed from their neighbours, the ô *Dif-
coll*'s, and ô *Flain*'s, by the epithet of ô *Colhtaicc*, *na N'ard-
Ccorn oir*, or ô *Cowhig* of the lofty gold drinking cup. Should
any doubt yet remain of the wealth of antient Ireland, the
Airigid-Sron, or Nofe-money, being an ounce of gold paid
annually by the head of every family, under the Danifh
power to thefe tyrants, may, furely, remove it.

When I firft propofed to myfelf the compilation of the following work, I did not intend the prefent fubject fhould extend beyond a general reference to a pamphlet which ought
to be dear to every Irifhman, I mean, Mr. Molyneaux's Cafe
of Ireland, &c. and a copy of the Irifh Magna Charta, which
laft, even to every difpaffionate reader, ought to be fufficient,
as ratified in the fame folemn manner, and containing the
fame facred privileges and immunities of the Englifh one, to
which they very juftly hold no law fuperior †. I fhall, however, claim the reader's indulgence, and proceed further:

All the charters and grants of liberties from Edward ‡ the
Confeffor's time down to the 9th of Henry the III. were but
confirmations one of another, and al of them declarations
and confirmations of the common law of England. And by
the feveral eftablifhments, which we have formerly mentioned,
of the laws of England to be of force in Ireland: Firft, in
the 13th of Henry II. Secondly, in the 12th of king John.

* Act. Sanctor. Hibern, p. 149

† Magna Charta is only an abridgment of our ancient laws and cuftoms; the King that fwears to it, fwears to them all, and is not admitted
to be interpreter of it, or to determine what is good or evil, fit to be obferved or annulled in it, and he can have no more power over the reft.
Lord Somers on the Rights of the people.

‡ Molyneux.

Thirdly,

Thirdly, in the 12th of Henry III. All thofe laws and cuftoms of England, which by thofe feveral charters were declared and confirmed to be the laws of England, were eftablifhed to be of force in Ireland. And thus Ireland came
to be governed by one and the fame common law with England ; and thofe laws continue as part of the municipal and
fundamental laws of both kingdoms to this day.

It now remains that we enquire, how the ftatute laws and
acts of parliament made in England, fince the 9th of Henry
III. came to be of force in Ireland ; and whether all or any
of them, and which, are in force here, and when and how
they came to be fo.

And the firft precedent that occurs in our books, of acts
of parliament made in Ireland, particularly mentioning and
confirming fpecial acts of parliament in England, is found in
a marginal note of Sir Richard Bolton's, formerly lord chief
baron of the Exchequer in Ireland, affixed in his edition of
the Irifh ftatutes, to ftat. 10 Hen. 7, cap. 22. to this purport,
That in 13 Ed. II. ' by parliament in this realm of Ireland
' the ftatutes of Merton, made the 20th of Henry II. and
' the ftatutes of Marlbridge, made the 25th of Henry III.
' the ftatute of Weftminfter the firft, made the 3d of Edward
' I. the ftatute of Gloucefter, made the 6th of Edward I.
' and the ftatute of Weftminfter the fecond, made the 13th
' of Edward I. were all confirmed in this kingdom, and all
' other ftatutes which were of force in England, were re-
' ferred to be examined in the next parliament ; and fo many
' as were then* allowed and publifhed, to ftand likewife for
' laws in this kingdom. And in the 10th of Henry
' IV. it was enacted in this kingdom of Ireland, " That
" the ftatutes made in England fhould not be of force in
" this kingdom, unlefs they were allowed and publifhed
" in this kingdom by parliament." ' And the like ftatute
' was made again in the 29th of Henry VI. Thefe fta-
' tutes are not to be found in the rools, nor any parliament
' roll of that time; but he (Sir Richard Bolton) had feen the
' fame exemplifyed under the great feal, and the exempli-
' fication remaineth in the treafury of the city of Waterford.'
Thus far the note. If we confider the frequent troubles and
diftractions in Ireland, we fhall not wonder that thefe, and
many other rolls and records, have been loft in this kingdom:
For from the 3d year of Edward the II. which was anno

* Vid. lib. rubr fcaccar. Dubl.

13 o, through the whole reigns of Edward the III. Richard II. Henry IV. and Henry V. and fo to the 7th year of Henry VI. anno 1428, which is about 118 years, there are not any parliament rolls to be found * ; yet certain it is, that divers parliaments were held in Ireland in thofe times †. The fame may be faid from Henry II's coming into Ireland, anno 1172, to the 3d year of Edward II anno 13,0, about 138 years.

Perhaps it may be faid, that if there were fuch ftatutes of Ireland as the faid acts of the 10th of Henry IV. and the 29th of Henry VI. as they fhew, that the parliaments of Ireland did think that Englifh acts of parliament could not bind Ireland ; yet they fhew likewife, that, even in thofe days, the parliaments of England did claim this fuperiority; or elfe to what purpofe were the faid acts made, unlefs in denial of that claim.

All which I hope may be readily granted without any pre-judice to the right of the Irifh parliaments : there is nothing fo common, as to have one man claim another man's right : and if bare pretence will give a title, no man is fecure : and it will be yet worfe, if when another fo pretends, and I infift on my right, my juft claim fhall be turned to my prejudice, and to the difparagement of my title.

We know very well, that many of the judges of our four-courts have been from time to time fent out of England; and fome of them may eafily be fuppofed to come over hither prepofeffed with an opinion of our parliament's being fubordi-nate to that of England. Or, at leaft, fome of them may be fcrupulous, and defirous of full fecurity in this point ; and on their account, and for their fatisfaction, fuch acts as afore-faid, may be devifed, and enacted in Ireland. But then, God forbid that thefe acts fhould afterwards be laid hold of to a clear other intent than what they were framed for ; and inftead of declaring and fecuring our rights, fhould give an handle of conteft, by fhewing that our rights have been quef-tioned of ancient time.

In conclufion of all, if this fuperiority of the parliament of England have been doubted a great while ago, fo it has been as great a while ago ftrenuoufly oppofed, and abfolutely denied by the parliaments of Ireland : and by the way, I fhall take notice, that from whencefoever this ancient pre-tence of Ireland's fubordination proceeded in thofe days, it did

* Annals of Ireland, at the end of Camden's Britain. Edit. 1637. page 195, 197, &c.
† Ibid. page 160. Pryn againft the 4th Inftit. chap. 76.

not arife from the parliament of England itfelf: for we have not one fingle inftance of an Englifh act of parliament exprefsly claiming this right of binding us: but we have feveral inftances of Irifh acts of parliament exprefsly denying this fubordination, as appears by what foregoes.

Afterwards, by a ftatute made in Ireland the 18th of Henry VI. cap. 1. All the ftatutes made in England againft the extortions and opprefsions of purveyors, are enacted to be 'holden and kept in all points, and put in execution in this 'land of Ireland.'

And in the 32d year of Henry VI. cap. 1. by a parliament in Ireland 'tis enacted, ' That all the ftatutes made againft 'provifors to the court of Rome, as well in England as in 'Ireland, be had and kept in force.'

After this, in a parliament at Drogheda the 8th of Edward IV. cap. 1. it was ratifyed, that the Englifh ftatute againft rape, made the 6th of Richard II. fhould be of force in Ireland, from the 6th day of March laft paft: ' And that 'from henceforth the faid act, and all other ftatutes and acts 'made by authority of parliament within the realm of Eng'land, be ratifyed, and confirmed, and adjudged, by the 'authority of this parliament in their force and ftrength, 'from the faid fixth day of March.' We fhall hereafter have occafion of taking farther notice of this ftatute upon another account.

Laftly, in a parliament held at Drogheda the 10th of Henry VII. cap. 22. it is enacted, ' that all ftatutes late' (that is as the * learned in the laws expound it, before that time) 'made 'in England, concerning the common and public weal of the 'fame, from henceforth be deemed effectual in law, and be 'accepted, ufed and executed within this land of Ireland in 'all points, &c.'

† And in the 14th year of the fame king's reign, in a parliament held at Triftle-Dermot, it was enacted, That all acts of parliament made in England for punifhing cuftomers, controulers, and fearchers, for their mifdemeanors; or for punifhment of merchants or factors, be of force here in Ireland, provided they be firft proclaimed at Dublin, Drogheda, and other market-towns.

Thus we fee by what fteps and degrees all the ftatutes which were made in England, from the time of Magna Charta, to the 10th of Henry VII. which did concern the public commonweal,

---

* Cook's 4th inftit. cap. 76, p. 351.   † Vid. Irifh Stat.

were received, confirmed, and authorized to be of force in Ireland; all which was done by affent of the lords fpiritual and temporal, and the commons in the parliament of Ireland affembled, and no otherwife.

We fhall not enquire, whether there are not other acts of the Englifh parliament, both before and fince the 10th of Henry VII. which were and are of force in Ireland, though not allowed of by parliament in this kingdom. And we fhall find, that by the opinion of our beft lawyers, there are divers fuch; but then they are only fuch as are declaratory of the ancient common law of England, and not introductive of any new law: for thefe become of force by the firft general eftablifh-ment of the common laws of England in this kingdom, under Henry II. king John, and Henry III. and need no particular act of Ireland for their fanction.

As to thofe Englifh ftatutes fince the 10th of Henry VIIth, that are introductive of a new law, it was never made a quef-tion whether they fhould bind Ireland, without being allowed in parliament here; till of very late years this doubt began to be moved; and how it has been carried on and promoted, fhall appear more fully hereafter.

I fay, till of very late years; for the ancient precedents which we have to the contrary, are very numerous. Amongft many, we fhall mention the following particulars.

In the 2.ft of Henry VIIIth, an act was made in England, making it felony in a fervant that runeth away with his mif-ter's or miftrefs's goods. This act was not received in Ireland till it was enacted by a parliament held here in the 33d of Henry VIIIth, c. 5. Sef. 1.

In the 21ft of Henry VIII. c. 19. there was a law made in England, that all lords might diftrain on the lands of them holden, and make their avowry not naming the tenant, but the land. But this was not of force in Ireland till enacted here in the 33d of Henry VIII. c. 1. Sef. 1.

An act was made in England, anno 31 Henry VIII. that joint-tenants and tenants in common fhould be compelled to make partition, as co-parceners were compellable at common law. But this act was not received in Ireland till enacted here, anno 33 Henry VIII. c. 10.

Anno 27 Henry VIII. c. 10. the ftatute for transferring ufes into poffeffion was made in England; but not admitted in Ireland till 10 Car. 2, Sef. 2.

In

In like manner, the Englifh ftatute 33 Henry VIII. c. 1. directing how lands and tenements may be difpofed by will, &c. was not of force in Ireland till 10 Car. 2. Sef. 2.

The act of uniformity of common prayer and adminiftration of the facraments was made in England the ift of Eliz. c. 2. but was not eftablifhed in Ireland till the 2d of Eliz. c. 2. And fo that of England 14 Car. 2. c. 14. was not received in Ireland till 17 & 18 Car. 2. c. 6.

The ftatute againft wilful perjury made in England 5 Eliz. c. 9. was not enacted in Ireland till 28 Eliz. c. 1.

So the Englifh act againft witchcraft and forcery made 5 Eliz. c. 16. And another act againft forgery 5 Eliz. c. 14. were neither of them in force in Ireland till the 28th of her reign, cap. 3, and 4.

The Englifh ftatute againft piracies was made the 28th of Henry VIII. c. 15. but not in, Ireland till the 12th of King James, c. 2.

In England an act was made the 27th of Eliz. c. 4. againft fraudulent conveyances ; but it was not in force in Ireland till enacted here the 10th of Charles, c. 3 Sef. 2.

In the 15th year of king Charles I. in a parliament held at Dublin, there were fix Englifh ftatutes made laws of this kingdom, with fuch alterations as beft fitted them to the ftate thereof, viz.

21 Jac. c. 14. For pleading the general iffue in intrufions brought by the king, by chap. 1 of the Irifh ftatutes.

31 Eliz. c. 2. For abridging of proclamations on fines, by chap. 2.

2 and 3 Edw. VI. c. 8. concerning offices before the efcheator, by chap. 4.

31 Eliz. c. 1. Difcontinuance of writs of error in the Exchequer chamber, by chap. 5.

8 Eliz. c. 4. and 18 Eliz. c. 7. concerning clergy, by chap. 7.

24 Hen. VIII. c. 5. concerning killing a robber, by chap. 9.

There are fix Englifh ftatutes likewife paffed in the time of king Charles II. upon and foon after the reftoration, fome of which were not paffed into laws in Ireland till a year, two or three, afterwards : as will appear by confulting the ftatute books *

* Irifh ftat. 13 C. 2, c. 2. 13 C. 2, c. 3. 14 & 15 C. 2, c. 1. 14 & 1_ C. 2, c. 19, 17 & 18 C. 2, c. 3. 17 & 18 C. 2, c. 11. Englifh ftat. 1_ C. 2, c. 12. 12 C. 2, c. 3. 12 C. 2, c. 14. 12 C. 2, c. 24. 12 C. 2, c. 3. 1_ & 17 C. 2, c. 5.

And

And in the first year of William and Mary, Sef. 2. c. 9. an act paffed in England, declaring all attainders and other acts made in the, late pretended parliament under king James at Dublin, void : but was not enacted here in Ireland till the 7th year of king William, c. 3. And this was thought requifite to be done upon mature confideration thereon before the king and council of England *, notwithftanding that the Englifh act does particularly name Ireland, and was wholly defigned for, and relates thereto.

The like may we find in feveral other ftatutes of England paffed fince his prefent majefty's acceffion to the throne, which have afterwards been paffed here in Ireland, with fuch alterations as make them practicable and agreeable to this kingdom, fuch as are amongft others, the act for difarming papifts. The act of recognition. The act for taking away clergy from fome offenders. The act for taking fpecial bail in the country, &c. The act againft clandeftine mortgages. The act againft curfing and fwearing.

Thefe, with many more, are to be found in our ftatute books in the feveral reigns of Henry VIII. Edward VI. queen Elizabeth, king James, king Charles I. and II. and king William. But it is not to be found in any records in Ireland, that ever any act of parliament, introductive of a new law made in England fince the time of king John, was by the judgment of any court, received for law, or put in execution in the realm of Ireland, before the fame was confirmed and affented to by the parliament in Ireland.

And thus I prefume we have pretty clearly made out, and plainly fhewn the feveral fteps by which the Englifh form of government, and the Englifh ftatute laws were received in this kingdom ; and that this was wholly by the people's confent in parliament, to which we have had a very ancient right, and as full a right as our next neighbours can pretend to, or challenge.

It were endlefs to mention all the records and precedents that might be quoted for the eftablifhment of the laws of England; I fhall therefore enter no farther into that matter but therein refer to lord chief juftice Cook, † Pryn ‡, Reyly §, &c.

---

* For we have had two feveral acts tranfmitted to us at different times, to this very purpofe. One we rejected in the lord Sidney's government, t'other paffed under the lord Capell.

† Fourth inft. ‡ Againft the fourth inft. § Placita parliamentaria.

m   The

The hand of Englifh power may be faid then to have grafped at Irifh freedom only, under the deteftable reign of Charles II*.

In the year 1663 the diftinctions † between the trade of England and Ireland ‡, and the reftraints on that of the latter commenced. By an Englifh act paffed in that year, intitled an act "for the encouragement of trade," a title not very applicable to the parts of it that related to Ireland, be- fides laying a duty nearly equal to a prohibition on cattle im- ported into England from that kingdom, the exportation of all commodities, except victuals, fervants, horfes, and falt for the fifheries of New England and Newfoundland, from thence to the Englifh plantations, was prohibited from the 25th of March, 1764. The exports allowed were ufeful to them, but prejudicial to Ireland, as they confifted of our people, our provifions, and a material for manufacture which we might have ufed more profitably on our own coafts.

In 1670 another act ‖ paffed in England, to prohibit from the 24th of March 1671, the exportation from the Englifh plantations to Ireland of feveral materials for manufactures §, without firft unloading in England or Wales. We are in- formed by this act that the reftraint of the exportation from the Englifh plantations to Ireland was intended by the act of 1663: but the intention is not effectuated, though the impor- tation of thofe commodities into Ireland *from England*, with- out firft unloading there, is, in effect, prohibited by that act.

The prohibition of importing into Ireland any plantation goods, unlefs the fame had been firft landed in England, and had paid the duties, is made general, without any exception, by the Englifh act of the 7th and 8th W. 3d, ch. 22.

* This I am fure of, that before thefe acts (cattle, tobacco, and navi- gation acts) in King Charles II. time, (the eldeft of which is not over thirty-feven years) there is not one pofitive full precedent to be met with in all the ftatute-book, of an Englifh act binding the kingdon of Ireland. And on this account we may venture to affert, that thefe are at leaft innovations on us, as not being warranted by any former precedents. And fhall proceedings only of thirty-feven years ftanding, be urged againft a nation, to deprive them of the rights and liberties which they enjoyed for five hundred years before, and which were invaded without and againft their confent, and from that day to this have been conftantly complained of? Let any Englifh heart that ftands fo juftly in vindication of his own rights and liberties, anfwer this queftion, and I have done. Moiyneux, p. 40.

† Commer. Reftr.
‡ 15 Ch. 2, ch. 7.   ‖ 22d and 23d Ch. 2d, ch. 26.
§ Sugar, tobacco, cotton, wool, indigo, fteel or Jamaica wood, fuftick, or other dying wood, the growth of the faid plantations.

By

By comparing the reftrictive law of 1699, with the fta- tutes which had been previoufly enacted in England from the 15th year of the reign of Charles the Second, relative to the Colonies, it appears that this reftrictive law originated in a fyftem of colonization. The principle of that fyftem was, that the Colonies fhould fend their materials to England, and take from thence her manufactures, and that the making thofe manufactures in the Colonies fhould be prohibited or difcour- aged. But was it reafonable to extend this principle to Ire- land ? The climate, growth and productions of the Colonies were different from thofe of their parent country. England had no fugar-canes, coffee, dying-ftuff, and little tobacco. She took all thofe from her Colonies only, and it was thought reafonable that they fhould take from her only the manufac- tures which fhe made. But in Ireland, the climate, foil, growth and productions are the fame as in England, who could give no fuch equivalent to Ireland as fhe gave to Ame- rica, and was fo far from confidering her, when this fyftem firft prevailed, as a proper fubject for fuch regulations, that fhe was allowed the benefits arifing from thofe Colonies equally with England, until the 15th year of the reign of King Charles * the Second. By an act paffed in that year, Ireland had no longer the privilege of fending any of her exports, except fervants, horfes, victuals and falt, to any of the Colo- nies; the reafons are affigned in the preamble, " To make " this kingdom a ftaple, not only of the commodities of thofe " plantations, but alfo of the commodities of other countries " and places for the fupplying of them, and it being the " ufage of other nations to keep their plantation trade to " themfelves †." At the time of paffing this law, though lefs liberal ideas in refpect of Ireland were then entertained, it went no further than not to extend to her the benefit of thofe Colony regulations; but it was not then thought that this kingdom was a proper fubject for any fuch regulations. The fcheme of fubftituting there, inftead of the woollen, the linen trade, was not at that time thought of. The Englifh were defirous to eftablifh it among themfelves, and by an act of parliament ‡ made in that year for encouraging the manu- facture of linen, granted to all foreigners who fhall fet it up in England, the privileges of natural born fubjects.

* 15 Ch. II. ch. 7.

† As other nations did the fame, Ireland was fhut out from the new world, and a confiderable part of the old in Afia and Africa.

‡ 15 Ch. II. ch. 15.

But

But it appears by the Englifh ftatute of the 7th and 8th
Will. III *. that this fcheme had not fucceeded ·in England ;
and from this act it is manifeft that England confidered itfelf,
as well as Ireland, interefted to encourage the linen manufacture there ; and it does not then appear to have been
thought juft, that Ireland fhould purchafe this benefit for
both, by giving up the exportation of any other manufacture.
But in 1698 a different principle prevailed ; in effect the fame,
fo far as relates to the woollen manufacture, with that which
had prevailed as to the commerce of the Colonies.   This is
evident from the preamble of the Englifh law † made in 1699,
" For as much as wool and woollen manufactures of cloth,
" ferge, bays, kerfies and other ftuffs, made or mixed with
" wool, are the greateft, and moft profitable commodities of
" this kingdom, on which the value of lands and the trade
" of the nation do chiefly depend; and whereas great quan-
" tities of like manufactures have of late been made and are
" daily encreafing in the kingdom of Ireland, and *in the*
" *Englifh plantations* in America, and are exported from thence
" to foreign markets, heretofore fupplied from England,
" which will inevitably fink the value of lands, and tend to
" the ruin of the trade and woollen manufactures of this
" realm ; for the prevention whereof, and for the encourage-
" ment of the woollen manufactures in this kingdom, &c."
The ruinous confequences of the woollen manufactures of
Ireland to the value of lands, trade and manufactures of England, ftated in this act, are apprehenfions that were entertained, and not events that had happened ; and before thofe
facts are taken for granted, I requeft the mifchiefs recited in
in the acts ‡ made in England to prevent the importation of
cattle dead or alive from Ireland, may be confidered.
Connecting this preamble of the act of 1699, with the
fpeech made from the throne to the parliament of Ireland
in the year 1698, with the addreffes of both houfes in England, and with the prohibition, by this and by other acts
formerly made in England, of exporting wool from Ireland
except to that kingdom, the object of this new commercial
regulation is obvious.   It was to difcourage the woollen
manufacture in Ireland, and in effect, to prohibit the exportation from thence, becaufe it was the principal branch of

* Ch. 39.
† 10th and 11th W. III. ch. 10.
‡ 15 Ch. II. ch. 7. 18 Ch. II. ch. 2. 20 Ch. II. ch. 7. 22d and
23d Ch. II. ch. 6. 3 Ch. II. ch. 2.

manufacture,

manufacture, and trade in England, to induce us to fend to them our materials for that manufacture, and that we should be supplied with it by them ; and to encourage, as a compensation to Ireland, the linen manufacture, which was not at that time a commercial object of any importance to England.

The supposed compensation was no more than what Ireland had before ; no further encouragement was given by England to our linen manufacture until six years after this prohibition, when at the request of the Irish house of commons, and after a representation of the ruinous state of this country, liberty was given by an English act of parliament * to export our white and brown linens into the colonies, which was allowing us to do as to one manufacture, what, before the 15th of king Charles the second, was permitted in every instance.

For several centuries before this period Ireland was in possession of the English common law †, and of magna charta. The former secures the subject in the enjoyment of property of every kind; and by the latter, *the liberties of all the ports of the kingdom are established.*

The statutes made in England for the common and public weal, are ‡ by an Irish act of the 10th of Henry the 7th, made laws in Ireland ; and the English commercial statutes, in which Ireland is expressly mentioned, will place the former state of commerce in this country in a light very different from that in which it has been generally considered in Great-Britain.

' By the 17th of Edward the 3d, ch. 1. all forts of merchandizes may be exported from Ireland, except to the king's enemies.

' By the 27th of Edward the 3d, ch. 18. merchants of Ireland and Wales may bring their merchandize to the staple of England ; and by the 34th of the same king, ch. 17. all kinds of merchandizes may be exported from and imported into Ireland, as well by aliens as denizens. In the same year there is another statute, ch. 18. that all persons who have lands or possessions in Ireland, may freely import thither,

---

* 3 and 4 Ann. ch. 8.
† 4 Inst. 349. Matth. Paris, anno 1172. p. 121, 220. Vit H. 2, Pryn, against the 4th Inst. 76, p. 250, 252. Sir. John Davis's Hist. 71. Lord Lyttleton's Hist. of H. 2. 3 Vol. 89, 90. 7 Co. 22. 23. 4th Black. 429.
‡ Cooke's 4th Inst. 351.

and export from that kingdom *their own commodities;* and by the 5cth of Edward the 3d, ch. 8. no alnage is to be paid, if frize ware, which are made in Ireland.

The reign of Edward the 4th furnishes still stronger instances of the *regard* shewn by England to the trade and manufactures of this country.

In the third year of that monarch's reign, the artificers of England complained to parliament that they were greatly impoverished and *could not live* by bringing in divers commodities and wares ready wrought *, An act passed reciting those complaints, and ordaining that no merchant born a subject of the king, denizen or stranger, or other person should bring into England or Wales any woollen cloths, &c. and enumerates many other manufactures, on pain of forfeiture; provided that all wares and " chaffers" made and wrought in Ireland or Wales, may be brought in and sold in the realm of England, as they were wont before the making of that act. †

In the next year another act ‡ passed in that kingdom, that all woollen cloth brought into England and set to sale, should be forfeited, except cloths made in Wales or Ireland.

In those reigns England was as careful of the commerce and manufactures of her ancient sister kingdom, particularly in her great staple trade, as she was of her own.

Of this attention there were further instances in the years 1468 and 1478. In two treaties concluded in those years between England and the duke of Bretagne, the merchandize to be traded in between England, Ireland and Calais on the one part, and Bretagne on the other, is specified, and woollen cloths are particularly mentioned §.

And in a treaty between Henry the 7th and the Netherlands, Ireland is included, both as to exports and imports ‖.

From this time until the 15th of king Charles the 2d, which takes in a period of 167 years, the commercial constitution of Ireland was as much favoured and protected as that of England; " the free enlargement of common traf-" fic which his majesty's subjects of Ireland enjoyed," is

* 3d Edw. 4. ch. 4.
† The part of this law which mentions that it shall be determinable at the king's pleasure, has the prohibition for its object, and does not lessen the force of the argument in favour of Ireland.
‡ 4th Edw. IV. ch. 1.   § Anderson on Commerce, 1 Vol. 285.
‖ Ib. 319

taken

taken notice of incidentally, in an Englifh ftatute, in the
reign of king James the 1ft* ; and in 1627 king Charles
the 1ft made a ftrong declaration in favour of the trade and
manufactures of this country. By feveral Englifh ftatutes in
the reign of king Charles the 2d, an equal attention was
fhewn to the woollen manufactures in both kingdoms; in
the 12th year of his reign † the exportation of wool, wool-
felts, fuller's earth, or any kind of fcowering-earth, was prohibited from both. But let the reafons, mentioned in the
" preamble, for paffing this law be adverted to: " For pre-
" venting inconveniencies and loffes that happened, and that
" daily do and may happen to the kingdom of England,
" dominion of Wales, and kingdom of Ireland, through the
" fecret exportation of wool out of and from the faid king-
" doms and dominions; and for the *better fetting on work the*
" *poor people* and inhabitants of the kingdoms and dominions
" aforefaid, and to the intent that the full ufe and benefit of
" *the principal native commodities* of the fame kingdom and
" dominion may come, redound, and be unto the fubjects and
" inhabitants of the fame.

The fhipping and navigation of England and Ireland were
at this time equally favoured and protected. By another act
of the fame year, no goods or commodities ‡ of the growth,
production or manufacture of Afia, Africa or America, fhall
be imported into England, *Ireland* or Wales, but in fhips
which belong to the people of England or *Ireland,* the dominion of Wales, or the town of Berwick upon Tweed, or
which are of the built of the faid lands, and of which the
mafter and three-fourths of the mariners are Englifh; and a
fubfequent ftatute § makes the encouragement to navigation
in both countries equal, by ordaining that the fubjects of Ireland and of the Plantations fhall be accounted Englifh within
the meaning of that claufe. Another law ‖ of the fame reign
fhews that the navigation, commerce and woollen manufactures of both kingdoms were equally protected by the Englifh
legiflature. This act lays on the fame reftraint as the above-
mentioned act of the 12th of Charles II. and makes the tranfgreffion ftill more penal. It recites that wool, wool-felts, &c.
are fecretly exported from England and Ireland to foreign
parts, to the great decay of the woollen manufactures and

* 3d James, ch. 6.   † 12th Ch. 2, ch. 32.
‡ 12 Ch. 2, ch. 18.   § 13th and 14th Ch. 2, ch. 11.
‖ 13th and 14th Ch. 2, ch. 18.

the

the deſtruction of the navigation and commerce of *theſe kingdoms.*

From thoſe laws it appears that the commerce, navigation and manufactures of this country were not only favoured and protected by the Engliſh legiſlature, but that we had in thoſe times the full benefit of their Plantation trade ; whilſt the woollen manufactures were protected and encouraged in England and Ireland, the planting of tobacco in both was prohibited, becauſe " it was one of the main products of ſeveral " of the plantations, and upon which their welfare and ſub" ſiſtence do depend*." This policy was liberal, juſt and equal ; it opened the reſources, and cultivated the ſtrength of every part of the empire.

This commercial ſyſtem of Ireland was enforced by ſeveral acts of her own legiſlature ; two ſtatutes paſſed in the reign of Henry VIII. to prevent the exportation of wool, becauſe, ſays the firſt of thoſe laws, " it hath been the cauſe of dearth " of cloth, and idleneſs of many folks †," and " tends to the " deſolation and ruin of this poor land." The ſecond of thoſe laws inforces the prohibition ‡ by additional penalties ; it recites, " that the ſaid beneficial law had taken little effect, but " that ſince the making thereof, great plenty of wool had been " conveyed out of this land, to the great and ineſtimable hurt, " decay and impoveriſhment of the King's poor ſubjects within " the ſaid land ; for redreſs whereof, and in conſideration that " conveying of the wool of the growth of this land out of the " ſame is one of the greateſt occaſions of the idleneſs of the " people, waſte, ruin and deſolation of the King's cities and " borough towns, and other places of his dominion within " this land." The 11th of Elizabeth § lays duties on the exportation equal to a prohibition ; and the reaſon given in the preamble ought to be mentioned ; " That the ſaid commodities " may be more abundantly wrought in this realm ere they ſhall " be ſo tranſported, than preſently they are, which ſhall ſet " many now living idle on work, to the great relief and com" modity of this realm ‖."

By the preamble of one of thoſe acts, made in the reign of Charles II. it appears that the ſale of Iriſh woollen goods

---

* 12 Ch. 2, ch. 27.   † Ir. act, 13 H. 8, ch. 2.
‡ 28 H. 8, ch. 17.   § Ch. 10.
‖ The neceſſity of encouraging the people of Ireland to manufacture their own wool, appears, by divers ſtatutes, to have been the ſenſe of the legiſlature of both kingdoms for ſome centuries.

in

in foreign markets was encouraged by England; "whereas
" there is a general complaint in *England*, France, and other
" parts beyond the seas, (whither the woollen cloths and other
" commodities made of wool in this his Majesty's kingdom of
" Ireland are transported) of the false, deceitful, uneven, and
" uncertain making thereof, which cometh to pass by reason
" that the clothiers and makers thereof do not observe any cer-
" tain assize for length, breadth and weight for making their
" cloths and other commodities aforesaid in this kingdom, as
" they do in the realm of England, and as they ought also to
" do here; by which means the merchants, buyers and users of
" the said cloth and other commodities are much abused and
" deceived, and the credit, esteem and sale of the said cloth and
" commodities is thereby much impaired and undervalued, to
" the great and general hurt and hindrance of the trade of
" clothing in this whole realm."

After the ports of England were shut against our cattle,
and our trade to the English Colonies was restrained, still
this commercial system was adhered to by encouraging the
manufactures of this country, and the exportation of them to
foreign countries. In 1667, when the power of the crown
was not so well understood as at present, the proclamation before mentioned was published by the Lord Lieutenant and
Privy Council of Ireland *, in pursuance of a letter from
Charles II. by the advice of his council in England, notify-
ing to all his subjects of this kingdom, the allowance of a
free trade to all foreign countries, either at war or at peace
with his Majesty.

In 1698 a most unjustifiable attack was made on the judicial privilege of the Irish House of Lords, by the English,
which gave birth to the following

ORDER of the HOUSE of LORDS in ENGLAND,

Die Martis, 24th Maij, 1698.

WHEREAS a petition and appeal was offered to the house
on the 7th of January last, of the society of the governor
and assistants of London, of the new plantation in Ulster,
in the kingdom of Ireland, against a judgment given by the
Lords Spiritual and Temporal of Ireland in parliament there
assembled, on the 24th day of September last, upon the petition and appeal of William, Lord Bishop of Derry, against

* Carte, 2 Vol. p. 344.

n   the

the decree or order made in the faid caufe in the court of
Chancery there : whereupon a committee was appointed, to
confider of the proper method of appealing from the decrees
made in the court of Chancery in Ireland, and that purfu-
ant to the order of the faid committee, and a letter fent to
the Lords Juftices of Ireland, by order of this houfe, feveral precedents have been tranfmitted by the Lords Juftices to
this houfe, copies whereof were ordered to be delivered to
either fide: after hearing counfel upon the petition of the
fociety of London, prefented to this houfe the 20th of April
laft, praying that they might be heard, as to the jurifdiction
of the houfe of lords in Ireland, in receiving and judging
appeals from the Chancery there, as alfo counfel for the bifhop
of Derry : after due confideration of the precedents, and of
what was offered by counfel thereupon ; it is this day ordered, adjudged and declared, by the lords fpiritual and
temporal in parliament affembled, that the faid appeal by the
bifhop of Derry, to the houfe of lords in Ireland, from the
decree or order of the court of Chancery there made, in the
caufe wherein the faid bifhop of Derry was plaintiff, and the
faid fociety of the governors and affiftants of London, of the
New plantation in Ulfter, in Ireland, were defendants, was
coram non judice, and that all the proceedings thereupon are
null and void ; and, that the court of Chancery in Ireland
ought to proceed in the faid caufe, as if no fuch appeal had
been made to the houfe of lords there ; and if either of the
faid parties do find themfelves aggrieved by the faid decree or
order of Chancery, they are at liberty to purfue their proper
remedy by way of appeal to this houfe.

Ordered, That the Lord Chancellor do write to the lords
Juftices of Ireland, and fend them this order.

MAL. JOHNSON, *Ckr. Parl*.

REASONS againft the foregoing ORDER,
By WILLIAM MOLYNEUX, Efq.*

1ft. Becaufe upon the conqueft † of Ireland by Henry
the IId. he introduced the laws of England in that kingdom,
and fent over the *Modus Tenendi Parliamentum in Terminis,* the

* Found in the hand writing of the author in blank leaves of one of
his cafes, &c. fent to the then bifhop of Meath, and now in the poffeffion
of John Evans, Efq; St. Stephen's-green, Dublin.
† Mr. Molyneux here ufes the word *conqueft,* in compliance with the
Englifh idea of Henry's invafion, in order, we may fuppofe, to render
his arguments more fubfervient to their object.

fame

same with that of **England**, in which record it is said that
such things may be examined and corrected, *in Pleno parliamento et non alibi.*

2dly. Because in the 20th year of king Henry the third, it
was provided, that all laws and customs which are enjoyed
in England, shall be also in Ireland, and that the land shall
be subject thereunto and governed thereby, *sicut Dominus Jo-
hannes Ker cum ultimo esset in Hibernia statuit et fieri mandavit et
quod brevia de communi jure quæ currunt in Anglia similiter currant
in Hibernia.*

3dly. Because king Edward III. in the 29th year of his
reign, ordained for the quiet and good government of the
people in Ireland, that in all cases whatsoever, errors in
judgment, in records, and proceedings in the courts of Ireland, shall be corrected and amended in parliament in Ireland.

4thly. Because it appears by other ancient records *quod terra
Hiberniæ intra se omnes et omnimodas habet curias prout in Anglia.*

5thly. Because a conqueror by the laws of England and
of nations, having power to introduce what laws he will in
the conquered country, and king Henry II. pursuant to that
power, having introduced the laws of England, and particularly that of holding parliaments in Ireland the house of
lords in parliament in Ireland, may proceed to hear and determine judicially such matters as shall be brought before them,
in the same manner as the lords in parliament in England.

6thly. Because pursuant to the many concessions made by
king Henry II. king John, king Henry III. and other kings
of England, the Lords in parliament in Ireland, have proceeded to correct and amend errors in judgment and decrees
in the courts of Ireland, (as appears by the several precedents certified over to your lordships) and their judgments
never before this called in question, many of them being very
irregular. It is therefore presumed to have been by a good
and lawful jurisdiction, otherwise they would have been by
our ancestors (who were zealous assertors of their rights) long
before this called in question.

7thly. The order declaring the appeal was *coram non judice,*
and null and void, will call all other judgments and decrees in
question, under which many estates have been purchased, set-
tled, and enjoyed, which will be of fatal consequence to
many families, and create great discontent and dissatisfaction
in that kingdom.

8thly. Because the declaring the said appeal to be *coram non
judice,* and null and void, strikes at and tends to the destruc-
tion

tion of the jurifdiction of this houfe, for Ireland having *omnes et omnimodus curias prout in Anglia*, muft include the high court of parliament, and if their high court of parliament, being an exact picture of the high court of parliament in England, cannot judicially hear and determine appeals, writs of error, and impeachments, it may from thence be alleged that this here cannot.

9thly. Becaufe this refolution ftrikes at and tends to abridge the king's prerogative in Ireland; all appeals and writs of error in parliament being *coram rege in parliamento*, and therefore thefe words *coram non judice* takes from the king the judicial power which is given to him there.

10thly. Becaufe the peers of Ireland have little elfe left them befide their judicature, which if taken away, they will be of little efteem there, and many of the peers of England have fome of their titles of honour from that kingdom.

11thly. Becaufe it is the glory of the Englifh laws, and the blefling attending Englifhmen, that they have juftice adminiftered at their doors, and not to be drawn as formerly to Rome, by appeals which greatly impoverifhed the nation; and by this order the people of Ireland muft be drawn from Ireland hither, whenfoever they receive any injuftice from the Chancery there, by which means poor men muft be trampled upon, not being able to come over to feek for juftice.

12thly. The danger of altering, changing, or leflening a conftitution, for above five hundred years unfhaken, or fo much as called in queftion in any one thing, (the cuftom and ufage of courts being the law of courts) may occafion the deftruction of the whole, for the judicial power of the houfe of peers in Ireland, in criminal caufes by way of impeachment or otherwife, may by the fame reafon be called in queftion, as their judicature in civil caufes, which will encourage evil difpofed men, efpecially thofe in employment in that kingdom (who are generally very arbitrary) to act wickedly; and the better we preferve the conftitution of Ireland, and of thofe plantations dependant on England, the better we fhall preferve our own; and they will be barriers to ours, to prevent any invafion of theirs; and fince the Kings of England have in all times in matters relating to their revenue, their grants by letters patent, and their minifters not only empowered the parliament of Ireland to hear, correct, reform and amend them, but alfo acquiefced in their judgment, it ought not now to be queftioned.

13thly.

13thly. Becaufe this taking away the juriſdiction of the lords houſe in Ireland, may be a means to diſquiet the lords there, and diſappoint the king's affairs.

14thly. Becaufe the judicial power of the houſe of peers in Ireland is in no reſpect altered by an act of parliament, the ſtatute of the 10th of Henry 7, c. 4, called Poyning's law, only directs a new form of paſſing bills into laws, but alters nothing of the judicial power, and their argument of their having the interpretation of all laws by a judicial power being allowed them, will enable them to make the laws what they pleaſe, will as well hold againſt the juriſdiction of this houſe, which ought not to be ſuffered.

Proteſt of the Iriſh Lords on the preceding Order.

Die Veneris 11° Februarii, 1703°

P R E S E N T.

Lord Chancellor, Speaker.

Lords Spiritual.

Lord Archbp. of Armagh,	Lord Biſhop of Killalla,
Lord Archbp. of Dublin,	Lord Biſhop of Oſſory,
Lord Archbp. of Caſhel,	Lord Biſhop of Dromore,
Lord Archbp. of Tuam,	Lord Biſhop of Clogher,
Lord Biſhop of Meath,	Lord Biſhop of Limerick,
Lord Biſhop of Kildare,	Lord Biſhop of Killalo,
Lord Biſhop of Kilmore,	Lord Biſhop of Raphoe,
Lord Biſhop of Ferns,	Lord Biſhop of Downe,
Lord Biſhop of Clonfert,	Lord Biſhop of Cork.

Lords Temporal.

Earl of Roſcommon,	Lord Viſc. Dungannon,
Earl of Londonderry,	Lord Viſc. Charlemont,
Earl of Meath,	Lord Viſc. Powerſcourt,
Earl of Cavan,	Lord Viſc. Laneſborough,
Earl of Inchiquin,	P. Pr. Ld. Viſc. Mountjoy,
Earl of Mount Alexander,	Lord Viſc. Strabane,
Earl of Longford,	Lord Viſc. Doneraile,
Lord Viſc. Ely,	Lord Baron of Kerry,
Lord Viſc. Skerrin,	Lord Baron of Santry,
Lord Viſc. Maſſareene,	Lord Baron of Shelburne.

Ordered on motion, That the petition of Edward earl of Meath, and Cecilia Counteſs of Meath, his wife, be read.

Read accordingly.

Ordered on motion, That the clerk of the rolls, do bring into this houſe, the roll of the acts of parliament of the 38th of Henry VI.'

Reſolved

Refolved on the queftion *nem con*. That by the ancient and known laws and ftatutes of this kingdom, her majefty hath an undoubted jurifdiction and prerogative in this her high court of parliament, in all appeals and caufes within this her majefty's realm of Ireland.

Refolved on the queftion *nem con*. That the determinations and judgments of this high court of parliament are final and concluf·ve, and cannot be reverfed or fet afide by any other court whatfoever.

Refolved on the queftion *nem con*. That if any fubject or refident within this kingdom, fhall hereafter prefume to remove any caufe determined in this high court of parliament, to any other court, fuch perfon or perfons, fhall be deemed betrayers of her majefty's prerogative and jurifdiction, and the undoubted ancient rights and privileges of this houfe, and of the rights and liberties of the fubjects of this kirgdom.

Refolved on the queftion *nem con*. That if any fubject or refident within this kingdom, fhall prefume to put in execution any order from any other court, contrary to the final judgment and determination of this high court of parliament, fuch perfon or perfons, fhall be deemed betrayers of her majefty's prerogative and jurifdiction, and the undoubted ancient rights and privileges of this houfe, and of the rights and liberties of the fubjects of this kingdom, &c.

In the Irifh Houfe of Lords, in the year 1703, upon the petition of Edward, then earl of Meath, and Cecilia, countefs of Meath, his wife, againft the lord Ward, complaining of their having been difpoffeffed of certain lands in the county of Tipperary, under a pretended order of the houfe of lords of Great Britain ; we find the lords of Ireland[*], unanimoufly adopt the refolutions on the foregoing appeal, in 1698.

On the 12th day of February, 1703, their lordfhips made the following order:

Whereas, upon hearing the complaint of the right hon. Edward, earl of Meath, and Cecilia, countefs of Meath, his wife, exhibited to this houfe on the 19th of October laft, it has appeared upon full proof, that they have been illegally difpoffeffed of the lands of part of Rocheftown, Corruta, Loughloughery, Keating, Milfield, Richardfon alias Richeftown, Cloughnecody, Ardfinane and Faren-Englifh, Rathcordane and Grumgill, Gortnecrannah, Drumtrafney, Kilnemaun, Gurtinebamagh, and Garriglifh, all lying and being

[*] Jour. Houfe of Lords, fol. 52.

in the county of Tipperary, the actual possession whereof was given them, pursuant to an order of this house, dated the 29th of October 1695: We the lords spiritual and temporal in parliament assembled, this 12th day of Feb. 705, do order, require, and command the Sheriff of the said county of Tipperary, for the time being, forthwith to put the said earl and countess of Meath into the actual, quiet and peaceable possession of all the aforesaid lands and premises, as he will answer the contrary at his peril.

From this period until the year 1717, we find the house of Lords of Great Britain did not attempt to interfere with the rights and privileges of the lords and people of this kingdom.

But about the year 1717, that house thought proper once more to endeavour the establishment of their usurped authority, and accordingly entertained an appeal from Maurice Annesly, Esq; against a decision of the lords of Ireland, reversed their decree, and ordered the sheriff of the county of Kildare to restore to Mr. Annesley the possession of certain lands, of which he had been dispossessed by the order of the Irish Lords.

And to enforce this order, the British lords had recourse to the authority of the Barons of the court of Exchequer here, who ordered the Sheriff of Kildare to restore Mr. Annesley to the possession of his lands, according to the order of the Lords of Great Britain.

The sheriff (Alexander Burrowes, Esq;) Hampden-like, refused obedience to this illegal order: the barons endeavoured to enforce it by the imposition of heavy fines; whereupon he petitioned the Irish Lords for relief, which having been referred to a committee of the house, they, on the 28th July, 1719, made the following report, and entered into the following resolutions and proceedings *.

On the 17th of October, 1719, the house proceeded on the order of the day, for reading the representation to his majesty of the proceedings of the house upon the petition of Alex. Burrowes, Esq; in the cause of Sherlock and Annesley †.

And the said representation was read, and agreed to by the house, and is as follows, viz.

To the King's most excellent Majesty.
The humble representation of the Lords spiritual and temporal in Parliament assembled.

* Lords Journals, Vol. II. fol. 621 to 625.
† Ib. 654.

Most

Moſt gracious Sovereign,

IT is with the greateſt concern that we, your Majeſty's moſt dutiful and loyal ſubjects, the lords ſpiritual and temporal in parliament aſſembled, do find ourſelves under a neceſſity of making this our humble repreſentation to your Majeſty.

It evidently appears, by many antient records, and ſundry acts of parliament paſſed in this kingdom, and particularly by one in the 11th of Queen Eliz. intitled, " An act for attainder of Shane O'Neil, &c." that the kings, with all the princes and men of value of the land, did, of their own good wills, and without any war or chivalry, ſubmit themſelves to your Majeſty's royal anceſtor, King Henry II. took oaths of fidelity to him, and became his liege ſubjects, who (as it is aſſerted by the Lord Chief Juſtice Coke and others *) did ordain and command, at the inſtance of the Iriſh, that " ſuch laws as he had in England, ſhould be of force and obſerved in Ireland." By this agreement the people of Ireland obtained the benefit of the Engliſh laws, and many privileges, particularly that of having a diſtinct parliament here, as in England †, and of having weighty and momentous matters, relating to this kingdom, treated of, diſcuſſed and determined in the ſaid parliament.

This conceſſion and compact thus made, and afterwards, by ſucceeding kings, confirmed to the people of this land, in proceſs of time, proved a great encouragement to many of the Engliſh to come over and ſettle themſelves in Ireland, where they were to enjoy the ſame laws and liberties, and live under the like conſtitution as they had formerly done in the kingdom of England ‡ ; which, thro' God's good providence, has proved a means of ſecuring this kingdom to the crown of England, and we truſt will do ſo to all futurity. By this happy conſtitution, and theſe privileges by us for ſo

---

* Coke, 4th Inſt. p. 349. Matt. Paris, anno 1172, p. 105.   † Ib. 350.
‡ Pryn, on 4th Inſt. p. 287 .Anno 31 Ed. III.
" Rex Juſtic. &c. Cancellar. ſuis Hibern. ſalutem, &c.—Item volumus
" & precipimus quod noſtra & ipſius terræ negotia præſertim majora
" & ardua in conſiliis perperitos conſiliarios noſtros ac prælatos, & mag-
" nates, & quoſdam de diſcretioribus et probrioribus hominibus de par-
" tibus vicinis, ubi ipſa conſilia teneri contigerit propter hoc evocandos.
" In parliamentis vero, per ipſos conſiliarios noſtros ac prælatos, & pro-
" ceres alioſque de terra prædicta prout nos exigit ſecundum juſtitiam,
" legem, conſuetu & dinem rationem tractentur, deducantur, & fide-
" liter, timore, favore, odio aut pretio, poſt poſitis diſcutiantur & etiam
" terminentur."

many

many years enjoyed, the Englifh fubjects of this kingdom
have been enabled faithfully to difcharge their duty to the
crown of England, and vigoroufly fet themfelves, upon all
occafions, to affert the rights thereof, againft all the rebellions which have been raifed by the Irifh enemies.   And therefore, we, your Majefty's loyal fubjects, do, with all fubmiffion to your Majefty, *infift* upon them, and hope, through
your Majefty's goodnefs, to have them preferved inviolable.

And we beg leave to reprefent to your Majefty, that though
the imperial crown of this realm was formerly infeparably
annexed to the imperial crown of England, and is now to
that of Great-Britain *, yet this kingdom being of itfelf a
diftinct dominion, and no part of the kingdom of England,
none can determine concerning the affairs thereof, unlefs authorized thereto, by the known laws and cuftoms of this
kingdom, or by the exprefs confent of the king †.

And as your royal anceftors have always enjoyed the right
and power of determining all matters that related only to
this kingdom, by their royal authority, in their parliaments
held here, fo we humbly hope your Majefty will always look
on this right as a moft valuable jewel of your crown, which
none fhould prefume to touch without your Majefty's confent :
and that your Majefty will gracioufly allow us to reprefent
it, as an invafion of your prerogative, and a grievance to
your loyal fubjects in this kingdom, that any court of judicature fhould take upon them to declare, that your Majefty
cannot determine all controverfies between your fubjects of
this kingdom, and about matters relating wholly to the fame,
by your royal authority, in your parliament fummoned to
meet here ; or that your fubjects of Ireland appealing to your
Majefty in your parliament in Ireland, in matters wholly
relating to this kingdom, do bring their caufe before an in-
competent judicature.

We have (may it pleafe your facred Majefty) endeavoured
with our utmoft care, to enquire into the grounds of all
fuch appeals or removals of caufes from this kingdom, as
have at any time been made into England, and are perfuaded
that fuch ufages have been introduced by flow degrees, at
firft the judges here being to determine the caufes that came
before them by the common laws of England, and fometimes
not knowing well the ufages there, applied to Henry III ‡,

* Anno 2 Eliz. p. 214, c. 5. c. 7. p. 218.
† Coke, 4th Inft. p. 350.
‡ 14th Henry III. ftat. Hibern. made at Weftminfter.

their

their then king, for information, who gave them an account
what the common law and cuſtom of England in like caſes
was, and this undoubtedly by the advice of the Juſtices of
the King's Bench, who then were obliged to attend the
King wherever he ſhould be * ; and in proceſs of time, when
his ſucceſſors had ſettled the court of King's Bench after
another manner, and had forborne to ſit there themſelves in
perſon, the application which formerly uſed to be made to
the King who perſided in that court, came of courſe to be
brought before the Juſtices of the court, although the King
was not there perſonally preſent. And this, as we conceive,
gave riſe to that cuſtom of removing cauſes, by writs of
error, from the King's Bench in Ireland to the King's Bench
in England ; but from hence to infer, that therefore appeals
from the Parliament of Ireland may be brought before the
Houſe of Peers in England or Great-Britain, is a conſequence
for which there appears to be no manner of ground.

As for the practice of appealing from the High Court of
Chancery in Ireland to the Lords of Great Britain, we can
find but two precedents of ſuch appeals before the late happy
Revolution, one in 1670, and the other in 1679; and we
can account for them no otherwiſe than by obſerving, that
they happened at a juncture when no oppoſition could be
given them from this kingdom, becauſe through the preva-
lency of a Popiſh intereſt, no parliament had been held here
for ſome years before, nor were we then in any likelihood of
having any called here for many years to come ; nor can we
find, that any like ſubſequent appeals from that court have
any other foundation than thoſe two precedents.

And ſuch appeals (though they had been of longer ſtand-
ing, and better founded) yet were never ſuppoſed to preclude
the King's Majeſty from his right of giving redreſs to his ſubjects of Ireland in his parliament, when aſſembled here, any
more than writs of error to the King's Bench in England
had hindered the like writs from being returnable in the parliament here.

And accordingly when, by God's bleſſing on the late happy
Revolution, this kingdom came to have a parliament, after
twenty-ſix years intermiſſion, complaints were heard, writs of
error and appeals were received, and proper orders were made
thereon as formerly ; nor were they, as far as we can find,
ever queſtioned, or their validity doubted, till the year 1699,
when two appeals from the parliament here were carried be-

* 28th Edward I. ch. 5.

fore

fore the Lords in England, though no pleadings to the jurif-diction of the parliament of Ireland had been offered or men-tioned by either party, on hearing the faid caufes here.

And though the parliament of Ireland could not then in-terpofe, or any way affert their jurifdiction, becaufe it was not fitting, yet the Lords of England declared the faid caufes to be *Coram non Judice*, and without hearing the merits of the caufes, reverfed the decrees that had been made here.

Upon which occafion, we cannot but obferve, that the parliament of Ireland (as the conftitution thereof has been for fome hundreds of years) being convened by the fame au-thority and writs of fummons, and confifting of like members and diftinct Houfes of Peers and Commons, and the former having the fame affiftance and attendance from the Judges of the feveral courts and Mafters of Chancery as in England or Great Britain, either fome record, act of parliament, or an-tient ufage muft be fhewn, whereby to make a difference (which has never yet been attempted) or elfe, from our very conflitution it muft, as we conceive, appear, that whatever power of judicature is lodged in the Englifh or Britifh parlia-ment, with refpect to that kingdom and its inferior courts, the fame muft alfo be allowed to be in the parliament of Ire-land, with like refpect to the kingdom and courts thereof. And if it be looked upon as illegal for any inferior court in Great Britain to act in direct oppofition to, or contempt of the orders and decrees of the Houfe of Lords in parliament there affembled, the fame muft alfo be concluded upon the like oppofition given, or contempt fhewn, to fuch parliamentary orders and decrees, as are or fhall be made within this king-dom.

And therefore, in the year 1703, when a parliament of Ireland met on a complaint of Edward, Earl of Meath, and Cecilia, Countefs of Meath, his wife, fetting forth, that dur-ing the interval of parliament they had, by order of the Lords in England, been difpoffeffed of the lands that had been here decreed them, the faid parliament *unanimoufly* re-ftored the faid Earl and Countefs to the lands they had been fo difpoffeffed of fo effectually, that neither they nor their heirs have been difturbed in the poffeffion of them.

And we may very juftly conclude, from the ftrong refolu-tions in which the parliament here did on that occafion affert their jurifdiction, that they would have proceeded as effectually in vindicating the decree on the other appeal, if the removal of the Lord Bifhop of Derry, the appellant here, and a com-
pofition

pofition made by his fucceffor with the Irifh fociety of Lon-
donderry, the appellants in England, had not prevented it.

After the time of thofe two appeals, feveral writs of error
and appeals were brought into your parliament in this kingdom, and among them an appeal wherein Maurice Annefley,
Efq; was refpondent, which were determined, and the judgment given on them took effect accordingly.   But the fame
Maurice Annefley being refpondent in an appeal brought lately
from the Chancery of the Exchequer, before the parliament
of Ireland, by Hefter Sherlock, appellant, after having appeared to the jurifdiction here, appealed to the Lords of
Great Britain, from a decree made here in juftice to the appellant Hefter Sherlock, and found fuch countenance there,
as has given your loyal fubjects juft reafon to complain of
much injury done both to your Majefty's prerogative and
their privileges.

For it having (after a full and fair hearing) been decreed
in your Majefty's parliament of Ireland, and accordingly ordered, that the appellant, Hefter Sherlock, fhould be put
into poffeffion of certain lands in the faid order named, until
fhe fhould receive thereout a certain fum of money to her decreed, to be due and chargeable on the faid lands.   And the
faid decree and order having accordingly been obeyed, and
put in execution by the then High Sheriff of the county of
Kildare, to whom the faid order was directed; and the faid
Hefter Sherlock being accordingly in the actual poffeffion of
the faid lands, the Lord Chief Baron, together with the
other Barons of your Majefty's court of Exchequer in this
kingdom, have taken upon them, in an illegal and unprecedented manner, to caufe the faid Hefter Sherlock to be difpoffeffed of the faid lands, and to lay feveral great fines upon
the late High Sheriff of the faid county of Kildare, for refufing to give obedience unto the orders of them, the faid
Barons, in that cafe iffued, although their faid orders were
manifeftly contrary to the laws, cuftoms, and antient ufages,
of this your Majefty's kingdom, as well as to the above-mentioned refolutions formerly made in the cafe of the late Earl
of Meath, and continuing upon record in the journals of parliament, of which refolutions, as well as of the feveral refolutions and decrees in like manner made upon the appeal of
the faid Hefter Sherlock, the faid Barons had fufficient and
timely notice before the iffuing of any of their above-mentioned illegal orders, as in a report of this whole proceeding,
now alfo entered in the Journals of parliament (a copy whereof

of we herewith humbly lay before your Majesty) may more fully and at large appear.

Hereupon we humbly crave leave to represent unto your Majesty, that although appeals from the courts of equity in this kingdom to the Lords of England or Great Britain, are but a very late practice, (as we have already set forth); yet in all such cases, it has been the constant and received practice here, that no copy of any order of the said Lords was ever allowed, or demanded to be allowed, as authentic in any such court, except the same were expressly directed unto the court which was to put the same in execution, and proved by a witness *viva voce*, upon oath, to be a true copy of the original order. Nor does it appear, that any such court ever claimed, or pretended to any authority, to supply any defects supposed at any time to be in any such order, or by virtue of such order in the least to go beyond what expressly and in words was in such order contained. And yet so it is, that although the only pretence of the said Barons for these their illegal proceedings, is grounded upon certain copies of orders, or pretended orders, from the Lords of Great Britain, yet neither were the said orders, or any of them, directed to the Court of Equity or Chancery-side of the Exchequer, (where the cause originally lay, and from whence the appeal was) but only to the Lord Chief Baron and other Barons, which is the stile of the common law-side thereof; nor were the said copies, or any of them, in manner aforesaid proved to agree with the original orders; neither were the names of any lands, or so much as of any county, inserted in the said copies, or any of them. And yet notwithstanding all these notorious defects and nullities of the said pretended orders, the said Barons have proceeded not only in their own names, to whom the said pretended orders were directed, but also in the names of the Chancellor and Treasurer of the court of Exchequer, (to whom the said orders were no way directed) to issue forth several injunctions and orders, and therein, without any warrant for so doing, to insert the names of lands, and of the county wherein they are supposed to lie, in order to dispossess the said Hester Sherlock of lands whereof she had been put into possession, as is herein above-mentioned.

And that your Majesty may be yet more fully apprised of the arbitrariness as well as the illegality of the proceedings of the said Barons, We further, in all humble manner, lay before your Majesty, that whereas, amongst other rules of practice in all your Majesty's courts throughout this your kingdom,

dom, by ancient law and cuftom eftablifhed, it is univerfally received, that every order or other rule of court ought to be made upon the motion of fome Counfel or Attorney, or other perfon by law or cuftom allowed to make fuch motion ; that no injunction or writ, ought to iffue out of any of your Majefty's courts, (except in the crown's caufe) without the name of a Six Clerk or Attorney, thereunto fubfcribed, who is to be accountable unto every perfon, who through any undue practice of his, fhall be aggrieved by fuch writ or injunction), and that no proceedings fhall be grounded upon any written affidavit, which is known to be either falfe, or defective in any material part thereof, (except fuch defect be firft fupplied or falfity expunged), the faid Barons in thefe their proceedings, have acted in open violation of thefe, as well as other rules, which by the law they ought to have obferved and ftrictly kept to. The Barons having ordered an injuction to iffue for the difpoffefing of the faid Hefter Sherlock, without any motion for the fame made either by Counfel or Attorney, or by any other perfon, except what was offered in court by the faid Lord Chief Baron himfelf; the faid injunction, alfo, having no name of any Attorney thereunto affixed or fubfcribed ; and the affidavit of John Annefley (upon which the faid Barons afterwards proceeded to fine the faid late High Sheriff) having feveral notorious falfities in it, of which, though the faid Barons were publicly advertifed at the time when the faid affidavit was read in open court, yet, they took on them to act thereupon, without caufing the fame to be rectified, or the faid falfities to be expunged or altered.

And, although the faid orders from the Lords in Great Britain exprefsly required no more, but that Maurice Annefley fhould be reftored to the poffeffion of thofe lands, of which the faid Maurice was difpoffeffed, pending the appeal before the faid houfe ; yet, the faid Barons in their faid injunction, not only ordered poffeffion of certain lands by name, to be given to the faid Annefley, as is already mentioned, but alfo, grounded this their injunction upon an affidavit, wherein it is not fo much as alledged that the faid Maurice was at all poffeffed or difpoffeffed of any lands whatfoever pending the faid appeal.

And whereas it is the duty of the Barons of your Majefty's Court of Exchequer in this kingdom, and a part of the oath by each of them taken at their entrance upon their faid office, " That where they may know any wrong or prejudice to be " done to the King, they fhall put and do all their diligence

" that

" that to redrefs. And if they may not do it, they fhall
" tell it to the king, or them of his council, or to the King's
" Majefty's Lieutenant, or other Chief Governor or Gover-
" nors of this Realm for the time being." So far have the
faid Barons in the prefent cafe been from doing all their diligence to redrefs the wrong or prejudice done to your Majefty's prerogative, of finally determining in your parliament
here, matters relating wholly to this your kingdom, that
they feem to have acted with great diligence and zeal in direct
oppofition thereto, and to have taken fuch meafures as will,
in effect, eftablifh a jurifdiction fuperior to that which your
Majefty undoubtedly has in your High Court of Parliament
in this kingdom ; nor does it in the leaft appear, or is it at all
pretended, that the faid Barons, or any of them, during all
the abovementioned proceedings, did ever tell, or make known
the fame, either to your Majefty's Lieutenant, or other Chief
Governor or Governors, or to your Majefty's Privy Council,
who, if they had been timely acquainted therewith, might
(according to their duty) have made the fame known to your
Majefty, or otherwife have done what was fit and proper for
the fupporting your Majefty's royal prerogative, and defending the juft rights and privileges of this your Parliament and
People.

And here we beg leave to lay before your Majefty fome of
the many evil confequences which we apprehend muft neceffarily follow from fuch exorbitant practices as thefe, if a timely,
and effectual ftop be not put to them.

It is the right and happinefs of the fubjects of this kingdom, as well as of thofe of Great Britain, that by their refpective conftitutions, the adminiftration of juftice is near at
hand, and within the kingdom whereunto they belong. So
that if any of your Majefty's liege people are at any time
wronged or oppreffed in any of the courts of law or equity,
they may, without any great trouble or expence, have recourfe
to your Majefty, in your high Court of Parliament, where
they may affure themfelves of fpeedy redrefs. But if this
your Majefty's Higheft Court within this kingdom is deprived
of the power of finally determining the caufes which come
before them, all fuch of your fubjects as do not abound in
wealth, and thereby are not able to follow their caufes, or
bear the expence of them in Great Britain, will be under a
perpetual neceffity of fitting down with the greateft wrong or
oppreffion which at any time, under the colour of juftice, or
by the management of rich and potent adverfaries may be
laid upon them, which (confidering the poverty that every
where

where prevails throughout this kingdom) muft, if not prevented in a fhort time, become a moft grievous and intolerable evil. And your Majefty's royal predeceffor, Edward the
III. was fo fenfible of the hardfhips that his loyal fubjects of
this kingdom fuffered for want of having a means of rever-
fing erroneous judgments within this kingdom, that by his
Charter, dated Auguft 30th, in the 29th year of his reign,
cn the complaint of his fubjects of Ireland, " he command-
" ed all his Judges and Minifters before whom any proceffes
" fhould be held at the profecution of the parties aggrieved,
" to return the Rolls of the Records, and proceffes into the
" Parliaments to be held in the kingdom of Ireland, and
" that the Records and Proceffes fhould be recited and
" examined, and the errors (if any fhould be found in them)
" duly corrected. *

It is, under God, the great fecurity of this your Majefty's
kingdom of Ireland, that by the laws and ftatutes thereof,
the fame is annexed and united to the Imperial Crown of
England, and declared to be depending upon, and for ever

* Pryn, on 4th Inft. pag. 286. Anno 29 Edw. III. " Edwardus Dei
" gratia, &c. Ex parte non nullorum fidelium noftrorum communitatis
" terræ noftræ Hiberniæ : nobis eft graviter conquerendo monftratum
" ut cum ipfi damna & gravamina quam plurima a magno tempore fuf-
" tinuerint ex hoc ; et etiam ex hoc, quod errores qui in Recordis &
" Proceffibus placitorum nec in Parliamentis in eadem terra corrig:
" nequeunt, nec alias juftitia inde fieri fine remedia in Anglia quærendo
" propter quod quidem propter labores & expenfas circa præmiffa appofi-
" tas ad maximam miferiam & inopiam deducuntur ; & quidam omnino
" ex hæredati exiftunt, per quod pro quiete & indemnitate populi noftri
" in terra predicta, fub noftro regimine exiftentis cui in exhibitione
" juftitiæ fumus debitores : Ordinamus quod, &c. et quod ad profecutio-
" nem omnium & fingulorum qui conqueri voluerint errores in Recordis
" & Proceffibus coram aliquibus juftic. feu aliis miniftris prædictis habitis
" interveniffe Rotuli eorundem Recordorum & Proceffuum in Parliamen-
" tis noftris in eadem terra tenend. per juftic. feu miniftros coram quibus
" Rocorda & Proceffus illa fuerint deferantur & ibidem eadem Recorda
" & Proceffus diligentur recitenter & examinentur; & errores, fi quos
" in eifdem inveniri contigerit debite corrigantur ; & ideo vobis manda-
" mus quod ordinationem prædictam in terra noftra prædicta teneri &
" partibus conquerentibus plenam & celerem juftitiam fieri fac. in forma
" prædicta quibufcunque mandatis vobis aut aliis in terra prædicta ante
" hæc tempora in contrarium directis non obftantibus ita quod aliquis
" materiam non habeat nobis pro defectu juftitiæ fuper cafibus prædictis
" de cætero conquerendi. Tefte apud Weftminfter, 30 die Augufti."
It appears from the latter end of this Record, that the original power
of Parliaments in Ireland, fettled by King Henry the Second, (as is
above fet forth) had afterwards been reftrained, as to writs of error, by
fome fubfequent Mandates of the Kings of England, which Mandates
are hereby recalled and made void.

belonging

belonging to the fame: but if all judgments, decrees, and determinations made in this your Majesty's High Court, within this your kingdom, are subject to be nulled and reversed by the Lords in Great Britain, the liberties and properties of all your subjects of Ireland must thereby become finally dependant on the British Peers, to the great diminution of that dependence which by law we always ought to have immediately upon the Crown itself.

That your Majesty has, by the constitution of this your realm of Ireland, the full power of judging and determining all causes that belong to it alone in Pleno Parliamento, is what no man hitherto has ventured openly to deny or doubt of.

But if in all cases that relate to this kingdom, the *dernier resort*, (as some of late have affected to speak) ought to be to the House of Lords in Great Britain, however this your Majesty's power may still in words be acknowledged, the force and effect of it is in reality taken away and wholly vested in the British Peers.

And we cannot but observe, with the utmost concern, that by this practice of the Peers of Great Britain, just and unjust causes will meet with equal encouragement. For however rightly such causes may be determined in Parliament here, the decrees will be annulled and reversed by the Peers of Great Britain, without hearing or entering into the merits of the cause, upon pretence that the proceedings were *Coram non Judice*.

The writs for summoning the Lords spiritual and temporal, and electing the Commons to assemble in parliament here, being the very same with those in England or Great-Britain, as has been before observed, either the respective powers in each kingdom must still be the same, or else the Peerage of this your Majesty's kingdom must remain little more than an empty title, and the Commons thereof stand for ever deprived of that most valuable privilege of impeaching in parliament, which cannot possibly be maintained if there be no such thing as a parliamentary judicature within this realm; *and if the power of the judicature may, by a vote of the British Lords, be taken away from the Parliament of Ireland, no reason can be given why the same may not, in like manner, deprive us of the benefit of our whole constitution.*

It is notorious, that the Lords of Great Britain have not, in themselves, either by law or custom, any way of putting their decrees in execution within this kingdom, of which they have

have given moſt undoubted evidence by their late application
to your Majeſty, to cauſe ſuch their decrees to be executed by
an extraordinary interpoſition of your royal power. And
ſhould your Majeſty think fit to yield to this their deſire, we
humbly preſume to think it would highly affect the liberty of
your Majeſty's loyal ſubjects of this kingdom.

In order to prevent the appellant, Heſter Sherlock, above-
mentioned, from making any further application to your Parliament here, your Majeſty's Deputy-receiver, John Pratt,
Eſq; thought fit to pay above £ 1800 to the ſaid Heſter Sherlock, which, on examination, he alleged to be his own money ; and that he made an agreement with the ſaid Heſter,
of himſelf, without any order from any perſon whatſoever ;
but that from ſome converſation which he had with perſons
of judgment, he thought he had reaſon to hope and expect,
that ſince what he had done was for the public good, the government would not permit him to be a ſufferer. What particular grounds the ſaid John Pratt had thus to hope and
expect, has not as yet been made known to us. But if ſuch
hopes and expectations as theſe are from time to time to be
ſatisfied, we leave your Majeſty, in your royal wiſdom, to
judge what the evil conſequences thereof may be.

And we farther humbly repreſent to your Majeſty, that
theſe proceedings of the Lords of England have greatly em-
baraſſed your Parliament, and diſquieted the generality of
your moſt loyal Proteſtant ſubjects of this your kingdom, and
muſt, of neceſſity, bring all ſheriffs and officers of juſtice
under great hardſhips, by reaſon of the claſhing of different
juriſdictions. Nor can we but with grief obſerve, that whilſt
many of the Peers and commons who ſat in Parliament were
Papiſts, their judicature was never queſtioned ; but of late,
ſince only Proteſtants are qualified to have a ſhare in the ligiſ-
lature, their power, and the right of hearing cauſes in Parliament, hath been denied, to the great diſcouragement and
weakening of the Proteſtant intereſt in Ireland.

And having thus, with all humility, laid before your Majeſty your undoubted power and prerogative within this your
kingdom of Ireland, the immediate dependence of the ſame
upon your Majeſty's crown, the right your Majeſty has to
hold Parliaments here, as in Great-Britain, and of finally determining therein all matters that wholly relate to this realm,
together with the great incroachments that of late have been
made upon your Majeſty's prerogative, and the rights of this
your Parliament, and the illegal unprecedented proceedings
of

of the Lord Chief Baron, and the other Barons of your Majefty's Court of Exchequer, whereby they have endeavoured
to fupport thofe encroachments with the evil confequences of
fuch proceedings, in cafe that a fpeedy and effectual ftop be
not thereunto put. We moft humbly hope, that all thefe
things being duly confidered and weighed with your Majefty's
ufual wifdom, will abundantly juftify us in the methods we
have taken, as well for the fupporting of your Majefty's royal
prerogative, as the prefervation of the juft rights and liberties
of ourfelves and our fellow fubjects, as the fame are fet forth
in the feveral refolutions we have come to, (a copy whereof
we have hereunto annexed,) with all humility affuring your
Majefty, that no difficulties which we may be laid under, fhall
hinder us from giving the utmoft difpatch to all your Majefty's affairs, or from moft chearfully demonftrating that
loyalty and affection to your Majefty's perfon, and attachment to your intereft, which becomes your Majefty's dutiful
and obedient fubjects, whereof we again, from our hearts,
make an humble tender to your moft facred Majefty.

Refolved, That a committee be appointed to draw up an
humble Addrefs to his Grace the Lord Lieutenant, to defire
his Grace to lay the faid Reprefentation before his Majefty, in
the beft and moft effectual manner.

The Declaratory Act of the 6th of George I. was formed
in confequence of thefe appeals, which ftatute exprefsly de-
clares, " That the kingdom of Ireland hath been, is, and
of right ought to be, fubordinate unto and dependent upon the
imperial crown of Great Britain, as being infeparately united
and annexed thereunto, and that the King, with the confent
of the Lords and Commons of Great Britain in parliament
affembled, hath power to make laws of fufficient force to bind
the kingdom and people of Ireland.

" And that the Houfe of Lords of Ireland have not, nor
ought of right to have, any jurifdiction to judge of, affirm,
or reverfe any judgment or decree made in any court within
the faid kingdom; and that all proceedings before the faid
Houfe of Lords upon any fuch judgment or decree, are void."

It is prefumed that no political cafuift, after a view of the
foregoing pages, will affect to talk of England's title to Ireland by *conqueft*.

The titles of the Kings of England to this kingdom appear to have been very precarious, even to Henry VIII.
as the very act which conftitutes him King of Ireland, exprefsly

prefsly fays " That the Irifhmen and inhabitants of this realm of
Ireland, have not bene fo obedient to the Kings highneffe and
his moft noble progenitors, and to their lawes, as they of right
and according to their allegeance and bounden duties ought
to have been*. Wherefore at the humble purfuit, &c." Befides,
what are all the papers in Bermingham and London 'lower,
but attempts to footh, foften, bribe and tame, by indulgence
and art, the fpirit of Irifh independence? What parties, divi-
fions, hatred, and animofities among the clergy! fometimes
acknowledging the power of the King, fometimes the Pope's,
and at others difavowing both! one time fomenting infurrections, and at others attempting to quell them. Pryn has preferved us a number of thefe tranfactions †, horrid picture of
ecclefiaftical tyranny, from which we are now, thank heaven, happily delivered! horrid picture of the minifters of that
gofpel, *which preaches peace on earth, and good will to all men!*
pious minifters, indeed! whofe feet, inftead of being fhod
with the preparation of the gofpel of peace, were rather fwift
to fhed blood!

Richard II. in perfon invaded this kingdom, for the purpofe of fubjugating it : Howes gives us the number of his
forces, and the lines following their fate.

Richard was at length prevailed on to march againft the
enemy commanded by Art. Mac-Murchad, who, notwithftanding the penfions he had received, and the fubmiffions he
had lately made, was ftill the inveterate enemy of the Englifh ; and in the violence of national pride, enflamed by the

---

* The following anecdote fhews the high ideas entertained by the Irifh
dynafts, of their own independence and dignity.
' Mac-Gillipatrick, 'the Irifh chieftain of Offory, had received fome
injury from the earl of Ormond, or at leaft found fome pretence of complaint againft the prefent deputy, better known among the Irifh by the
name of *Piers the Red*. In all the dignity of offended grandeur, he determined to apply to the king of England for redrefs ; but not with the
humility of a fuppliant or a fubject. His ambaffador was fent to the
court of England to obtain juftice, or elfe to denounce the vengeance of
an injured potentate. He appeared at the chapel door, when the king was
going to his devotions, and advancing with a compofed undifmayed
gravity of deportment, delivered his commiffion in thefe words—" Sta
" pedibus! Domine Rex! Dominus meus Gillapatricius me mifit ad te
" juffit dicere, quod fi non vis caftigare Petrum Rufum, ipfe faciet bel-
" lum contra te." Stand on your feet! lord King! my lord Gillipatrick
has fent me to tell you, that if you do not chaftife Peter Rufus, he himfelf will make war againft you.
† II Vol. Eccl. Jur. p. 372, 373, 378, 382, 393, 397, 422, 423,
458, 474, 475, 480, 481, 482, 559, 603, 616, 632, 633, 634, 635,
690, 719, 735, 756, 768, 784, 807, 808, 810, 827, 828, 857, 858,
859, 957, 939, 956, 990, &c. &c.

profpect of fuccefs, vowed the moft defperate vengeance against his invaders. To fecure himfelf from the fuperiour numbers of the enemy he retired to his woods; and at their approach, appeared at the head of three thoufand men fo well armed and appointed, and with fuch an appearance of determined valour, as were perfectly aftonifhing to the Englifh, who had been taught to defpife their rude and undifciplined violence. The royal army was drawn out in order of battle, expecting a vigorous attack ; but the Irifh forces, who thought of nothing lefs than a regular engagement in the field, fuddenly difappeared ; and Richard, elevated by this retreat, ordered the adjacent villages and houfes to be fet on fire, and the royal ftandard to be advanced, under which he created feveral knights, and among thefe the young Lord Henry the fifth, who on this occafion gave the firft proofs of his diftinguifhed valour.

To facilitate the purfuit of an enemy who appeared to fly, a large body of peafants was employed to open a paffage through the woods, which the Irifh had by every means endeavoured to render impaffable. As the king's army marched through all the difficulties of an encumbred road, perpetually impeded, and fometimes plunged into deep and dangerous moraffes, the enemy frequently affailed them with loud and barbarous ululations; caft their darts with fuch force as no armour could withftand, flaughtered their detached parties, retired, and advanced with aftonifhing agility, fo as continually to annoy and harrafs the Englifh forces, though they could not be brought to a general engagement. Some of the Irifh lords, lefs penetrating than their fubtile chieftain, and among thofe his uncle, were indeed terrified by the numbers of the king's forces, and with all the marks of humiliation fubmitted to Richard. They appeared before him with halters round their necks, fell at his feet, imploring peace and forgivenefs, and were gracioufly received. Art Mac-Murchad was fummoned to make the like fubmiffions ; and, to prevail upon him to accept of grace, and return to his allegiance, Richard was weak enough to promife large rewards, territories, and caftles in Leinfter. The Irifhman, who well knew the difficulties to which the King's army was reduced, and the impoffibility of their fubfifting for any time in their prefent fituation, returned a haughty anfwer of defiance, and declared his refolution of oppofing the King of England to the utmoft. Richard had the mortification to find, that the diftrefs of his foldiery, which had encouraged the adverfary to this infolence, could

could no longer be concealed, and every day grew more intolerable. Numbers of his men perished by famine; their horses, from want and severity, grew incapable of service; a general gloom spread through his camp, and his bravest Knights murmured at their fate, who were to perish in a service attended with so little honour, and such severe distress. A few ships laden with provisions from Dublin having landed on the neighbouring coast, the famished soldiers plunged into the sea, seized and rifled them, shedding each others blood in a furious contest for relief. The necessity of decamping was too apparent, and too urgent to admit of the least delay. Richard, with his numerous forces, was compelled to retire before an inconsiderable band of enemies whom he had despised, who pursued, and incessantly harrassed him in his retreat *.

It is universally acknowledged, that no prince ever brought into this kingdom such an army as Richard II. for reducing it, and we see he did not succeed therein †.

After reading this account, I know not how it can be said that the Irish chieftains submitted to Henry II. ‡ through fear, an affection they appear not to be much influenced by; the most probable causes for this transaction was pride, malice, and, above all, the hopes of revenging public and private insults, or supposed insults, to the impressions of which they were exceedingly susceptible; to this assertion the following letter and answer, which passed in the 14th century, authenticated by Cox, will bear no inconsiderable testimony.

O'Nial to O'Donnell.

" Pay me your tribute, or if you don't"——

O'NIAL.

O'Donnell to O'Nial.

" I owe you no tribute, and if I did"——

O'DONNELL.

The strength of the kingdom thus divided at first, became an easy prey to every invader.

* Story of Richard II. his last being in Ireland. By the Earl of Tothnes.

† It is not in memory, that ever any king of England made such provision for any journey into Ireland, nor such a number of men of arms nor archers.   HOWES.

‡ Henry II. brought with him into this kingdom a train of 500 Knights, the Kings of the land, &c. of *their own good wills*, without any war or chivalry, submitted and took oaths of fidelity to him.

Parliam. debates, vol. 7, p. 274, &c.

To

To this caufe was owing the firft invafion of Greece by Darius with a numerous and mighty army, the deftruction of which, by the few intrepid troops of the Athenians, will ever be remembered.

The following are the three principal charges brought againft the earl of Strafford by Mr. St. John, which plainly fhew that he did not confider Ireland as a *conquered nation.*

1. There at Dublyn, the principal city of that kingdome whither the fubjects of that country came for juftice, in an affembly of Peeres and others of greateft ranke, upon occafion of a fpeech of the Recorder of that city thouching their Franchifes and legal rights, he tels them, that *Ireland was a conquered nation, and that the king might do with them what he pleafed.*

2. Not long after, in the *parliament* 10 *Car.* in the chaire of ftate, in full parliament againe, That *they were a conquered nation, and that they were to expect laws as from a conqueror ; before the King might do with them what he would ; now, they were to expect it, that he would put this power of a conqueror in execution.*

3. Upon like occafion of preffing the lawes and ftatutes, that he would make *an act of counfell board in that kingdom binding as an act of parliament.*

My Lords, continued he, I have done with the three treafons within the ftat. of 25 Ed. III.

-◄►►•►►►◄◄•►►►►◄◄◄◄◄◄◄◄►►►-

From a perufal of the collections of Pryn [*], Rymer, &c. it will plainly appear that the Monarchs of England paid every attention to the welfare of their fubjects in this kingdom till Char. time. Henry II. we fee gave them a *Modus tenendi Parliamenta,* in the fame terms with that of England, and confidering it as a *diftinct kingdom,* fettled it on his fon John for an appenage, who confirmed to the Irifh, by charter, his father's grant of the *Common Law* of England, and a free parliament with immunities to the city of Dublin [†] and Waterford [‡], even beyond thofe of London, which Henry VI. farther confirmed. Henry III. granted us a Magna Charta.

In the fifth of Edward I. the Englifh laws were confirmed to the Irifh [§].

[*] Animad. p. 7, 11, 50, 59, 60, 111, 120, 121, 123, 127, 143, 415, 146, 160, 229, 248 250, 254 to 327, 408 to 414. See alfo index to 4 Inft. under Ireland.

[†] Charta Johanni regis Angl. et dom. Hibern. civib. Dub. facta 30 die Julii reg. 17. Ex lib nig. eccl. S. Trin. Dub. A. D. 1214.

[‡] Pat. 9, Hen. VI. No. 7.

[§] De legibus Anglicanis Hibernis concedendis ex bundella literarum in Turr. Lond. Pryn, tom. 3, p. 1218.

The ftatutes of force in England, which, in the time of Edward II. were referred to be examined in the next parliament, fo many as were then allowed and publifhed to ftand likewife for laws in this kingdom *.

Edward III. ordained that the affairs of the land (Ireland) efpecially the weightieft, fhould be handled, difcuffed, and determined by the Prelates, Nobles, and other difcreet men of the King's Council there ; and by his Council, Prelates, and others in parliaments according to juftice, law, cuftom, reafon, &c †.

Richard III. on ufurping the Englifh crown, expreffed thefe words : " From this moment, I take upon me the govern-" ment of the two kingdoms of *England* and *France;* the " former to be governed and defended ; and the latter, by. " God's help, and my peoples' affiftance, to be fubdued." That he in no wife confidered Ireland as annexed to that crown, which certainly at this time was a feparate and diftinct nation, wherein the ftate of *England* had not leifure or abilities to bring about a reformation, till their own civil diffentions were appeafed.

The Declaratory Act in the reign of Henry IV. exprefsly fays, " That Englifh ftatutes bind not, unlefs retracted here ‡," and the fimilar one of Henry VI. fpeaks its attention to this great object ; in the 18 of Henry VI. ceffing of horfe or foot upon the King's fubjects here is made treafon ; even the act of Poyning in the time was intended as falutary to the fubject, as may appear from the following copy of it.

An act that no Parliament be holden in this land, until the acts be certified into England.

Item, At the requeft of the Commons of the land of Ireland, be it ordained, enacted and eftablifhed, That at the next parliament that there fhall be holden by the king's commandment and licence, wherein amongft other the king's grace entendeth to have a general refumption of his whole revenues fith the laft day of the reign of King Edward II. no parliament hereafter be holden in the faid land but at fuch feafon as the king's lieutenant and counfaile there firft do certifie the king under the great feale of that lande the caufes and confiderations, and all fuch acts as to them feemeth fhould pafs in the fame parliament, and fuch caufes, confiderations and acts

* See marginal note of Sir Richard Bolton, in his edit. of the Irifh ftatutes. See alfo, Pryn 264, 265, 266. An. 20, Edw. 2.
† Pat. ftat. 31 Edw. III. m. 11, 12, exemplified likewife in Pat. 17, R. 2, m. 34. See likewife Rylye's appendix, p. 582, &c. Pryn 287.
‡ See p. lxxxvii of thefe Facts.

affirmed

affirmed by the king and his counſaile to be good *and expedient for that land*, and his licenſe thereupon, as well in affirmation of the ſaid cauſes and acts, as to ſummon the ſaid parliament under his great ſeal of England had and obtained, that done, a parliament to be had and holden after the form and effect afore rehearſed, and if any parliament be holden in that land hereafter, contrary to the form and proviſion aforeſaid, it be deemed void and of none effect in Law.

Ir. Stat. 28 H. 8. cap. 4 & 20. 11 El. cap. 1 and 8.

In the Iriſh act paſſed 28 Henry VIII. it is fully aſſerted, and enacted, " That the ſaid *Engliſh* act, and every thing and
" things therein contained, ſhall be eſtabliſhed, affirmed, taken,
" obeyed, and accepted within this land of *Ireland*, as good
" and perfect law, and ſhall be within the ſaid land of the
" ſame force, effect, quality, condition, ſtrength and virtue
" to all purpoſes and intents, as it is within the realm of
" *England*, and that all ſubjects and reſidents within this ſaid
" land of *Ireland*, ſhall obſerve, keep, obey, accompliſh and
" execute the effects and contents ſpecified in the ſaid *Engliſh*
" act, and ſhall have and enjoy the profit and commodity of
" the ſame, as the *Engliſh* ſubjects are thereby bound, or in-
" tituled, &c."

Notwithſtanding that it is allowed, that there were a few Engliſh ſtatutes reſtraining our commerce before 1663 [*], yet they appear to have been ſo little felt, that our commercial reſtriction may properly be ſaid to have commenced at the foregoing period, when an Engliſh act was formed to prevent exportation from Ireland to the Engliſh Colonies, and in 1670, another act was made to prevent importation from thence.

Let the hiſtories of both kingdoms [†], and the ſtatute-books of both parliaments be examined, and no precedent will be found for the act of 1699 [‡], or for the ſyſtem which it intro- duced.

The whole tenor of the Engliſh ſtatutes relative to the trade of this country, and which by our act of the 10th of Henry VII. became a part of our commercial conſtitution, breath a ſpirit totally repugnant to the principle of that law, and it

[*] Stat. Hib. 14 Hen. III. Ordin. Iriſh ſtat. Hib. 17 Edw. I. 2 Hen. VI, &c.
[†] Commer. Reſtr.
[‡] When the act paſſed in England reſtraining the exportation of all woollen manufactures from Ireland, which was then the ſource of in- duſtry in that kingdom, and the diſcouragement of them, the principal cauſe of her diſtreſs, the encouragement of the linen manufacture was not an equivalent at this time, and if it was, has long ſince ceaſed to be ſo.

is

is therefore with the utmoſt deference ſubmitted to thoſe who
have the power to decide, whether this law was agreeable to
the commercial conſtitution of Ireland, which for 5co years
has never produced a ſimilar inſtance.

It might be naturally ſuppoſed, by a perſon not verſed in
our ſtory, that in the ſeventeenth century * there had been
ſome offence given, or ſome demerit on our part.   He would
be ſurprized to hear, that during this period our loyalty had
been exemplary, and our ſufferings on that account great.   In
164 , great numbers of the proteſtants of Ireland were
deſtroyed, and many of them were deprived of their property, and driven out of their country from their attachment

---

* 6 Geo. I. cap. 21. ſect. 49.   If any tobacco entered out for foreign
parts and exported, ſhall afterwards be landed in *Ireland*, the ſame and
double the drawback ſhall be forfeited, and every debenture for the drawback ſhall become void, as if the tobacco were relanded in *Great Britain;*
which forfeitures may be recovered in any of the courts of record of
Weſtminſter or *Dublin*, or in the Exchequer of *Scotland*.

Brit. ſtat. 5 Geo. I.   No wrought ſilks, Bengals, ſtuffs mixed with ſilk
and herba, or muſlins or other callicoes, of the manufacture of *Perſia*,
China, or *Eaſt India*, ſhall be imported into *Ireland*, from any place other
than *Great Britain*, on forfeiture of the goods or value thereof, as alſo
of the ſhip, with all her guns and tackle, &c. &c.

. Brit. ſtat. 6 Geo. I. cap. 21. § 52.   Where any ſhip or veſſel of the
burthen of fifty tons or under, laden with cuſtomable or prohibited goods,
ſhall be found at anchor, or hovering on the coaſts of Ireland, within
two leagues of the ſhore, and not proceeding on her voyage (wind and
weather permitting), it ſhall be lawful for any Officer of his Majeſty's
cuſtoms of that kingdom, to go on board every ſuch ſhip, &c.——The
Britiſh parliament regulating his Majeſty's cuſtoms in *Ireland!*   It is but
a ſtep, one ſmall ſtep, from the regulation of revenue to the impoſition
of taxes.——See the remainder of that ſection, and alſo the following
one.   The ſtat. 11 & 12 W. III. cap. 7; 4 Geo. I. cap. 11. § 7; and 8
Geo. I. cap. 24. for the puniſhment of piracies.——And 2 Geo. II. cap.
28. 19 Geo. II. cap. 12. ſect. 23. no perſon ſhall import into *Ireland* any
crown plate, flint, or white glaſs; or any common bottles, or other
green glaſs; or glaſs of any kind or denomination, other than the manufacture of *Great Britain*.   And if any kind of glaſs, other than the manufacture of *Great Britain*, ſhall be landed out of any veſſel in *Ireland*,
it ſhall be forfeited and deſtroyed within ten days after condemnation
thereof; and the veſſel alſo, with her tackle and furniture, &c. ſhall be
forfeited; and the maſter of the veſſel, and every other perſon concerned
in importing or landing the ſame, ſhall forfeit ten ſhillings for every
pound weight thereof, and ſo in proportion for any quantity.

7 Geo. II. cap. 19.   If any foreign hops, other than of *Britiſh* growth,
ſhall be landed in *Ireland*, all ſuch hops ſhall be forfeited and burnt within ten days after the ſame ſhall be lawfully condemned; and the perſons
concerned in importing of the ſame, or that ſhall have aſſiſted in landing
the ſame, ſhall forfeit five ſhillings for every pound weight thereof.

to

to the Englifh government in this kingdom, and to that religion and conftitution which they happily enjoyed under it. At the Revolution they were conftant in the fame principles, and fuccefsfully ftaked their lives and properties againft domeftic and foreign enemies, in fupport of the rights of the Englifh crown, and of the religious and civil liberties of Britain and of Ireland. They bravely fhared with her in all her dangers, and liberally partook of all her adverfities. Whatever were their rights, they had forfeited none of them. Whatever favours they enjoyed, they had new claims, from their merit and their fufferings, to a continuance of them. They now wanted more than ever the care of that foftering hand, which by refcuing them twice from oppreffion (obligations never to be forgotten by the proteftants of Ireland) eftablifhed the liberties, confirmed the ftrength, and raifed the glory of the Britifh Empire.

Befides our exclufion from foreign markets, England had two objects in the difcouragement of our woollen trade.

It was intended that Ireland fhould fend her wool to England, and take from that country her woollen manufactures *. It has been already fhewn that the firft object has not been attained ; the fecond has been carried fo far as, for the future, to defeat its own purpofe. Whilft our own manufacturers were ftarving for want of employment, and our wool fold for lefs than one half of its ufual price, we have imported from England in the years 1777 and 1778 woollen goods to the enormous amount of 715,740l. 13s od. as valued at our cuftom-houfe, and of the manufactures of linen, cotton and filk mixed, to the amount of 98,086l. 1s. 11d. making in the whole in thofe two years of diftrefs 819,826l. 14s. 1 d. Between 20 and 30,000 of our manufacturers in thofe branches were, in thofe two years, fupported by public charity. From this fact it is hoped, that every reafonable man will allow the neceffity of ufing our own manufactures. Agreements

---

* The commiffioners of trade, in their reprefentation, dated the 10 of November, 1697, relating to the trade between England and ir... advife a duty to be laid upon the importation of oil, upon ... whether imported or growing there, and upon all the utenfils exp...y the making any woollen manufactures ; on the utenfils of worfted...en... and particularly a duty by the yard upon all cloth and woollen ... except frizes, before they are taken off the loom. Eng. Com. Journ. v. 428.

amon,

among our people for this purpofe are not, as it has been fuppofed, a new idea in this country. It was never fo univerfal
as at prefent, but has been frequently reforted to in times of
diftrefs. In the feffions of 1703, 1705 and 1707 *, the
Houfe of Commons refolved unanimoufly, That it would
greatly conduce to the relief of the poor and the good of
the kingdom; that the inhabitants thereof fhould ufe none
other but the manufactures of this kingdom in their apparel
and the furniture of their houfes; and in the laft of thofe
feffions the members engaged their honours to each other,
that they would conform to the faid refolution. The not importing goods from England, is one of the remedies recommended by the council of trade in 1676, for alleviating fome
diftrefs that was felt at that time †; and Sir William Temple,
a zealous friend to the trade and manufactures of England,
recommends to Lord Effex, then Lord Lieutenant, " to in-
" troduce, as far as can be, a vein of parfimony throughout
" the country, in all things that are not perfectly the native
" growths and manufactures ‡."

The Englifh law ‖ of 1663, reftraining the exportation
from Ireland to America, was at that time, and for fome
years after, fcarcely felt in this kingdom, which had then
little to export, except live cattle, not proper for fo diftant a
market.

The act of fettlement paffed in Ireland the year before this
reftrictive law, and the explanatory ftatute for the fettlement
of this kingdom, was not enacted until two years after. The
country continued for a confiderable time in a ftate of litiga-
tion, which is never favourable to induftry. In 1661 the people muft have been poor; the number of them of all degrees,
who paid poll money in that year was about 360,000 §. In
1672, when the country had greatly improved, the manufacture beftowed upon a year's exportation from Ireland, did not
exceed eight thoufand pounds **, and the clothing trade had
not then arrived to what it had been before the laft rebellion.
But ftill the kingdom had much increafed in wealth, tho' not
in manufactured exports. The cuftoms which fet in 1656
for 12,000l. yearly, were in 1672 worth 80,000l. †† yearly,
and the improvement in domeftic wealth, that is to fay, in

* Com. Journ. 3 vol. 348, 548.
† Sir W. Petty's Political Survey, 312.
‡ Sir W. Temple, 3 v. 11.
‖ Ib. 9. and 110.   § Sir W. Petty, p. 9.
** 15 Ch. II.   †† Ib. 89.

building,

building, planting, furniture, coaches, &c. is faid to have advanced from 1652 to 1673 in a proportion of from one to four, Sir William Petty in the year 1672 complains not of the reftraints on the exportation from Ireland to America *, but of the prohibition of exporting our cattle to England, and of our being obliged to unlade in that kingdom † the fhips bound from America to Ireland ; the latter regulation he confiders as highly prejudicial to this country.

The immediate object of Ireland at this time, feems to have been to get materials to employ her people at home without thinking of foreign exportations.   When we advanced in the export of our woollen goods, the law of 1663 ‡, which excluded them from the American markets, muft have been a great lofs to this kingdom; and after we were allowed to export our linens to the Britifh colonies in America, the reftraints impofed by the law of 1670 upon our importations from thence became more prejudicial, and will be much more fo if ever the late extenfion of our exports to America fhould, under thofe reftraints, have any effect ; for it is certainly a great difcouragement to the carrying on trade with any country, where we are allowed only to fell our manufactures and produce, but are not permitted to carry from them directly to our own country their principal manufactures or produce. The people to whom we are thus permitted to fell, want the principal inducement for dealing with us, and the great fpring of commerce, which is mutual exchange, is wanting between us.

As the Britifh legiflature has thought it reafonable to extend, in a very confiderable degree, our exportation to their colonies, and has doubtlefs intended that this favour fhould be ufeful to Ireland, it is hoped that thofe reftraints on the importation from thence, which muft render that favour of little effect, will be no longer continued.

From thofe confiderations it is evident, that many ftrong reafons refpecting Ireland are now to be found againft the continuance of thofe reftrictive laws of 1663 and 1670, that did not exift at the time of making them.

Ireland was by thofe laws excluded from almoft all the trade of three quarters of the globe, and from all direct beneficial intercourfe with her fellow-fubjects in thofe countries, which were partly ftocked from her own loins.   But ftill, though deprived at that time of the benefit of thofe colonies,

* Sir W. Petty, p. 9 and 10.   † Ib. 34, 71, 125.   ‡ 15 Ch. II. ch. 7.

fhe was not then confidered as a colony herfelf; her manufacturers were not in any other manner difcouraged, her ports
were left open, and fhe was at liberty to look for a market
among ftrangers, though not among her fellow-fubjects in
Afia, Africa or America *.

By the proceedings in the Englifh parliament in the year
1698, and the fpeech of the Lords Juftices to the Irifh parliament in that year it appears, that the linen was intended to
be given to this country as an equivalent for the woollen manufacture. The opinion that this fuppofed equivalent was
accepted of as fuch by Ireland is miftaken. The tempera-
ment, which the commons of Ireland in their addrefs faid
they hoped to find, was no more than a partial and a temporary duty on the exportation, as an experiment only, and not
as an eftablifhed fyftem, referving the exportation of frize,
then much the moft valuable part to Ireland †. The Englifh
intended the linen manufacture as a compenfation, and declared they thought it would be much more advantageous to
Ireland ‡ than the woollen trade.

This idea of an equivalent has led feveral perfons, and
among the reft two very able writers §, into miftakes, from
the want of information in fome facts which are neceffary to
be known, that this tranfaction may be fully underftood, and
therefore ought to be particularly ftated.

The Irifh had before this period applied themfelves to the
linen trade. This appears by two of their ftatutes, in the
reign of Elizabeth, one laying a duty on the export of flax
and linen yarn ‖, and the other, making it felony to fhip

---

* Sir William Petty mentions that " the Englifh who have lands in
" Ireland were forced to trade only with ftrangers, and became unac-
" quainted with their own country, and that England gained more than
" it loft by a free commerce (with Ireland', as exporting hither three
" times as much as it received from hence;" and mentions his furprize
" at their being debarred from bringing commodities from America di-
" rectly home, and being obliged to bring them round from England
" with extreme hazard and lofs.—Political Survey of Ireland, p. 143.

† The Lords commiffioners of trade in England, by their report of
the 31ft of Auguft 1697, (Eng. Com. Jour. 12 vol. p. 428) relating to
the trade between England and Ireland, though they recommend the
reftraining of the exportation of all forts of woollen manufactures out of
Ireland, make the following exception, " except only, that of their frize,
" as is wont, to England."

‡ See before fpeech of Lords Juftices.

§ Mr. Dobbs, and after him Dr. Smith.   ‖ 11 Eliz. feff. 3, ch. 10.

them without paying fuch duty *.   In the reign of Charles I.
great pains were taken by Lord Strafford to encourage this
manufacture; and in the fucceeding reign † the great and
munificent efforts of the firft Duke of Ormond were crowned
with merited fuccefs.   The blafts of civil diffentions nipped
thofe opening buds of induftry, and when the feafon was
more favourable, it is probable that, like England, they
found the woollen manufacture a more ufeful object of national purfuit; which may be collected from the addrefs of the
Englifh houfe of commons, "that they fo unwillingly promote
" the linen trade ‡;" and it was natural for a poor and exhaufted country to work up the materials of which it was
poffeffed.

In 1696 the Englifh had given encouragement to the manufactures of hemp and flax in Ireland, but without ftipulating
any reftraint of the export of woollen goods.

In 1699, there was no equivalent whatever given for the
prohibition of the export of our woollen manufactures.

But perhaps it may be neceffary to inform the reader, that
the foregoing privileges at firft extended only to the Englifh
adventurers in the pale ‖ and five Irifh families, the O'Briens,
the O'Cavanaghs, the O'Neals, the O'Conors, and O'Mea
Loughlins of Meath, the reft were deprived of their lives,
lands, and liberties by the Englifh with impunity; and, to
compleat their misfortunes, the celebrated ftatute of Kilkenny, which here follows, was paffed in 1365, which proved a
more refpectable and numerous affembly than had hitherto
been convened in Ireland.   The prelates of Dublin, Cafhel,
Tuam, Lifmore, Waterford, Killalloe, Offory, Leighlin,
Cloyne, obeyed the fummons of the king's fon. The temporal
peers and commons chearfully attended. Both eftates fat together: and the refult of their deliberations was, that the Englifh of the realm § of Ireland, before the arrival of the duke

* 13 Eliz. feff. 5, ch. 4.
† 17 and 18 Ch. 2, ch. 9, for the advancement of the linen manufacture.   Carte.   ‡ See before.
‖ Which included Dublin, Meath, Uriel, now Louth, the cities of
Kildare, Waterford, Cork, and Limerick.
" Tho' a Prince affume the title of Sovereign of an entire country,
(as our Kings did of Ireland,) yet if there be two-thirds of that country,
wherein he cannot punifh treafon, or murder, or theft, if the jurifdiction
of his ordinary courts of juftice doth not extend to thefe parts; if he
have no certain revenues, no efcheats or forfeitures, I cannot fay, that
fuch a country is conquered.   Davis's Hift. of Ire. p. 9.
§ MSS. Lamb. G. No 608. fol. 1.

of Clarence, were become mere Irish in their language, names, apparel, and manner of living; had rejected the English laws, and submitted to those of the Irish, with whom they had united by marriage-alliance, to the ruin of the general weal. It was therefore enacted, that marriage, nurture of infants, and gossipred with the Irish, should be considered and punished as high-treason. Again, if any man of English race shall use an Irish name, the Irish language, or the Irish apparel, or any mode or custom of the Irish, the act provides that he shall forfeit lands and tenements, until he hath given security in the court of Chancery, to conform in every particular to the English manners; or, if he have no lands, that he shall be imprisoned until the like security be given. The Brehon law was pronounced, to be a pernicious custom and innovation lately introduced among the English subjects *. It was therefore ordained that in all their controversies they shall be governed by the common law of England; and that whoever should submit to the Irish jurisdiction, was to be adjudged guilty of high-treason. As the English had been accustomed to make war and peace with the bordering enemy at their pleasure, they were now expressly prohibited from levying war upon the Irish, without special warrant from the state. It was also made highly penal to the English, to permit their Irish neighbours to graze their lands, to present them to ecclesiastical benefices, or to receive them into their monastries or religious houses; to entertain their bards, who perverted their imaginations by romantic tales; or their news tellers, who seduced them by false reports. It was made felony to impose or cess any forces upon the English subject against his will. And as the royal liberties and franchises were become sanctuaries for malefactors, express power was given to the king's sheriffs to enter into all franchises, and there to apprehend felons or trai-

---

* *Finglas*, chief Baron of the Exchequer in King H. VIII. time says, " That the English statutes passed in Ireland, are not observed above eight days after passing them; whereas those laws and statutes made by the Irish on their hills, they keep firm and stable, *without breaking them for any favour or reward.*" Baron Finglas's Breviate of Ireland.

" There is no nation under the Sun, that love equal and indifferent justice, better than the Irish, or will rest better satisfied with the execution thereof, although it *be against themselves.*" Sir J. Davice's Hist. Ire.

" I have been informed by many of them that have had judicial places there (in Ireland) and partly of mine own knowledge, that there is no nation of the Christian world, that are greater lovers of justice than they are; which virtue must of necessity be accompanied by many others. Cooke's Inst. chap. 76.

tors. Laftly, becaufe the great lords, when they levied forces for the public fervice, acted with partiality, and laid unequal burdens upon the fubjects, it was ordained, that four wardens of the peace in every county fhould adjudge what men and armour every lord or tenant fhould provide. The ftatute was promulgated with particular folemnity; and the fpiritual lords, the better to enforce obedience, denounced excommunication on thofe who fhould prefume to violate it in any inftance.

Voltaire, whofe acquaintance with Irifh hiftory appears to be very flight, afferts, " That the Irifh always behaved fhame-fully at home." I am confident, with all his ingenuity, he would not be able to fupport this on any principle of philofo-phy or common fenfe: he fhould, however, firft have recol-lected the celebrated battle of Clontarf, which was the 99th in which Boroimhe was victorious over the Danes; he fhould alfo have recollected the battle of Aughrim, * where 15000 Irifh, ill-paid, and worfe cloathed, fought with 25000 men, highly appointed, and the flower of all Europe, compofed of *Englifh, Dutch, Flemings* and *Danes*, vying with each other. That after a moft bloody fight of fome hours, thefe began to fhrink on every fide; and would have received a moft complete over-throw, but for the treachery of the commander of the Irifh horfe, and the death of their general, killed by a random fhot.

At the firft fiege of Limerick, a fmall party of Irifh, headed by the gallant *Sarsfield*, cut off a confiderable body of thefe aliens near Cullen, and deftroyed all the cannon and amu-nition, intended for the expediting this work; and in this en-terprife it is difficult to determine which to admire more, the wifdom of the plan, or the intrepidity with which it was executed. Soon after this, when a breach was made in the walls 40 feet wide, which the Englifh, with their accuftomed bravery, mounted, and poured into the city, the Irifh rallied in the centre of the Irifh-town; in their turn attacked the enemy, beat them back to the difmantled walls, and from thence to the Foffe. They did not ftop here: they purfued them to their camp with great flaughter; and though they did not fet fire to the Englifh hofpital, where the wounded, unable to fly, were perifhing in the flames, yet, it is a known fact, that they partly prevented the effects of this unnatural order, by quenching the fire, and faving numbers of thefe half-expiring wretches. The cenfure which King William paffed on his troops, after this defeat, is too glorious for the Irifh to be here omitted: " *Had I* (faid he) *but the handful of*

* O'Halloran, page 270.

r   " men

" *men who defended this city, and that you were all shut up in it,*
" *I would take it in spite of you.*" M. de Voltaire makes but a
poor atonement to this injured nation, when he rapidly
tells us, " that they behaved well abroad." He knew that
their valour abroad was such, that in many capital defeats
of the French armies they alone remained conquerors. Witnefs the battle of the *Woods*, where Clare's regiment alone cut
to pieces one of two battalions, so that none but the colonel
(Gore) and a very few survived the action. While the whole
army were complimenting the *great Marlborough*, on this signal
victory, he alone appeared melancholy and dejected. *I wish*,
(said a young colonel) *that my regiment had been on that service.*
I wish they had (answered this officer, cooly) *for then I should be*
at the head of 1500 *brave fellows, and you not have ten.* The
affair of Cremona, were there no other instance, one should
think would secure them immortality in France, were gratitude the characteristic of the French nation; and the remark
of a senator, in the British house of commons the winter following, shews how sensibly the high allies felt the check:
" Two Irish regiments (said he) have done at Cremona
" more real injury to the high allies, than the fee-simple of
" all their forfeited estates is worth!"
   If time and the limits of this work permitted, numerous
examples of Irish prowefs and disinterested generosity could
be adduced, but every invidious remark to the contrary may
be overthrown, from the bare transactions of the great *Hugh*
O'Nial, and his intrepid followers:

Ō sacred LIBERTY! shall faction's train
Pervert the reverend archives of thy reign?
Shall slaves traduce the blood thy votaries spilt,
Blaspheming glory with the name of guilt?
And shall no son of thine, their wiles o'erwhelm,
And clear the story of *our* injur'd realm?
To this bright task some *Irish* spirit raise,
With power surpassing even a Livy's praise;
Thro' this long wilderness his march inspire,
And make thy temperate flame his leading fire!
Teach his keen eye, and comprehensive soul,
To pierce each dark recefs, and grasp the whole!
Let truth's undoubted signet seal his page,
And glory guard the work from age to age;
That *Irish* minds from this pure source may draw
Senfe of thy *rights*, and passion for thy *law*;
Wisdom to prize, and honour that inspires,
To reach that virtue which adorns our fires.   HAYLEY

Approaching to a clofe, I prefume, my endeavours may at leaft lay fome claim to the laudable verfes of old Ennius:

Anteiqua fepolta vetufta,
Quai faciunt mores vetercfq. novofque tenentem,
Moltarum veterum legum divomque hominumque.

And though accuracy may be difappointed in arrangement, judgment in feleétion, and indulgence wearied with length ; to balance thefe, difcernment may difcover a defire to paufe, where candour feemed fatisfied, till hurried on by frefh information to eftablifh truth, or difpel prejudice, repetition confequently following : however, fhould the former prevail, youth, hafte, and avocation to neceffary bufinefs, could be produced in my favour, if the pleafing refleétion of having endeavoured to ferve my country, did not at leaft, though at the fame time with every poffible refpeét to public opinion, prepare my feelings againft every ill-natured attack ; in confidence of which, I fhall add a few remarks, unwilling to quit a fubjeét which has left fuch pleafing impreffions on a heart, which only laments the inability of a head to gratify its warmeft wifhes.

Videmus quid deceat non affequimur.   *Cicero.*

It is plain, *then*, that Ireland *never was* conquered by the Englifh ; it is not probable to fuppofe, that Strongbow with 400, and Henry II. with 500 Knights, fhould prevail where 60,000 and upwards, ignominioufly failed. In addition to what has been faid on this fubjeét, the following may not be deemed inappofite.

The very beft view of the political ftate of this kingdom (from the reign of Henry the fecond to that of James the firft) is given by Sir John Davies, Attorney-General, who was fent hither in that charaéter, foon after his royal mafter's acceffion to the throne of Great Britain. His book bears the title of ' Hiftorical colleétions: or, a difcovery of the ' true caufes why Ireland was never entirely fubdued, nor ' brought under obedience to the crown of England, until ' the beginning of the reign of king James.' The caufes are affigned under two general heads : 1ft. The faint profecution of the war. Both Henry the fecond and his fon (King John) contented themfelves with gaining a fuperficial homage from the kings of three provinces; and Sir John Courcy, earl of Ulfter, made little more impreffion on the fourth. No force fufficient to fupport the Englifh intereft, appeared before the thirty-fixth of Edward the third ; and this was reckoned an intolerable burden upon the treafury of England. So was Richard the fecond's expedition in the latter end of his reign ;

from

from which time, to the 39th of queen Elizabeth, there never
was a competent ftrength fent over. The author, in this part of
his difcourfe, fhews at large what hindrances every preceding reign was cloged with, running through the moft material occurrences in each. 2. The other chief caufe of this
flow progrefs he attributes to the defects and loofnefs in the
civil adminiftration. There was from the beginning, he obferves, a fhew of giving Englifh laws and franchifes to the
natives in general; but, in fact, thefe privileges were only allowed, by the courts of judicature, to five Irifh fepts, the
reft being always treated as aliens and enemies. In proof of
this, he entertains his reader with feveral curious cafes and
pleadings in faid courts. A like fault in policy was the paffing
of exhorbitant grants, whole countries and provinces, to the
firft adventurers, who, inftead of winning over the natives to
the obedience of their Sovereign, fell into endlefs quarrels among
themfelves. Thefe ftruggles put them under a neceffity of
living under the old Irifh fafhion, for, to increafe the numbers and powers of their refpective families and clans, they
obferved the laws of Tainiftry and Gavelkind; and, as their
forces grew numerous, they were fubfifted by the wicked ex-
tortion of Buanachd, Coigna and Livery. The ftatutes of
Kilkenny made fome provifion for the cure of this epidemic
diftemper : and thefe enacted by Sir Edward Poyning, under
king Henry the feventh, feemed to fecure an univerfal obfer-
vance of the Englifh laws. Yet, in the very next reign, there
was room enough for a farther reformation both in church
and ftate : when the Lord Grey, having (among other wholefome acts of parliament) procured an eftablifhment of the
king's fupremacy, firft difcovered that the Irifh made no fcru-
ple in renouncing the Pope, when they had once refolved to
obey the king. However, the advances that were afterwards
made by the Earl of Suffex under Queen Mary, feconded by
thofe of Sir H. Sidney, and Sir Charles Blount (Lord Mount-
joy) under Queen Elizabeth, finifhed the martial part of a
plenary reduction of the whole kingdom; leaving only the
peaceful diftribution of juftice, and the fettlement of trade and
commerce, to the miniftry of King James. This is the fum
and fubftance of that excellent treatife, which abounds with
fuch a mafterly knowledge in the hiftory and ftate of Ireland,
as is truly incomparable.

It is plain then that we enjoyed all the commercial liberties of England, until the 15th of Charles II. * In 1663, our

---

* Additionl proofs to thofe I have already advanced in favour of this
affertion, fee 3d James I. ch. 6, 12 Ch. II. ch. 32. Matth. Paris.

exportation to the Colonies was prohibited. In 1670, our importation thence. In 1699, King William III. declared he
would restrict our wool trade as *far as in him lay*, which he
accordingly did.

As, nine-tenths of the present inhabitants of this kingdom are allowed to be descended from those English settlers,
and the natives; who from time to time were permitted the
use of the English laws *; it is clear, beyond contradiction,
that *we* were as FREE as the English during 500 years.
Our liberties were first infringed by the detestable Strafford,
but the cries of this oppressed country pursued, and overtook him †.
Since that period, you have borne " the whips and scorns of
" time ‡, the oppressor's wrongs, the proud man's contumely,

anno. 1172, p. 121, 220. Vit. H. 2. Pryn 4 Inst. 349. Against the
4 Inst. c. 76, p. 250, 252. Lord Lyttleton's hist. H. II. 3d vol. 89, 90.
7 Co. 22,23. Sir J. Davis's hist. 71. 4th Black 439. Cooke's 4th Inst.
351. Lucas's works. Irish Hist. Lib. p. 136, &c.
* De legibus ab Anglicanis in Hibernia usitatis meri Hibernicis concedendis. A. D. 1280, Pryn, an. 257, Pat. 8, Ed. I. m. 12.
† See Mr. Flood's speech, December 18, 1781.
‡ Lucæ De Linda, Descriptio Orbis. Amsterdam 1665. p. 385.
Mores Hibernorum nostri temporis. Baptizatis infantibus nomina impo-
nunt profana matrimonia contrahunt, non de præsenti, sed de futuro,
ideo facile divortium admittunt, ubi sine negotio maritus aliam quærit
uxorem et mulier alterum maritum silvestres Irlandi in genua procum-
bunt, cum novilunium spectant frumentum pro equis, quorum ingentem
gerunt curam, servant, urgente nimium fame etiam crudas carnes comedunt,
vaccæ sanguinem coagulatum butyro superfundunt, et ita comedunt.
Adhæc Anglo-Hiberni adeo ab antiquis illis Hibernis sunt seperati ut
colonorum omnium ultimus qui in Anglica provincia habitat, filiam suam,
vel nobilissimo Hibernorum principi in matrimonium non daret, Tales
vero lites æstimare solent certi homines quos *Brebonios* appellant, qui tam
juris civilis, quam Britannici ignorantes sunt, judicantque solum ex do-
mesticis consuetudinibus, quæ usu et frequentia actuum receptæ sunt. In
suam et montanis velut feræ oberrent locis quod illorum spectat eruditio-
suam, illa valde exigua est. Medicos ibi hæreditas, non doctrina facit
satisque se doctos putant, si illud Hippocratis, *ars longa vita brevis* recitare
queant.   Grafton.
     Manners of the Irish of our days. Their baptismal names are prophane;
they wed for the future, not the present, whereby divorces are easily obtained, and the husband at liberty to chuse another wife, and the wife another husband; the savage Irish fall on their knees at sight of the new moon;
they pay great attention to their horses, feeding them with corn; pressed
by great hunger, they eat raw flesh, they likewise eat cow's blood,
covered with butter. The English Irish as yet are separated from the old
natives, and the English who inhabit the Pale, being the last of all the colonies, would not give one of their daughters in marriage to the noblest
Prince of the Irish. Their disputes are determined by certain men, called
Brebons, who are as ignorant of the civil law as of the British; they
judge wholly from domestic customs, which, confirmed by frequency of
                                                        acts

," and the laws delay ;" your hiftory confidered as fable, your courage fool-hardinefs, and your hofpitality intemperance.

And now, my countrymen and fellow-fubjects, fince ye have fet fo bright an example to pofterity in the redemption of your liberties, continue to preferve them inviolate; watch them with the eye of circumfpection and caution; truft not to the fpecious profeffions of national friendfhip and generofity, they are the words only of fpeculation and fophiftry. The dreams of Puffendorf and Montefquieu may amufe in the clofet, but they vanifh in the field. Power only is the law of nations: when affured of the confidence of Britain, yield her every confiftent aid; one of her fons had the prefumption already to ring the fhackles ye have nobly broken in your ears, and to brand ye with difcontent; the voice of your unanimity has already reached the throne; ye have given the higheft marks of gratitude for a *fimple act of juftice*. What would Britain require?

acts, are received; they live in mountains and woods like wild beafts; they fcarcely poffefs any learning; their phyficians are hereditary, and illiterate; they conceive themfelves learned enough, if they are able to repeat the fentence of Hippocrates, *Ars longa, vita brevis*, art is long, life fhort.

Lucæ de Linda Amfteldam. 1665.

In Irelande there be two kinde of men, one foft, gentle, ciuile, and curteous: And to thefe people, as to the moft richeft, and beft nurtured perfons, doth many merchantmen of the Countryes adjoynyng, dayly refort. But becaufe the moft refort thether is of the Englifhe nation, the Irifhe men folow and counterfeyt their ciuile manners, and honeft conditions. And by reafon of the the common trade and entercourfe betwene them, they have learned the Englifh tongue, and can both fpeake and underftand it. And all this kind of people is under the fubjection and dominion of the king of England. The other kinde is cleane contrary from this, for they be wylde, rufticall, foolifhe, fierce, and for their unmanerly behauier, and rude fafhions are called wilde and fauage Irifhemen. And thefe men have many gouernours and feuerall rulers, which kepe continuall battaile, and dayly warre amongeft themfelues, for the which caufe they be more fierce, more bolde and hardie then the other Irifh men, and they be uery defyrous of newe thinges, and ftraunge fights and gafyngs, and after robery, theft, and rapine, and in nothing fo much delightyng as with tumulteous fedition and continuall ftrife. And to thefe wilde Coltes, Perkyn fhewed himfelfe firft, eafily perfwadyng them to beleue that he was the fame very perfon whom he falfly fained and counterfeited. ·   Grafton.

" Some nations feem formed for fubjection to others. The Englifh always had a fuperiority over the Irifh, in genius, as well as arms and riches, nor has Ireland ever been able to fhake off the yoke, *fince fhe was firft fubdued by an Englifh baron*." · ·   Voltaire.

" The Irifh, from the beginning of time, had been buried in the moft profound barbarifm and ignorance." ·· ··   Hume.

See more on this fubject, particularly in the introduction to Dr. Curry's hift. of the Civil Wars of Ireland. ··

" Let the favour received be what it will, liberty is too
" dear a price for it. A ftate that has been *obliged*, is not
" therefore to be *enflaved*. It ought, if poffible, make an
" adequate return for the fervices done to it ; but to fuppofe
" that it ought to give up the power of governing itfelf, and
" the difpofal of its property, would be to fuppofe, that in
" order to fhew its gratitude, it ought to part with the power
" of ever afterwards exercifing gratitude." Dr. *Price.*

Aroufe! be awakened and guard the freedom that is juftly
your due! guard the precious fruit of your own exertions
with *breathing fire*. Place your confidence, therefore, in Heaven and *yourfelves* alone.

Wifdom and moderation have already marked your councils ; ye have proceeded, and may ye continue fo to do, with
the firmnefs of men refolved to be FREE.

It is not my wifh to awaken difcontents or jealoufies. Englifhmen cannot blame ye for adoring what themfelves admire :
they are generous, fo are ye; they are brave, fo are ye. May
Britain—but a favourite Poet conveys my wifh, &c.

> May Britain foon her better intereft know,
> Nor fpurn the good Ierne can beftow ;
> Her paltry pride, her mean fufpicions chace,
> And win, by bounteous acts, a grateful race.
> In many a maze, while commerce flows around,
> New force and value fhall to her redound ;
> Wide, and more wide, the genial currents born,
> With rifing herbage fhall their banks adorn ;
> And fcatter plenty, as their path they fweep,
> Then fink in her, as in their parent deep :
> Or like the blood, with heat informing roll,
> Strength to the limbs, and fpirit to the foul.

VOLUNTEERING, &c.

.«‹·‹·‹·‹·‹·‹·‹·‹·‹·‹·‹·‹❁❁❁❁·»·»·»·»·»·»·»·»·»·»·»·

BEFORE we enter on the unexampled period that muſt ever raiſe the page of Iriſh hiſtory ſuperior to all others, let us take a ſhort view of this iſland immediately preceding it; happily ſituated, placed beneath one of the fineſt climates, behold the richeſt ſoil no longer entruſted with the hopes of harveſt, but conſigned to the ſuſtenance of cattle as the only marketable commodity; a ſpiritleſs peaſantry, ill-lodged, worſe cloathed, and coarſely fed; a ruined tenantry; every heretofore crowded hamlet and village experiencing the real miſeries of Doctor Goldſmith's *Deſerted One;* the ſpirit of freedom broken by oppreſſion into deſpondence; the languid eye only lifted to take in freſh images for ſorrow; life meaſured by length; and death or emigration, the living death of population, preſented as the only reſource from miſery; every ſpecies of induſtry blaſted in the bud; public credit failed, merchants became bankrupts, our artificers begged in our ſtreets, the numbers of our poor grew greater as the means of relieving them grew leſs; our charity only was not chilled, but our hands could not obey the warm dictates of our hearts; wool reduced one half in its uſual price; wheat one third; black cattle of all kinds in the ſame proportion, and hides in a much greater; buyers not had without difficulty at thoſe low rates, and from the principal fairs men commonly returned with the commodities they brought there. Many faithful pictures of our miſery * were given,

* Were I, ſays the ingenious Dr. Campbell, to deviſe an emblematic figure of Ireland, in her preſent ſtate, it ſhould not be a Manerva-like figure with her ſpear and harp, nor ſhould it be a Diana with her wolf dogs, coupled, and the mooſe deer in the back ground; but my picture of Ireland ſhould be *Mulier formoſa ſuperne,* a woman exquiſitely beautifully,

even the voice of verse arose to aid *slighted truth*, a piece of cloth of Irish manufacture, presented to the Queen by Lord Clare, was accompanied by the following lines, so truly descriptive of our situation, that an apology for their insertion must be needless.

And O! might poor Ierne hope,
In sober freedom's liberal scope,
To ply the loom, to plough the main,
Nor see Heaven's bounties pour'd in vain;
Where starving hinds, from fens and rocks,
View pastures rich with herds and flocks;
And only view, forbid to taste—
Sad tenants of a dreary waste;
For other hinds our oxen bleed,
Our flocks for happier regions feed;
Their fleece to Gallia's looms resign,
More rich than the Peruvian mine;
Her fields with barren lillies strown,
Now white with treasures not her own:
In vain Ierne's piercing cries
Plaintive pursue the golden prize;
While all aghast the Weaver stands,
And drops the shuttle from his hands.
Barter accurst! but mad distress
To ruin flies from wretchedness.
Theirs be the blame, who bar the course,
Of commerce from her genuine source,
And drive the wretch his thirst to slake
With poison, in a stagnant lake.

Hence ports secure from ev'ry wind,
For trade, for wealth, for pow'r design'd;
Where faithful coasts and friendly gales
Invite the helm and court the sails;
A wide deserted space expand,
Surrounded with uncultur'd land.
Thence Poverty, with haggard eye,
Beholds the British streamers fly;
Beholds the Merchant doom'd to brave,
The treacherous shoal, and adverse wave;

fully, with her head and neck richly attired, her bosom full, but meanly drest, her lower parts lean and emaciated, half covered with tattered weeds, her legs and feet bare with burned shins, and all the squalor of indigent sloth. Philosop. Survey

Conftrain'd to rifk his precious ftore,
And fhun our interdicted fhore.
Thus Britain works a Sifter's woe ;
Thus ftarves a friend, and gluts a foe.

So fhackled were we in our trade, by the interefted policy
of England, and by the power fhe had affumed of making
laws to bind us, that we even ftooped to follicit the liberty
of fome trifling manufactures, and they were refufed, though,
the requeft was founded in juftice, and begged as a favour ;
in fo low an eftimation were we held in the fcale of the empire,
that the trivial intereft of every infignificant town was preferred to the juft rights of an extenfive nation, and every
attempt to eftablifh any manufacture their jealous avarice
deemed injurious, met with immediate oppofition, and the
attempt itfelf was treated as an infolent violation of the rights
of Britain; nay, to complete our mifery, the landed property of the kingdom was fhaken, the principal export trade
ruined by a repeated embargo *, to ferve the low corrupt in-
trigues of an Englifh minifter, to bribe a vote, and fill the
pockets of a contractor. To add, if poffible, a further dif-
grace, we were made the inftruments of our humiliation ;
we were upbraided with a langour, and inattention, of which
England alone was the caufe ; and while every exertion and
every art were ufed to forge and rivet our chains, we were
charged with the vices that refult from a ftate of defpendent
fervitude, and they were made the infolent plea for refufing
our juft demands. It muft however, be acknowledged, that
in the midft of tyranny, they thought on mercy ; and, when
they had loft America, they were pleafed, with all the
kindnefs of infulting condefcenfion, to indulge us in the unfollicited favour of cultivating tobacco ; and, to give the laft
gloomy finifhing to the picture of our diftrefs, the property
of the kingdom, feverely injured and threatened with total
and immediate deftruction, by a combination of fecret vil-
lains, hardened in iniquity, and made defperate by want.

It is a juft obfervation that there are moments big with the
fate of nations, as well as of perfons : 1779 appears to be
peculiarly fo with refpect to Ireland ; the combination of

* By a proclamation, dated the 3d of February, 1776, on all fhips and
veffels, laden in the ports in this kingdom, with provifions of any kind,
but not to extend to fhips carrying falted beef, pork, butter and bacon
into Great-Britain, or provifions to any part of the Britifh empire, except the Colonies mentioned in the faid proclamation. 4th of January,
1779, taken off as far as it relates to fhips carrying provifions to any of the
ports of Europe.

several happy circumstances, happily attended, produced the
desired effect; several literary luminaries arose on our hitherto
almost darkened hemisphere; the re-illumined mind recog-
nized her long lost liberties, and determined to reclaim them;
the thunder of Britain died at a distance, and the sea only
trembled beneath the flight of her fleet; informed in the language of confidence that we were unjustly oppressed by a
sister kingdom, whose extent of territory exceeded ours only
in one-third, and her inhabitants one-half, and if a narrow
sea divided us, a still narrower divided her and France, which
must ever be her enemy, let her be the ally of whom she
will; we smiled at our strength and the justness of our cause;
the sparks of liberty were still alive, and only required to be
fanned; the flame caught even the pulpit, the hallowed lip
touched with fire, the manly exertions for our liberty, as a
grand principle of the social and moral duties, was warmly
ushered on the wings of religion.

And hark! *Ierne* calls her sons to arms,
From plain to plain we hear the glad alarms!
On ev'ry breeze the sacred banners stream;
From hill to hill the marshall'd squadrons beam!
Not shepherd's carrol, now, nor hunter's horn,
But piercing fifes awake the ling'ring morn!
Not rural sports the village throng delight,
But warlike lessons, and the mimic fight!
See, gayly dread, the virtuous bands appear,
Dear to their country, and to freedom dear!
No venal slaves, by some poor stipend led,
To sell their worthless blood for daily bread;
No ready engines, at a tyrant's word,
'Gainst human rights to draw the guilty sword:
Awake, alive, possest with glory's charms,
'Tis virtue, virtue calls the host to arms.
They blend the citizen's and soldier's name,
And reason sanctifies the martial flame.
Each sacred pledge that human life endears,
Each awful call that sounds to virtuous ears:
The rising energies of free-born mind,
The glorious ties that honour loves to bind;
And last, the promise of a deathless meed,
See prompts, nor vainly prompts th' heroic deed,
What honest flames from ev'ry eye-ball dart!
What god-like transports heave the bursting heart!
Now virtue reigns, sublime, supreme, confest;
A nation feels her like a single breast!

Lord Nugent, whose name Irish gratitude should remember, on the 19th of January, 1779, called the attention of the British senate to the situation of our affairs, by moving for " an account of the imports from Ireland, and the exports to that kingdom, from the year 1768." His motion, he said, would, if carried, enable gentlemen to see at once the rapid decay of trade in Ireland ; and to judge whether the bills passed last session in favour of Ireland, had been productive of that good which the house, at the time of passing them, intended to do. He assured gentlemen, that the situation of the Irish was truly deplorable ; want and poverty were visible every where throughout the kingdom ; manufactures were at a stand ; and famine had so overspread the country, that nothing but the miseries of our people at Calcutta, during the dreadful scarcity of provisions there, could equal the present situation of the Irish. The whole revenue of the kingdom was scarcely adequate to the support of the military establishment, and the payment of interest for the debts contracted in the *cause* of Britain. The value of estates had sunk to 17 and 14 years purchase ; and even at that low rate no purchasers were to be found, and for want of trade there was no money in circulation. The loyalty of the Irish in such a distracted condition was eminently conspicuous ; no sooner was France leagued with America, than the parliament of Ireland voted 300,000l. for the service of his Majesty ; and actually pays the enormous interest of seven and a half per cent. because the poverty of the nation prevented it from settling a loan filled upon easier terms.

He offered to produce a letter from Sir George Saville to confirm what he advanced, and still farther appealed to Lords North, and Germaine, as *they knew what he had said was too true.*

The narrow policy of confining the trade of an empire to one part, and excluding all the others from a participation in it, was no less absurd than prejudicial to the whole. It was singular and unparalleled in Europe. There was no Prince on the continent, whose dominions were composed of different states, who absurdly cherished the interest of one to the ruin of the rest. The house of Austria possesses Austria, the Netherlands, the Milanese, Hungary and Bohemia, and finds it her interest in granting the benefit of a free and equal trade to all France, makes no distinctions between the ancient possessions of the crown and its newly acquired dominions, Alsace, Franche Gomte, Lorraine, and what are called Les Pays

Reconque

Reconques, all participate in trade equally with the other provinces of the kingdom. Spain acted formerly as we do now; but our misfortunes had made them wise. Cadiz was the only port in Spain allotted for American commerce: but that foolish system had been lately exploded; and now that all the Spanish ports are opened, the Spaniards find their manufactures revived; but above all, they see their navy raised to a degree of strength unknown to Spain at any other period. We in our turn ought to learn from them. Ireland had always been our best customer; she had taken our manufactures off our hands, and gave bread to our workmen. To disable her from continuing to do so, is to rob our manufacturers of the means of subsisting. Our tanning-bark, which was formerly sold in Ireland at four guineas a ton, brought at present only half that sum: The other commodities of this kingdom had sunk in proportion. Was that policy? Was that justice either to English or Irish? The prosperity of one country he always understood to be beneficial to the other; and as their interests were inseparable, so their advantage should be mutual. Ireland, situated as it is, would be still more advantageous to Great Britain, than if it was placed in the very centre of England; because from the situation it must always be of service to our navigation.

Mr. T. Townshend, lord Newenham, lord Beauchamp, and latterly Mr. Burke, appeared equally warm in the cause of Ireland. Sir George Yonge, our *worthy* vice-treasurer, indeed appeared wholly averse to the inquiry, and insisted, that our distress arose from indolence, and not from the restraints we lay under.

His Excellency John Earl of Buckinghamshire, Lord Lieutenant General, and General Governor of Ireland, his Speech to both Houses of Parliament, at Dublin, on Tuesday the 12th Day of October, 1779.

" *My Lords and Gentlemen,*

" AT a time when the trade and commerce of this kingdom are, in a more particular manner, the objects of public attention, it were to be wished, that the general tranquility, ever desireable, had been restored, so as to have left you entirely at liberty to deliberate on those great and important subjects. But I am persuaded, you will not permit any interests, however dear to you, to impede your efforts or disturb your unanimity at this most important period: and I have it expresly in command from his majesty to assure you, that the cares and solicitudes, inseparable from a state of hostility, have

have not prevented him from turning his royal mind to the interests and diftreffes of this kingdom with the moft affectionate concern; of which the money remitted to this country for its defence, when England had every reafon to apprehend a moft formidable and immediate attack, affords a convincing proof. Anxious for the happinefs of his people, his majefty will moft chearfully co-operate with his parliaments, in fuch meafures, as may promote the common intereft of all his fubjects.

" I have the pleafure to inform you of an acceffion to his majefty's family, fince the laft feffion of parliament, by the birth of another prince. May the fame Providence, that continues to increafe his domeftic felicity, protect the honour of his crown, and the happinefs of his people.

" *Gentlemen of the Houfe of Commons,*

" It is with great concern, I am to inform you, that on account of the extraordinary decline of the revenues, the very liberal fupplies of the laft feffion have proved inadequate to the exigencies of government; fo that, contrary to my moft fanguine expectations, and moft earneft endeavours, there is a confiderable arrear now to be provided for.

" His majefty, from his paternal attention to the interefts of his people, and his folicitude to obviate, to the utmoft, the neceffity of increafing their burdens, has gracioufly commanded me to declare to you, that the greateft œconomy fhall, in every inftance, be exerted, as far as may be confiftent with the honour of his crown, and the real interefts of the nation.

" I have ordered the public accounts and other neceffary papers to be laid before you: and I have no doubt that your known loyalty to your king, and attachment to your country, will induce you to go as far, as the national abilities will admit, in making a provifion fuitable to the exigency of the times, and the honourable fupport of his majefty's government.

" *My Lords and Gentlemen,*

" The united efforts and great military preparations of the houfe of Bourbon, feem only to have rouzed the courage and called forth the exertions of his majefty's brave and loyal fubjects of this kingdom. I have only to lament, that the exhaufted ftate of the treafury, has hitherto put it out of my power to give thofe exertions the moft extenfive and conftitutional operation, by carrying the militia-law into execution.

" I am perfuaded, you will not fuffer any dangers, that may be threatened from abroad, to draw off your attention from wife and neceffary domeftic regulations; and that, among the many fubjects worthy of your confideration, the Proteftant charter fchools and linen manufacture, will continue to be objects of your ferious attention.

"In promoting thefe, and in all other meafures, that may tend to increafe the profperity and improve the true interefts of this kingdom, I am bound to co-operate with you by a double tie, of inclination and of duty. Nothing can ever effect me with more real fatisfaction, than the exerting my beft endeavours for the welfare of Ireland; nor can I ever render a more acceptable fervice to my fovereign, than in promoting the happinefs of his people."

Houfe of Lords, Wednefday, October 13. Committees fat upon the addreffes to his majefty and the lord lieutenant, which were reported and agreed to unanimoufly, and ordered to be prefented. That to his majefty contained a paragraph fimilar to the one introduced into the commons one, relative to a free trade.

Houfe of Commons, Tuefday October 12. As foon as the Speaker had, according to cuftom, read the lord lieutenant's fpeech,

Sir Robert Deane arofe, and after an exordium, lavifh in its encomiums on the lord lieutenant's adminiftration, and the good difpofitions of his majefty and the British miniftry toward this kingdom, moved for an addrefs to the throne, expreffing in the warmeft terms the greatful fenfe the houfe entertained of the above difpofitions, and, in the ufual language of thefe addreffes, eechoing the fpeech. He was feconded by

Mr. R. H. Hutchinfon, who faid this was a great, critical, and important period, in which the declarations of the king, the beft of princes, and the British legiflature, left us no room to doubt but every good was defigned for Ireland; that his majefty's fpeech in the British houfe, at the clofe of the laft feffion, was the harbinger of good tidings and great events, which was this day confirmed in the lord lieutenant's fpeech, who fays he has it in command to declare his wifh to co-operate in fuch meafures as may beft promote our interefts, interefts which, in the hands of the prefent adminiftration, muft be well managed, as their defigns are pure; that under fuch an adminiftration the general benefit of the empire would be attended to, above all partial and felfish confiderations; and the veil of calumny, which fo long traduced them, would difappear, and the factious calumniators, touched with truth, as with the

fpear

fpear of Ithuriel, would ftart into fhape. What thanks were
due to our chief governor, who fo refpectfully mentions the
focieties of armed patriots throughout the kingdom? What
muft our opinion be of a chief governor who fpeaks fo honourably of that great bulwark of conftitutional liberty, a
national militia? though our diftreffes are great, from them
profperous days may fpring, like that fair flower the fabling
poets tell of, which fprung from a hero's blood.

Mr. Grattan faid, the fpeech contained nothing explicit,
nothing fatisfactory; it meant to quiet the minds of the people without any declaration whatever. After his majefty had
been addreffed by his Irifh fubjects for a free export trade,
did fuch addreffes require no anfwer? Were the people of Ireland undeferving the notice of the Britifh minifters? Was there
no refpect for the interefts of thefe kingdoms among the fervants of the crown on this fide of the water? Were not thefe
fervants of the crown alfo reprefentatives of the people?
Why not then fpeak out? Are our diftreffes of fo private a
nature that they muft not be mentioned? [Here he gave an
eloquent and pathetic picture of the miferable condition of
this kingdom.] It is plain we have nothing to expect, fince
applications from the people, backed with the fame from the
officers of the crown, are not attended to. Ireland, then, has
nothing to depend upon but her fpirit; no redrefs of grievances, no extenfion of trade, but from the efforts of her
people! and will it be politic, will it be fafe, here or elfewhere,
to oppofe thefe efforts? Why does not our addrefs alfo fpeak
out? Why have we lefs fpirit than the people? Shall the commons of Ireland fhew lefs fpirit than the moft infignificant
corporation? Are we fo fallen, fo defpicable, as to be more
afraid of England's cenfure, than of the cries of our ftarving
manufacturers.

The diftreffes of this kingdom are two fold, the beggary of
the people, and the bankrupcy of the ftate. The firft he
would afk the commiffioners of the revenue to prove, but he
would afk them upon oath, whether the reftrictions on our
trade was not the caufe? whether the prohibitions laid on by
England againft the exports of woollen clothes did not
occafion it? Whether there were not too many inhabitants in
this kingdom, though not half peopled; whether to thofe inhabitants was the American continent ftill open, would
they not have migrated thither rather than pine in their native land, the victims of Englifh tyranny, rather than ftarve
in it by an Englifh act of parliament? And laftly, was there
one

one rich merchant in the kingdom? This kingdom, (he continued) ruined by a balance of trade againſt her for ſo many years, and the drain of abſentees, owes its preſent exiſtence to aſſociations; it is but a temporary expedient, and ſomething more effectual muſt be done.

As to the bankruptcies of the ſtate, they are the conſequence of a ſyſtem of boundleſs prodigality, profligacy, and violence; a boundleſs prodigality, while our means were limited, a profligacy and violence uniformly maintained. One inſtance will ſuffice, where the late attorny general obliged the merchants of Cork to ſign an illegal bond, as a collateral ſecurity to an illegal oath. The peace eſtabliſhment of this poor country amounts to one-ſixth of that of England; what proportion is there in our means? What is this eſtabliſhment? infamous penſions to infamous men! [here he launched into ſome perſonalities] and will thoſe men, whom we pay, vote againſt an extenſion of our trade? vote againſt the means of ſupporting them! To what paſs have theſe profligate adminiſtrations reduced this kingdom! to be inſulted with our poverty in the ſpeech from the throne; to be told of our beggary; that the officers of the crown here have begged 50,000l. from England, or the troops could not have marched into camp; when it is known, that it is this profligacy that has unnerved the arm of government, and made the ſword of defence fall in its hand.

He then moved an amendment to the addreſs, to be inſerted in the following words:

"That we beſeech your majeſty to believe, that it is with the utmoſt reluctance we are conſtrained to approach you on the preſent occaſion; but the conſtant drain to ſupply abſentees, and the unfortunate prohibition of our trade, have cauſed ſuch calamity; that the natural ſupport of our country has decayed, and our manufacturers are dying for want. Famine ſtalks hand in hand with hopeleſs wretchedneſs, and the only means left to ſupport the expiring trade of this miſerable part of your majeſty's dominions, is to open a free export trade, and let your Iriſh ſubjects enjoy their natural birthright." Lord Weſtport ſeconded Mr. Grattan's motion for the amendment. Mr. Flood conſidered the addreſs as inexplicit.

Sir Henry Cavendiſh declared he would vote againſt the amendment, apprehending (with a view we may ſuppoſe to inefficacy and procraſtination) that this buſineſs would be better effected by opening a committee on purpoſe, or rather fol-

lowing

lowing a precedent in the year 1661, when the Lords and
Commons of Ireland appointed commiffioners to attend the
King, to *fupplicate* the redrefs of grievances.

Mr. Ogle, in a ftrain of honeft indignation, reprobated the
idea of entering into a committee on the fubject of our
grievances; he was fick, he faid, of that mode of trifling with
the nation in order to gain time; that the ghoft of the committee on the embargo haunted him every time he heard a
committee mentioned; and laftly, if we did not mention
fomething in the addrefs, the miniftry might again fhelter
themfelves under the old excufe, " That truly they did not
" know what the Irifh wanted, as their parliament was filent
" on the head," and fo go on with the old fyftem of duplicity.

Sir Edward Newenham, in a fpirited and warmly decided
ftrain, conjured the houfe, by all they held dear, to re-affume
their wonted dignity and power, the early claims to which
he happily and unanfwerably traced; charged the Britifh miniftry with contempt and neglect to the nation, and called on
their warmeft advocate to deny the affertion; faid he perfectly
agreed with Mr. Flood, that the addrefs did not go far
enough, and that he thought the original addrefs a fervile
echo to the fpeech.

The Provoft drew a moft pathetic picture of the melancholy
fituation of his native country, declaring, on this queftion,
that no adminiftration fhould bias him from the welfare of
his country.

The Attorney General, without arguments to fupport, or
art to deceive, delivered a ftudied eulogium on the fenfibility
of the King, and the humanity of his minifter.

The debate now took a new turn; feveral of the minifterial
party declared, that though they thought this bufinefs might
have come more properly otherwife, yet, that there might be
an unanimity, they would not oppofe the amendment.

Hon. Henry Flood declared for the amendment, and entered largely into a juftification of his political conduct,
which, he faid, had unfortunately been much mifreprefented;
that the office he held was the unfollicited gift of his Sovereign, which he had received with gratitude, and held with
honour; that when a time came that he could no longer do
it, he would gladly throw the bracelet into the common
cauldron.

Mr. Prime Serjeant, after expaciating on the neceffity of
immediately laying, in an unequivocal manner, the ftate of our
diftreffes at the foot of the throne, moved in lieu of the
amendment propofed, " that it is not by temporary expedi-

" ents,

" ents, but by a Free Trade alone, that this nation is now to
" be faved from impending ruin."

The amendment was carried *nem. con.* as was alfo the addrefs to the Lord Lieutenant.

We fhall here give a flight review of this feffion: every
object now wore the appearance of beauty, contrafted with
the deformity we have defcribed; our liberties reftored!
our commerce emancipated! a people, no longer divided
by religious prejudice and factious animofity, but, endeared
to each other by the firmeft ties of gratitude and affection;
united to her fifter kingdom, in the ftrongeft bonds of intereft and amity; content and fatisfaction diffufed on every
countenance; the loweft individual taught, by experience, to
know his own importance, and actuated by a fpirit of emu-
lation, to attain a higher rank amongft his fellow-citizens.
The acts of commerce encouraged by the rich, and purfued
with induftry by the poor; convinced that their activity will
now be followed by fuccefs; the nation itfelf, roufed from
indolence, governed folely by a fpirit of freedom, and elevated to the moft exalted fituation in the opinions of mankind,
which, while it gratifies their pride, infures its ftability; her
natural rank in the political fcale of Europe afcertained: no
longer confidered a meer appendage to Great Britain; fupported wholly by that confequence, to which the fertility of
her foil, the peculiar happinefs of her fituation, and the fpirit of her people intitle her.

Immediately previous to this, the patriotic town of Gal-
way entered into a non-importation agreement, which was
inftantly followed over all the kingdom, now clothed in her
native manufacture :   ——with ruftic air,

Blooming fhe ftands, and innocently fair.
Let polifh'd arts the bafhful nymph refine,
In filken raiment let her beauties fhine;
Th'admiring world fhall own her peerlefs charms,
And diftant bofoms pant with foft alarms.

Military affociations arofe unnumbred over the land. England,
indeed forgetful, or pretending to be fo, of the liberal plan
on which the majefty of the people ftept forth. affected to defpife them; and even Lord Shelburn, who draws a very confiderable part of his fources from our ifle, had the prefumption
in the Britifh houfe to call us an *enraged mob*,* but an opportunity foon offered, which convinced our enemies of the eftimation in which we were to be held.

* See his fpeech in the Houfe of Lords, May the 11th, 1779.

Late

Late in the fummer of the year 1779, while the combined fleet of our enemies rode triumphant in the channel, and menaced the kingdom with immediate invafion, the affrighted maratime towns made application to government for protection, the eftablifhed forces of the nation having been called away to fupport the war in America; the chief governor was forced to confefs himfelf unable to afford any effectual affiftance in this alarming ftate of urgent neceffity; the people of Ireland refolved to defend themfelves; government, forgetting their jealoufy in their fears for the fafety of the empire, yielded to the impulfe of the nation, and, with reluctant confidence, placed arms in the hands of men, that fhewed themfelves worthy of the important truft. The fleets of the enemy, alarmed at our military preparations, beheld the banners of defiance, and fled precipitate from our coafts.

For this never to be forgotten fervice, the Duke of Leinfter, and Mr. T. Conolly moved, " That the thanks of the " houfe be given to the feveral Volunteer Corps, for their " fpirited exertion at this time fo neceffary in defence of this " country," (which paffed *nem. con.*)

This the Lord Chanceller and Lord Annally feemed defirous to oppofe, by wifhing to know under what authority the Volunteers arofe; forgetful, it feems, that power only originates from the people, which, once for all, that they may perfectly know, I have fubjoined the plain, but truly fenfible remarks of Mr. Locke hereon, &c.

The reafon why men enter into fociety, is the prefervation of their property; and the end why they chufe and authorize a legiflative, is, that there may be laws made, and rules fet, as guards and fences to the properties of all the members of the fociety; to limit the powers, and moderate the dominion of every part and member of the fociety; for fince it can never be fuppofed to be the will of the fociety, that the legiflative fhould have a power to deftroy that which every one defigns to fecure by entering into fociety, and for which the people fubmitted themfelves to legiflators of their own making, whenever the legiflators endeavour to take away, or to deftroy the property of the people, or to reduce them to flavery under arbitrary power, they put themfelves into a ftate of war with the people [*i. e.* Rebellant, they bring back the ftate of war] who are thereupon abfolved from any farther obedience, and are left to the common refuge which God hath provided for all men againft force and violence.

Whenfoever,

Whensoever, therefore, the legislative shall transgress this
fundamental rule of society, and either by ambition, fear,
folly, or corruption, endeavour to grasp themselves, or put
into the hands of any other, an absolute power over the
lives, liberties and estates of the people; by this breach of
trust they forfeit the power the people had put into their
hands for quite contrary ends, and it devolves to the people again, who have a right to resume their original liberty;
and by the establishment of a new legislative (such as they
shall think fit) to provide for their own safety and security,
which is the end for which they are in society.   What I have
said here concerning the legislative in general, holds true also
concerning the supreme executor, who having a double trust
put in him, both to have a part in the legislative and the
supreme execution of the law, acts against both when he
goes about to set up his own arbitrary will as the laws of the
society.   He acts also contrary to his trust when he either
employs the force, treasure, and office of the society, to corrupt the representatives, and gain them to his purposes, or
openly pre engages the electors, and prescribes to their choice
such whom he has, by solicitations, threats, promises or
otherwise, won to his designs, and employs them to bring
in such who have promised beforehand what to vote and what
to enact.   Thus to regulate the candidates and electors, and
new model the ways of election, what is it but to cut up the
government by the roots, and to poison the very fountain of
public security? for the people, having reserved to themselves
the choice of their representatives, as the fence to their properties, could do it for no other end but that they might
always be freely chosen, and so chosen, freely act and advise,
as the necessity of the common wealth and the public good
should, upon examination and mature debate, be judged to
require.   This those who give their votes before they have
heard the debate, and have not weighed the reasons on all
sides, are not capable of doing. To prepare such an assembly
as this, and to endeavour to set up the declared abettors of
his own will for the true representatives of the people, and
the law-makers of the society, is certainly as great a breach of
trust, as perfect a declaration of a design to subvert the government, as is possible to be met with; to which if one shall
add, rewards and punishments visibly employed to the same
end, and all the arts of perverted law made use of, to take
off and destroy all that stand in the way of such a design,
and will not comply and consent to betray the liberties of

their

their country, it will be paſt doubt what is doing. What power they ought to have in the ſociety, who thus employ it contrary to the truſt that went along with it in its firſt inſtitution, is eaſy to determine; and one cannot but ſee, that he who has once attempted any ſuch thing as this cannot any longer be truſted.   Locke on Gov. chap. 19, § 222.

The fears of an invaſion ſubſided; but the people, now accuſtomed to aſſociate in arms, and ſenſible of their importance, conferred, began to ſpeak and think with more freedom of that ſtate of ſubjection, in which they had too long been held, and which was aggravated by the diſtreſs felt at this time, in a peculiar degree, convinced of their rights, and conſcious they were now in a ſituation to demand a reſtitution of them, they looked forward to redreſs, and they thought it juſt, that whilſt they protected Ireland from the enemies of Britain, it ſhould be made of ſome value to themſelves. The fire of Liberty ſpread through their different aſſociations; their union ſerved to ſtrengthen and diffuſe the flame; they talked amongſt themſelves of their preſent degenerate ſtate; wondered at their puſillanimous conduct, and reſolved to redeem themſelves in the eyes of mankind; at this critical period, the ſeſſion of 79 opened:—The Secretary entered on the buſineſs of government with the uſual confidence of ſucceſs; a confidence authorized by the experience of the former ſeſſion, in which, aſſiſted by a numerous and *corrupt* majority in parliament, he had triumphed over the efforts of the virtuous part of the people, and by continuing an odious embargo, had brought the nation to the verge of bankruptcy; how great then muſt have been the ſurprize of the miniſter to meet with unaccuſtomed oppoſition! to feel himſelf obliged to give way to an unanimous reſolution of the Houſe of Commons, inſerted even in the addreſs to the throne; " That, it was not by temporary expedients, but by a Free Trade alone, this country could be ſaved from impending ruin." This great reſolution, in the opinions of the repreſentative, can be attributed only to that ſpirit of liberty, which the armed aſſociations had diffuſed through the whole nation; they ſeemed ſenſible of this, and gave a ſanction to their aſſemblies, by voting them *unanimouſly*, an addreſs of thanks; the words, " *Free Trade*" echoed through the kingdom, and the people pledged themſelves to ſupport the requiſition of the commons; the nation however had not yet learned to ſpeak out, nor had the gal-

lant

lant affociations yet infpired or affumed that confidence, their
refpectability of character eminently entitled them to. A remarkable inftance of this occurs in the printed debates of the
houfe in the early part of this feffion ; on a motion for re-
trenchment, it being fagaci fly infinuated by Sir Benjamin
Chapman, that, it would be prudent in government to comply chearfully with the reafonable demands of the people, now
with arms in their hands, determined to defend their rights.
He was anfwered by Luke G—r, and John D—n, Efqrs.
that, the Volunteers had taken up arms, *only*, for the purpofe of defending the country from external violence, and
internal infurrection, and not, by any means, with the
view fuggefted. So little was the true fpirit of the Volunteer
combinations at that time underftood or afferted in parliament. A Free Trade, with the acquiefcence of England, was
the confequence of thofe fpirited meafures ; the people were
not to be refufed, but England, while fhe was forced to yield
to the ftrong remonftrances of the nation, endeavoured (and
in a great meafure effected her plan) to make the acquifition
of little value, by forcing, through the weight of parliamentary influence, fuch regulations as were inapplicable and
injurious to the purpofes of commerce. Thefe attempts to
evade our requifitions awakened the attention, and confirmed the fpirit of Ireland ; fhe began to fee, that it was idle
and in vain to expect, that the freedom of trade would be
inviolate, while the freedom of the conftitution remained
ftill unafferted ; thefe wife and generous fentiments fo worthy
of a great people, fhe was taught to feel and maintain in a
manner becoming her dignity, by one of the firmeft and moft
diftinguifhed patriots a grateful nation was ever bleffed with :
Mr. Grattan directed the efforts of the Volunteers to the at-
tainment of an object that merited all their exertions ; a total
emancipation from the intruded power of England, and a
perfect reftoration of that freedom to which they were entitled by Magna Charta. While he infpired the armed forces
of the nation with an idea of their own confequence, he at
the fame time fupported their claims in parliament with fuch
purfuafive eloquence, fuch power of argument, that each
individual of the commons abjured for himfelf, the fupremacy
of Great Britain ; and, it cannot be faid he was defeated,
though he did not, at that time, prevail in carrying his motion for a parliamentary declaration of rights. He fucceeded
however in eftablifhing the idea in the minds of every individual in the kingdom. He was looked up to as their leader

in

in the glorious work of liberty; he deferved the honourable
ftation, and was regarded by all parties, as the glory, ornament, and faviour of his country. The people having now
difclaimed all obedience to the acts of the Englifh legiflature,
as we had no law of our own, to regulate the conduct of the
army, it was neceflary that a mutiny bill fhould be immediately enacted; it paffed here, and was fent to England for
the royal affent: here fhe again fhewed, how tenacious fhe
was ftill of the power fhe had affumed; the bill was altered,
and the law made *perpetual* though it had been limited by
our parliament to two years only. Still the arts of venality,
which had triumphed with fuch avowed fuccefs in the former
feffions, again prevailed, and the bill was paffed in its prefent
difgraceful form: arguments were not wanting to fupport or
palliate corruption; it was attempted to be proved, that a
perpetual law was of equal fervice to the nation, and that the
alteration of the Englifh council ought not to alarm the jealoufy of this kingdom, as their admitting at all, the neceffity of a new law was a fufficient relinquifhment of their
right to bind Ireland. This flimfy reafoning however did
not fatisfy the people; they faw with aftonifhment and contempt the interefted venality of their reprefentatives: the
Volunteers entered inftantly into the moft fpirited and decided refolutions expreffive of their difcontent, and difappro-
bation; and the parliament was prorogued while the nation
remained thus unfatisfied. The general diffatisfaction had
fpread itfelf into the remoteft corners of the kingdom; every
man was called upon to lend his affiftance, and enlift under
the banner of freedom. If any before remained inatten-
tive, they were now convinced of the neceffity of uniting in
the general caufe: fcarcely was one individual found indo-
lent or bafe enough to look on an idle fpectator. Reviews
were appointed; new corps were added; provincial mufters
were directed; encampments were formed; inftructions came
from the conftituents to their reprefentatives, and the people
waited in military array, until the hour came, when they
could with firmnefs and dignity demand from parliament a
legal fanction to their claims.

April 20, 1780, Mr. Grattan, uninfluenced by power,
ftrengthening from defeats, and brightening from minifterial
collifion, moved, " that the King's moft excellent Majefty, and
" the Lords and Commons of Ireland, are the only power
" competent to make laws to bind Ireland: " yet fuch, at
this time, was the corruption of the fenate, that this moft

falutary

salutary motion was negatived, though urged with the clearest arguments, and delivered with the warmest pathos.

It was originally intended that this work should close with the last session, (in 1782,) but finding on a closer view, the transactions from this to that period numerous, deeply interesting, and worthier of higher discussion than time has hitherto permitted, they are reserved for the continuation of a second volume; and as the principle design of this work is to diffuse information, and convey, to the latest moment, those important determinations which the unanimous voice of a whole nation has uttered, and their transactions conformed, a few observations and extracts are added, as a mirror in which the subject may view his own importance, &c. as a member of the empire; the duty he owes to, and in return expects from his sovereign; the futility of kings reigning by *divine right*, so frequently urged by sleepy church dignitaries, court sycophants, and the gilded pen of ministerial hirelings.

The King is chosen as head of the community, to preside in their councils, and to execute their laws in times of peace; not to controle the one, or make the other; and to conduct and command their armies, in times of war. This *supreme Magistrate*, and *chief General* they dignified with the *honours* and *title* of KING. All the rights, powers and privileges necessary to support the regal rank, and sovereign dignity of this great officer, consistent with the great end of the institution, now called prerogatives of the crown, were annexed; with an absolute freedom and exemption to his person, from all coercive or offensive acts of violence whatsoever; except on his committing a breach of the *implied* or *written* CONTRACT between KING and PEOPLE; in which case, they have reserved to themselves, and constantly exercised, the power of dethroning their King, and that of appointing and limiting the succession to the throne.

The legislative power of the Lords extends to the framing, and passing bills, for all purposes of good government; excepting the granting *taxes*, or *subsidies*; such bills must take rise in the Commons only, their assent and consent, being of *original right*, first to be obtained.   LUCAS.

The *election* of commoners, to be immediate trustees and apt representatives of the people in parliament, is the hereditary and indefeasible privilege of the people. It is the privilege which they accepted, and which they retain, in exchange of their originally inherent and hereditary right of sitting with the King and Peers, *in person*, for the guardianship of their own liberties, and the institution of their own laws.

u   Such

Such reprefentatives, therefore, can never have it in their
power to give, delegate, or extinguifh the whole, or any part
of the peoples infparable and undiftinguifhable fhare in the legiflative power; neither to impart the fame to any one of the
other eftates, or to any perfons or perfon whatever, either in
or out of parliament.   Where plenepotentaries take upon
them to abolifh the authority of their principals; or where
any fecundary agents attempt to defeat the power of their
primaries; fuch agents and plenepotentaries defeat their own
commiffion, and all the powers of the truft neceffarily revert
to the conftituents.

The perfons of thefe temporary truftees of the people, during their feffion, and for fourteen days before and after
every meeting, adjournment, prorogation, and diffolution of
parliament, are equally exempted, with the perfons of peers,
from arreft and durefs of every fort.

They are alfo, during their feffion, to have ready accefs
to the King or Houfe of Lords, and to addrefs or confer
with them on all occafions.

No member of the Houfe of Commons, no more than of
the Houfe of Peers, fhall fuffer, or be queftioned, or compelled to witnefs or anfwer, in any court or place whatfoever,
touching any thing faid or done by himfelf, or others, in
parliament; in order that perfect freedom of fpeech, and
action, may leave nothing undone for the public weal.

They have alfo (during feffion) an equal power with the
Houfe of Lords, to punifh any who fhall prefume to traduce
their dignity, or detract from the rights or privileges of
any Member of their Houfe.

They commons form a court of judicature, diftinct from the
judicature of the Houfe of Lords.   Theirs is the peculiar
privilege to try and adjudge the legality of the election of
their own members.   They may fine and confine their own
members, as well as others, for delinquency or offence againft
the honour of their houfe.   But, in all other matters of judicature, they are merely a court of *inquifition* and *prefentment,*
and not a tribunal of *definitive judgment.*

In this refpect, however, they are extremely formidable.
They conftitute the *grand inqueft* of the nation; for which
great and good purpofe, they are fuppofed to be perfectly
qualified, by a perfonal knowledge of what hath been tranf-
acted throughout the feveral fhires, cities, and boroughs,
from whence the affemble, and which they reprefent.

Over and above their inquiry into all public grievances,
wicked Minifters, tranfgreffing Magiftrates, corrupt Judges and

Infic'aries, who fell, deny, or delay juftice; *evil Counfellors*
of the crown, who attempt or devife the fubverfion or alteration of any part of the conftitution; with all fuch overgrown
malefactors as are deemed above the reach of inferior courts,
come under the particular cognizance of the Commons, to be
by them impeached, and prefented for trial at the bar of
the Houfe of Lords. And thefe inquifitory and judicial powers of the two Houfes, from which no man under the crown
can be exempted, are deemed a fufficient allay and counterpoife to the whole executive power of the King by his Minifters.

The legiflative department of the power of the Commons
is, in all refpects, co-equal with that of the peers. They
frame any bills at pleafure for the purpofes of good government. They exercife a right, as the Lords alfo do, to pro-
pofe and bring in bills, for the amendment or repeal of old
laws, as well as for the ordaining or inftitution of new ones.
And each houfe alike hath a negative on all bills that are
framed and paffed by the other.

But the capital, the incommunicable privilege of the Houfe
of Commons, arifes from that holy truft which their conftituents repofe in them; whereby they are impowered to borrow from the people a fmall portion of their property, in
order to reftore it threefold, in the advantages of peace,
equal government, and the encouragement of trade, induftry, and manfactures.

To impart any of this truft would be a breach of the conftitution: and even to abufe it, would be a felonious breach
of common honefty.

By this fundamental truft, and incommunicable privilege,
the Commons have the fole power over the money of the people; to grant or deny aids, according as they fhall judge them
either reqifite, or unneceffary to the public fervice. Theirs is
the province, and theirs alone, to enquire and judge of the
feveral occafions for which fuch aids may be required, and to
meafure and appropriate the fums to their refpective ufes.
Theirs alfo is the fole province of framing all bills or laws
for the impofing of any taxes, and of appointing the means
for levying the fame upon the people. Neither may the firft
or fecond eftate, either King or Peerage, propound or do
any thing relating to thefe matters, that may any way interfere with the proceedings of the Commons, fave in their
negative or affent to fuch bills, when prefented to them, without addition, deduction, or alteration of any kind.

After

After fuch aids and taxes have been levied and difpofed of, the Commons have the further right of enquiring and examining into the application of the faid aids; of ordering all accounts relative thereto, to be laid before them; and of cenfuring the abufe or mifapplication thereof.

The royal affent to all other bills is expreffed by the terms, *Le Roy le veut, the King wills it.* But, when the Commons prefent their bills of aid to his Majefty, it is anfwered, *Le Roy remercier fes loyal fubjeds et ainfi le veut, The King thanks his loyal fubjeds and fo willeth.* An exprefs acknowledgment that the right of granting or levying monies for public purpofes, lies folely, inherently, and incommunicably, in the people and their reprefentatives.

This capital privilege of the Commons, conftitutes the grand counterpoife to the King's principal prerogative of making peace or war; for how impotent muft a warlike enterprize prove, without money, which makes the finews thereof; and thus the people and their reprefentatives ftill retain in their hands the *grand momentum* of the conftitution, and of all human affairs.

Diftinguifhed reprefentatives! Happy People! Immutably happy, while *worthily reprefented.*

As the fathers of the feveral families throughout the kingdom, nearly and tenderly comprize and reprefent the perfons, cares, and concerns of their refpective houfhoulds; fo thefe adopted fathers immediately reprefent, and intimately concentrate, the perfons and concerns of their refpective conftituents, and in them the collective body, or fum of the nation. And while thefe fathers continue true to their adopting children, a fingle ftone cannot lapfe from the *great fabric of the conftitution.*

The Three Eftates in Parliament.

With the King, Lords, and Commons, in parliament affembled, the people have depofited their *legiflative* or *abfolute power, in truft* for their whole body; the faid King, Lords, and Commons, when fo affembled, being the *great* reprefentative of the whole nation, as if all the people were then convened in one general affembly.

As the inftitution, repeal, and amendment of laws, together with the redrefs of public grievances and offences, are not within the capicity of any of the three eftates, diftinct from the others, the *frequent holding of Parliaments* is the vital food, without which the conftitution cannot fubfift.

The three eftates originally, when affembled in parliament fat together confulting in the open field. Accordingly, a

Running

Running Mead, five hundred years ago. King John passed the great charter, (as therein is expressed) by the advice of the Lords Spiritual and Temporal, by the advice of several Commoners (by name recited) *et aliorum fidelium,* and of others his faithful people. And in the twenty-first clause of the said charter, he covenants, that, " For having " the Common Council of the kingdom to assess aids, he will cause " the Lords spiritual and temporal to be summoned by his writs ; " and, moreover, he will cause the principal Commoners, or " those who held from him in chief, to be generally summoned " to said parliaments by his Sheriffs and Bailiffs."

In the said assemblies, however, the concourse became so great and disorderly, and the contest frequently so high between the several estates, in assertion of their respective prerogatives and priviliges, that they judged it more expedient to sit apart, and separately to exercise the offices of their respective departments.

As there is no man, or set of men, no class or corporation, no village or city, throughout the kingdom, that is not virtually represented by the delegates in parliament, this *great body politic,* or *representative of the nation,* consists, like the body natural, of a head and several members, which, being endowed with different powers for the exercise of different offices, are yet connected by one main and common interest, and actuated by *one life or spirit of public reason,* called the *laws.*

In all steps of national import, the King is to be conducted by the direction of the parliament, his great national council ; a council on whom it is equally encumbent to consult for the King with whom they are connected, and for the people by whom they are delegated, and whom they represent. Thus the King is constitutionally to be guided by the sense of his parliament ; and the parliament alike is constitutionally to be guided by the general sense of the people. The two estates in parliament are the constituents of the King ; and the people, mediately or immediately, are the constituents of the two estates in parliament.

Now, while the three estates act distinctly, within their respective departments, they effect and are reciprocally affected by each other. This *action and re-action* produces that general and *systematic controul* which, like *conscience,* pervades and superintends the whole, checking and prohibiting evil from every part of the constitution. And from this confinement of every part of the rule of *right reason,* the great *law of liberty to all* ariseth.

For instance, the King has the sole prerogative of making war, &c. But then the means are in the hands of the people and their representatives.

Again, to the King is committed the whole executive power. But then the minifters of that power are accountable to a tribunal, from which a criminal has no appeal or deliverance to look for.

Again, to the King is committed the cognizance of all caufes. But fhould his Judges or Jufticiaries pervert the rule of righteoufnefs, an inqufition, impeachment, and trial impends, from whofe judgment the Judges cannot be exempted.

Again, the King hath a negative upon all bills, whereby his own prerogatives are guarded from invafion. But fhould he refufe the royal affent to bills tending to the good of the fubject, the Commons can alfo with-hold their bills of affeff-ment, or annex the rejected bills to their bill of aids: and they never failed to pafs in fuch agreeable company.

Laftly, to the King is committed the right of calling the two eftates to parliament. But, fhould he refufe fo to call them, fuch a refufal would be deemed *an abdication of the conftitution ;* and no one need be told, at this day, *that an abdication of the conftitution is an obdication of the throne.*

Thus, while the King acts in confent with the parliament and his people. he is limitlefs, irrefiftable, omnipotent upon earth; he is the free wielder of all the powers of a free and noble people; a King throned over all the Kings of the children of men. But fhould he attempt to break bounds, fhould he caft for independence, he finds himfelf hedged in and ftraightened on every fide ; he finds himfelf abandoned by all his powers, and juftly left to a ftate of utter impotence and inaction.

Hence is imputed to the fovereign head, in the conftitution of Great Britain, the high and divine attribute, *the King can do no wrong ;* for he is fo circumfcribed from the poffibility of tranfgreffion, that *no wrong can be permitted te any King in the conftitution.*

While the King is thus controuled by the Lords and Commons; while the Lords are thus controuled by theCommons and the King, and while the Commons are thus controuled by the other two eftates, from attempting any thing to the prejudice of the general welfare, the three eftates may be aptly compared to three pillars divided below at equidiftant angles, but united and fupported at top, merely by the bearing of each pillar againft the others. Take but any of thefe pillars away, and the other two muft inevitably tumble. But while all act on each other, all are equally counteracted, and thereby affirm and eftablifh the general frame.

How

How deplorable then would it be, fhould this elaborate ftructure of our happy conftitution, within the fhort period of a thoufand years hence, poffibly in half the time, fall a prey to effeminacy, pufilanimity, venality, and feduction; like fome ancient oak, the lord of the foreft, to a pack of vile worms that lay gnawing at the root; or, like Egypt, be contemptibly deftroyed by *lice and locufts.*

Should the morals of our conftituents ever come to be debauched, *confent*, which is *the falt of liberty*, would then be corrupted, and no falt might be found wherewith it could be feafoned. Thofe who are inwardly the fervants of *fin*, muft be outwardly the fervants of *influence.* Each man would then be as the Trojan *horfe* of old, and carry the enemies of his country within his bofom. Our own appetites would then induce us to betray our own interefts; and ftate policy would feize us a *willing facrifice to our own perdition.*

Should it ever come to pafs, that corruption, like a dark and low-hung mift, fhould fpread from man to man, and cover thefe lands. Should a general diffolution of manners prevail. Should vice be countenanced and communicated by the leaders of fafhion. Should it come to be propagated by minifters among legiflators, and by the legiflators among their conftituents. Should guilt lift up its head without fear of reproach, and avow itfelf in the face of the fun, and laugh virtue out of countenance by force of numbers. Should public duty turn public ftrumpet, Should fhops come to be advertifed, where men may difpofe of their honour and honefty at fo much per ell. Should public markets be opened for the puachafe of confciences with an *oyez!* We bid moft to thofe who fet themfelves, their trufts, and their country to fale! If fuch a day, I fay, fhould ever arrive, it will be doom's-day, indeed, to the virtue, the liberty, and conftitution of thefe kingdoms. It would be the fame to Great Britain, as it would happen to the univerfe; fhould the laws of of cohefion ceafe to operate, and all the parts be diffipated, whofe orderly connection now forms the beauty and *commonwealth of nature.* Want of fanity in the material, can never be fupplied by any part in the building. A conftitution of *public freemen* can never confift of *private proftitutes.*

BROOKE.

We here fee the harmoney of the whole arifes from the mutual connection, and the mutual oppofition of the feveral conftituent parts. The three different orders which compofe the fyftem, including every part of the community, and poffeffing felling the unlimited authority of the whole, are connected together by a power of ordaining belonging jointly to them all; they are oppofed to one another by a power of hindering. belonging feparately to each; by the former, they are enabled to provide for the good of the community in general; by the latter, they are difabled from encroaching on each others rights, or oppreffing any part. The legiflative power, which requires much council and mature deliberation, is very properly placed in the hands of the many; the executive power, which requires immediate action, is, with equal propriety, committed to the one. How hath the wifdom of nature been ftretched! how have the veins of the valiant been exhaufted, to form, fupport, reform, and bring to maturity this unexampled conftitution, this coalefcence and grand effort of every human virtue, *Britifh Liberty!*

If it was poffible for any man who hath the leaft knowledge of our conftitution, to doubt in good earneft, whether the prefervation of public freedom depends on the prefervation of parliamentary freedom, his doubts might be removed, and his opinion decided, one would imagine, by this fingle obvious remark, that all the defigns of our Princes againft liberty, fince parliaments began to be eftablifhed on the model ftill fubfifting, have been directed conftantly to one of thefe two points; either to obtain fuch parliaments as they could govern, or elfe to ftand all the difficulties, and run all the hazards of governing without parliaments. The means principally employed to the firft of thefe purpofes have been, undue influences on the elections of members of the Houfe of Commons, and on thefe members when chofen. When fuch influences could be employed fuccefsfully, they have anfwered all the ends of arbitrary will; and when they could not be fo employed, arbitrary will has been forced to fubmit to the conftitution.

Bolingbroke's Differtat. Letter XI page 15.

The King at his coronation folemnly fwears to the following effect: " That he will govern the people of the realm according to the ftatutes in parliament made, that is by the reprefentatives of the people; and agreeable to the laws, and cuftoms by them eftablifhed; that he will caufe law and juftice in mercy and equity to be difpenfed and executed; that he will protect and maintain, to the utmoft of his power, the laws of God, the true religion and profeffion of the gofpel, and the general rights and liberties of all the people, whether clergy or laity, without diftinction."

It

www.ingramcontent.com/pod-product-compliance
Lightning Source LLC
Chambersburg PA
CBHW020548270326
41927CB00006B/761